FINDING GOOD NEWS IN (
AND PARABLES OF JUDGMENT

AD 70

— AND —

THE END OF THE WORLD

PAUL ELLIS

KINGSPRESS
Birkenhead, New Zealand

AD70 and the End of the World

ISBN: 978–1–927230–41–1

Copyright © 2017 by Paul Ellis. Published by KingsPress, Birkenhead, New Zealand. This title is also available in ebook form. Visit www.KingsPress.org for information.

Cover layout and design by tatlin.net.

Version: 1.1 (September 2017)

ENDORSEMENTS

Paul Ellis has written another book for the ages. *AD70* will undoubtedly become a resource to help multitudes sort out the oft-confusing interpretations of end-time events, especially Matthew 24, in light of the finished work of Jesus. This book is gripping in its scholarship and refreshing in its hopeful conclusions. Paul is a voice of confidence and clarity for a generation coming out of the shadows of an angry God mentality.

    – KEN SPICER
       Lead Pastor, New Creation Church, Beaumont, CA

Matthew 24 finally makes sense! Paul has done a masterful job of interpreting a difficult passage of Scripture through the lens of grace. Thank you, Paul!

    – CLARK WHITTEN
       Pastor, Grace Church, Orlando, FL, and author of *Pure Grace*

A great book. Very insightful look at church history and that time period. A must-read for every teaching pastor.

    – CHRIS BLUE
       Pastor, Faith City Church, Palm Harbor, FL

I wholeheartedly commend Paul Ellis for courageously publishing his perspectives on a subject many authors consider too confronting, challenging, complex, and controversial. He has done so with kindness, thoroughness, and a clear desire to honor the Lord. Reader, should you approach this book in the same spirit with which it was written, I am confident you will experience both a strengthening of your convictions and a stirring of your curiosity.

    – CHAD M. MANSBRIDGE
       Pastor, Bayside Int. Church, South Australia and author of *He Qualifies You*

I have read Paul Ellis' book AD70 carefully. As a long-time futurist, I would ask both futurists and preterists to give serious consideration to his presentation. Each side of this discussion has inherent problems, and Paul clearly and methodically removes many of them with this readable and sensible book. He shows us that this is not an either/or topic. It is possible for us to stand in awe of what has been fulfilled while still looking forward to what is coming.

    – DAVID ORRISON, PhD,
       Pastor, The Chapel, Loveland, CO

I read this book and all confusing end time theology disappeared!

    – JUN YU
       Senior pastor Jesus Faith Christian Fellowship, the Philippines

I can't say I'm surprised after reading *AD70*, but I will say I'm impressed. Since the day the Lord revealed to me his gospel of grace, I have wondered how anyone could reconcile the fear-inducing message of Christ's return with a God that is forgiving, loving, and empowering. Paul Ellis has done an excellent job of opening our eyes to the fact that that blessed day will truly be a blessed day! Thank you, Paul, for undertaking such a contentious subject and making it clear, as does the gospel, that there is no fear in love.

    – REVEREND OSCAR RIOS
        Founder, It's Grace Ministries, Fremont, OH

It can be difficult to wade through the mire of conjecture, myth, and wild predictions that so often fill the pages of modern end-time interpretation, without coming away with a sense of fearful dread. Paul Ellis' latest book is a breath of fresh air, bringing insight into often-neglected historical fact mixed with clear exegesis of scripture, presented in a unique and entertaining way. The gospel is good news; it is not a message of doom and gloom but one of hope and peace. Paul Ellis has done much here to dispel the fear of end times, a very helpful and recommended read.

    – TONY IDE
        Senior Pastor, Freedom Life, Perth, Australia

Responsible, fair, and fun, Paul Ellis' new book, *AD 70 and The End of the World*, provides a detailed and fascinating look at one of the most debated sections of scripture – Matthew 24. I recommend this book for anyone looking to expand their understanding of grace in light of the past fall of Jerusalem and the future return of Christ.

    – LUCAS MILES
        Author of *Good God: The One We Want To Believe In But Are Afraid To Embrace*

This book cuts through the current narrative of eternal conscious torment vs universalism and full preterism vs the anti-Christ showing up any minute now. While I still haven't taken a full stance on the tribulation, I have great value for Paul's reading of Matthew 24. It has personally helped me be able to give a more responsible answer to those who pay attention to my ministry. This book won't answer all your questions about the return of Jesus but it could very well allay your fears of a coming doomsday.

    – CLINT BYARS
        Pastor, Forward Church, Sharpsburg, GA

CONTENTS

INTRODUCTION

When I was a young boy, a prominent speaker came to our church to preach on the end times. He had charts and maps, and he had me convinced that the world was going to end in 1984. Right there and then I was ready to quit school. Phone the principal because I was never going back. What was the point of homework and exams if Jesus was about to return? Thankfully, wisdom intervened, and I didn't ruin my life.

Eschatology, or the study of end times, is a subject that is susceptible to abuse. The speaker I heard painted a terrifying vision of the future. He had us convinced we were on the verge of a great tribulation where our choices were either starvation or damnation. He told us secret organizations ran the world and that a one-world government would fall under the sway of a charismatic antichrist. Soon Christians would be hated by all. We wouldn't be able to get jobs or buy food unless we were laser-tattooed with the mark of the beast.

With any luck, we'd be raptured before we starved to death, but there was a risk we would be left behind. To insure against this possibility, we were exhorted to stay abreast of current events and share the good news about the awful future a loving God had in store for us.

I laugh about it now, but at the time it was scary as hell. I honestly wondered why my parents had been so reckless in having children in such troubled times.

As it turned out, Jesus didn't return in 1984. The world didn't blow up, and if there was a great tribulation, I must've missed it. On reflection, the only bad end-times event that happened to me in the '80s was that sermon.

Perhaps it is because of this experience that I have always been intrigued by the disciples' questions to Jesus: What will be the sign of your coming? When is the end of the world?

These are good questions to which Jesus provides brilliant answers. But they're not exactly plain answers.

Jesus doesn't say anything like, "I'll be back in 2025," or "When America gets a female president I shall return."

When Jesus comes

The Bible says much about the coming of the Lord, but a lot of what it says can appear confusing. Take his first coming, for example. The Jews had been waiting for the Messiah for centuries, but where would he appear? One Old Testament prophet said he would come from Bethlehem; another said he would come out of Egypt, while others said he would come from Nazareth. Imagine the arguments!

Of course, we now know that all three prophecies were on the mark, for Jesus spent his formative years in all three places. But that was only the first coming of Jesus, and the Bible speaks of at least five. (Yes, five; I list them in Chapter 31.) It's easy to latch onto one scripture and build a story around it, but there are hundreds of scriptures about the different comings of the Lord. The potential for confusion is high.

If we wish to make sense of what the Bible says, we'd better drink deep or not drink at all. But the Bible is a big book, which is why this book will focus on the words of Jesus. In particular, we will examine his parables and prophecies of judgment and the end of the world.

Christ's longest and most astonishing prophecy is the one recorded in Matthew 24. It's known as the Olivet Discourse, because Jesus was on the Mount of Olives when he gave it. This prophecy contains the words of life and death, but these words can seem mystical and weird to our 21st-century minds. What are we to make of darkening suns, eastern lightning, and loud trumpets? What do nursing mothers have in common with fig trees and drunk servants? Thankfully these questions are explained by the context, namely the times in which Christ lived and the Old Testament prophecies which he quoted. Context does not come from *Newsweek* or *Al Jazeera* or charts linking the Freemasons with ISIS. When reading the Bible, it's always safest to let scripture interpret scripture, which is what we shall do here.

Although the emphasis is on Jesus, we won't ignore the eschatological visions of Daniel, John, and the other prophets. (More than 500 scriptures are indexed at the back of the book.) However, we will filter all we read through the lens of Jesus.

This book has two parts. In Part A we will wander verse-by-verse through the prophetic treasures of Matthew 24. Then in Part B, we will ask hard questions about the meaning of life and how to live with the end in mind. This is not a book you need to read from cover to cover, but you'll get a good sense of the Big Picture if you do. If you just want the highlights, you'll find them in the chapter summaries in the final chapter.

Why I wrote this book

Fear-based eschatology is dangerous. It binds the free and makes the church look foolish. Worse, it distorts the gospel and portrays God as something other than our heavenly Father who loves us.

Buy into a doom-and-gloom view of the future and you'll be a bad advertisement for Jesus. Instead of shining in dark places, you'll dismiss evil as a sign of the times. "Sure, this is bad, but it needs to happen so Jesus can come back." You'll hunker down in the proverbial lifeboat while the rest of the world goes to hell in a handbasket. "Thank God I'm saved. I'm going to sit tight until Jesus returns."

Thankfully, fear-based eschatology is falling out of fashion. Today many have embraced an optimistic end-times perspective, which is a good thing. But the view looking back is less encouraging. For 2,000 years scholars and theologians have put a dark slant on Christ's words, and the result is a mixed message. "God loves you, but if you don't love him back he'll destroy you. Just look at what happened to Jerusalem."

I am no end-times expert; my passion is the gospel. I write so that you might trust the One who speaks the words of life. But over the past few years, a growing number of people have asked for my views on the events of AD70.

AD70 was the year that Israel almost ceased to exist. (By Israel, I mean the Galilee and Judea that the apostles knew.) Israel has gone through dark times in its long and rich history, but AD70 was arguably the darkest year of all.

What does AD70 have to do with us? Quite a lot, as it turns out. Many intelligent people believe that God was behind the disaster that befell Israel. But if God destroyed Jerusalem in the summer of AD70, this is bad news for you and me, as we shall see.

When Jerusalem was destroyed, it was pretty much the end of the Jewish world, at least for a time. But I'm also interested in the end of our world, and Jesus talks about that too. Indeed, the two events share things in common, and our understanding of one will shape our understanding of the other. So although we'll begin by looking at the past, the insights we glean will help us go forward into the future.

Our lives reflect our beliefs. If you are worried that a powerful anti-christ is about to take control of the United Nations and that a great tribulation is imminent, it will affect the choices you make today. Personally, I believe the future is bright. Yes, there will be dark times, but Jesus is on the throne. It is his story that shapes history.

This book offers a radical departure from tradition in that it provides a grace-based version of Christ's parables and prophecies of judgment. I wrote it to give you a confident and cheerful expectation of the future. God put you on this earth to make a splash and leave a legacy, and the four men who were with Jesus on the Mount of Olives did just that. You can too.

Disturbing discoveries

Full disclosure: I have never attended seminary, and I don't have a degree in Jewish history. But before I was a writer I was a university professor, which means I like to read and study. It also means I'm not dazzled by jargon, and I can tell when the emperor's wearing no clothes.

In reading about AD70, I made a couple of disturbing discoveries. Although most Bible commentaries are written by highly educated experts, I found some authors rely on earlier commentators to such an extent that rumors and speculations offered by the former are accepted as gospel truths by the latter. In my research, I found cautious guesses, invented claims, even outright errors were repeated again and again until they were embraced as factual. This is poor scholarship because bad facts lead to bad conclusions.

How did I know they were bad facts? Because when it comes to the destruction of Jerusalem, there is only one firsthand source: a Jewish historian named Flavius Josephus.

Josephus was hardly an unbiased writer, but he was there when it happened. In some ways, Josephus was the perfect chronicler because he played for both teams. He began the war as a Jewish general and ended it as a Roman emissary. He knew the key players on both sides, and he literally stood between the two armies.

His is an eyewitness account which puts it miles ahead of oral traditions and made-up stories. I have no wish to recycle hearsay and speculation, so in this book I will rely heavily on Josephus' original accounts. And I'll list my sources, so you can verify everything I say.[1]

Flavius Josephus: "I was there"

Here's another unsettling discovery. While I found many commentators who said God destroyed Jerusalem, I found none who said he didn't. Not one. Every commentator I read said, "The Jews had it coming," or they maintained a thunderous silence.

This is unacceptable. The marginalization of the Jews by some Bible scholars is contrary to the gospel of Jesus Christ. Jesus died for the Jews; they didn't die for him. As far as I know, no other author in 2,000 years has spoken against this injustice, which means either I'm the first to do so or I'm a first-rate heretic.

And I'm open to that. I could be wrong about everything. To help insure against this possibility, it is important to give a fair hearing to alternative points of view. To that end I have recruited a couple of knowledgeable characters: Mr. Preterist, whose name derives from the Latin word for past, believes Biblical prophecies have been fulfilled, while Mr. Futurist believes they are yet to be fulfilled. These gentlemen are smart, and they know the scriptures. They also have strong convictions, which they are not afraid to express, so don't be surprised if an argument breaks out. I'll try and keep it civil, but you have been warned. All right, here we go.

A futurist and a preterist walk into a bar...

---

[1] In particular, I will draw upon two works by Josephus: *The Wars of the Jews* (c.75) and *The Antiquities of the Jews* (c.94). Both works are in the public domain and can be found online. Just as there are different translations of the Bible and some are better than others, there are different translations of Josephus. I relied on two: Whiston's (1737) classic word-for-word translation (my version is the 1987 edition of *The Works of Josephus: Complete and Unabridged*, published by Hendrickson), and Maier's shorter and reader-friendly translation (*Josephus: The Essential Works*, published in 1988 by Kregel). Each translation complements the other. Maier gives you the story, while Whiston gives you the details. Since I did not wish to pepper this book with distracting notes, you will find most of the references to Josephus' works listed in the timeline found in Appendix 1.

1. NOT ONE STONE

Jesus came out from the temple and was going away when his disciples came up to point out the temple buildings to him. And he said to them, "Do you not see all these things? Truly I say to you, not one stone here will be left upon another, which will not be torn down." (Matthew 24:1–2)

Jesus was steaming. He had just delivered one of the biggest verbal smackdowns in history. Using some of the angriest words recorded in the Bible, he had torn shreds off the scribes and Pharisees. God's Son told God's men that they were blind fools. Hypocrites, he called them, and sons of hell.

No one had ever spoken to the religious leaders like that. Never. The disciples didn't know whether to grin or run for cover.

Jesus' last visit to the temple of Jerusalem was one for the ages. He had charged the law teachers and Pharisees with all sorts of misdeeds before blaming them for the murders of every righteous man from Abel to Zechariah. Then, walking away from the temple, never to return, Jesus said the strangest thing of all. "These stones are coming down."

The temple was the grandest building in Israel. It was God's house, built by an army of priests atop a plateau carved out of Mount Moriah. The temple plaza was large enough to accommodate the million or so pilgrims who regularly flocked to Jerusalem for various feasts and festivals. Built of white marble and gold, the temple appeared on the horizon as a snow-covered mountain. Surrounding the temple were shady porticoes lined with 162 Corinthian columns.

Since Herod the Great had funded its construction, it was known as Herod's Temple. It was also known as the Second Temple in contrast with the original built by King Solomon. But second didn't mean inferior for Herod's Temple was bigger and shinier, an engineering marvel for the ages. Made of massive stones, some weighing many tons, it was built to last forever. It would've impressed the socks off illiterate Galilean fishermen.[1]

"Lord, isn't this the most awesome building in the world? Check out these massive stones!"

"*Pshaw!* This building's coming down. Mark my words."

What? When? How?

Herod's shiny temple

Such questions would have flooded their minds, but this was not the place to ask them. Jesus was in enough trouble with the religious authorities. So the disciples kept quiet until they were a safe distance away. Then their questions came rushing out.

> As he was sitting on the Mount of Olives, the disciples came to him privately, saying, "Tell us, when will these things happen, and what will be the sign of your coming, and of the end of the age?" (Matthew 24:3)

How many questions did the disciples put to Jesus?

Mr. Preterist: "Count the question marks. They asked one question."

Mr. Futurist: "Nope. They asked three."

It's a safe bet the disciples thought they were asking one question. They wanted to know about the long-awaited day of the Lord when God would intervene in Jewish history, end evil, and set things right. They had been waiting for Jesus to reveal his true colors. So when Jesus rips into the Pharisees and starts talking about the destruction of the temple, they figure he's about to do it. Finally, he's going to deliver the Jews from Roman and religious oppression.

Isn't that why Jesus had come to Jerusalem at the Feast of Passover?

Nope. The disciples were mistaken for Jesus hadn't come to wield the sword but to die on a cross. He hadn't come to seize the keys of the kingdom from Rome and restore them to Israel (Acts 1:6), but to usher in a new and heavenly kingdom.

The disciples may have thought they were asking one question, but they were really asking two or possibly three.

"When will these things happen?" Meaning the things Jesus has just been discussing. They are on the Mount of Olives with the temple in front of them. Apparently, it's coming down. The disciples want to know when.

"What will be the sign of your coming?" In other words, "When are you going to reveal yourself as you truly are?" This could be a reference to Christ coming into his kingdom, his coming in judgment on Israel, his Second Coming to earth, or a mix of all three.

"And when will be the end of the age?" By which the disciples might have meant the end of the old covenant age or the end of the world.

Mr. Preterist: "These divisions are pointless. The disciples did not ask three questions but one to which Jesus gave one answer. Study history and you will see that his words were fulfilled during the siege of AD70 when the Romans destroyed the temple."

Mr. Futurist: "No, Jesus is talking about Judgment Day. The destruction of the temple was a prophetic picture of that greater calamity."

As you can see, Mr. Preterist and Mr. Futurist hold different views. Mr. Preterist reads Matthew 24 as pointing to a chain of catastrophes that befell Israel in AD70, while Mr. Futurist reads it as a series of cataclysmic events associated with the Second Coming of Christ. One says it's ancient history ("No need to panic"), while the other says it's yet to happen ("Watch the signs!").

Which is it? As we will see, some parts of Matthew 24 seem to point directly to the fall of Jerusalem, but other parts are not so clear-cut. Regardless of how many questions the disciples asked, Jesus seems to give several answers. Yet his answers are connected, as we shall see. Each forms part of an astonishing prophetic picture that is as relevant for us as it was for them.

---

[1] Shelley Cohney, "The Jewish Temples: The Second Temple," *Jewish Virtual Library*, website: www.jewishvirtuallibrary.org/jsource/History/secondtemple.html, accessed August 9, 2016. Josephus' descriptions of Herod's temple can be found in *Wars*, 1.21.1 and 5.5.

2. BIRTH PANGS

And Jesus answered and said to them, "See to it that no one misleads you. For many will come in my name, saying, 'I am the Christ,' and will mislead many." (Matthew 24:4–5)

Mr. Futurist: "Jesus is talking about these last days in which we live, for there are many self-appointed gurus and false messiahs. Just the other day I read about a man claiming to be Jesus."

Mr. Preterist: "Jesus is speaking about the many false messiahs of the first century. The Jews had been waiting for the Messiah for hundreds of years. If Jesus wasn't the Messiah – as many of them thought – the real Messiah could show up at any moment. Jesus is saying, 'Don't be misled.'"

When we hear the word "Christ", we think "Son of God," so someone claiming to be the Christ is claiming to be God's Son. That's a big blasphemous claim.

But Jesus is talking about false *messiahs*. In a Jewish context, a messiah is not necessarily the Son of God. A messiah could be anyone who delivers Israel from oppression. For instance, Cyrus the Great, who delivered Israel from the Babylonians, was called "God's anointed" (Isaiah 45:1). So Cyrus was a kind of messiah.[1]

Were there false messiahs in the years following Jesus' death and resurrection, as claimed by Mr. Preterist? There were many. Some of these, such as Simon Magus, and Judas of Galilee, are listed in the Bible. Others are recorded by the Jewish historian Josephus and the Christian historian Eusebius. Several of these false messiahs claimed to come in the name of God. What did these false messiahs do? For the most part, they picked fights with the Romans and died young.

About fifteen years after Christ's prophecy, a man named Theudas, to give one example, convinced the crowds to follow him to the Jordan River. This self-appointed prophet promised to part the river and led the Jews to freedom. However, Cuspius Fadus, the Roman governor at the time, pursued him with cavalry and chopped his head off. Theudas was just one of many who tried and failed to deliver the Jews from Roman oppression.[2]

You will be hearing of wars and rumors of wars. See that you are not frightened, for those things must take place, but that is not yet the end. For nation will rise against nation, and kingdom against kingdom, and in various places there will be famines and earthquakes. (Matthew 24:6–7)

Mr. Futurist: "Jesus is describing the last and most violent century in history, the only century with two world wars. These days you can't turn on the news without hearing about wars or earthquakes or political upheavals."

Mr. Preterist: "Yet the decades following Christ's death were possibly the most violent in history, at least as far as the Jews were concerned. Josephus wrote a book about it called *The Wars of the Jews*, and it records how the Jews and their Greek-speaking neighbors slaughtered each other. The Parthians, Samaritans, Syrians, and Egyptians all hated the Jews, and the Jews hated them back. It was nation against nation. King Herod lost his entire army in a battle against King Aretas of Petra. It was kingdom against kingdom. But these were mere birth pangs compared to the brutal three and a half years of Jewish-Roman warfare that climaxed in the destruction of Jerusalem."

Mr. Futurist: "Okay, so the first century had a few wars ..."

Mr. Preterist: "And bear in mind that Jesus predicted these wars during the *Pax Romana*, a period of unprecedented peace. It was a remarkable prophecy, like predicting snow in summer."

Mr. Futurist: "So what about the *rumors* of wars? Surely that's a reference to social media and WikiLeaks."

Mr. Preterist: "A few years after Christ's death, the emperor Caligula decided that the Jews should bow to the cult of Rome. He ordered statues of Roman gods to be erected in their temple and sent Publius Petronius with an army to do the job. But the army was met by tens of thousands of protesting Jews. 'Don't do it,' they said. 'This idolatry is against our religion.' Petronius told the Jews that if he didn't deliver the statues that Caligula would go to war against them. The Jews didn't budge. They neglected their crops and prepared for death. Eventually, Petronius backed down and war was averted. He had no stomach for slaying women and children. But when Caligula heard about this, he was furious, and the war was back on. Then Caligula was assassinated, and the war was off again. For a while, the whole nation was on tenterhooks. The economy ground to a halt because of the rumors about the on-again, off-again war."

Mr. Futurist: "Well, how do you explain the famines and the earthquakes?"

Mr. Preterist: "Because of the faceoff with Caligula, the Jews neglected their harvest, and this brought a food shortage to neighboring Tyre and Sidon. You can read about in in Acts 12:20."

Mr. Futurist: "A food shortage? Doesn't sound like much of a famine."

Mr. Preterist: "Then how about the great worldwide famine predicted by Agabus in Acts 11? According to Josephus, many people in Jerusalem died as a result of it. In fact, their suffering was one of the reasons why Paul collected funds from other churches."

Mr. Futurist: "I did not know that. Okay, what about earthquakes? I suppose you're going to tell me there were some prior to AD70."

Mr. Preterist: "Well, there was one when Jesus died and another when he rose. There was a violent earthquake the night Paul and Silas were freed from prison. And yes, historians tell us there were many earthquakes in the first century in places like Crete, Laodicea, Rome, and Pompeii. There was even one in Jerusalem on the eve of the Roman siege."[3]

The Roman siege. We're building up to that, but, long story short, AD70 was arguably the single worst year in the history of Israel. In the opening verses of Matthew 24, Jesus predicted five signs – false messiahs, wars, rumors of wars, famines, and earthquakes – that all came to pass in the buildup to this catastrophic year. Does that mean Jesus was prophesying about the destruction of Jerusalem? Or are these events merely coincidental?

Recall that Jesus was speaking to his disciples. He said that they would hear of wars and rumors of wars, and they did. His exhortation not to be misled by false messiahs or frightened by current events would be meaningless if these things didn't happen to them. Jesus was describing events that the disciples would personally experience.

In Luke's account of Christ words, there are a couple of additional signs:

> When you hear of wars and disturbances, do not be terrified; for these things must take place first, but the end does not follow immediately … Nation will rise against nation and kingdom against kingdom, and there will be great earthquakes, and in various places **plagues** and famines; and **there will be terrors and great signs from heaven**. (Luke 21:9–11)

Were plagues or pestilences experienced before the fall of Jerusalem? Tacitus, the Roman historian, records that a plague swept through Rome in AD65, filling the houses with dead "and the streets with funerals." And shortly after the Romans besieged Jerusalem in AD70, the city suffered a pestilential destruction as a consequence of the confined masses. This outbreak of disease filled the streets with so many dead that those who went to battle with the Romans had to tread upon their bodies.[4]

What about terrors and heavenly signs? According to Josephus, numerous signs and prodigies were seen before and during the siege of Jerusalem. These included: a star resembling a sword (possibly Halley's Comet); a bright light that shone on the temple for half an hour one night; a cow that was about to be sacrificed gave birth to a lamb; the heavy eastern gate of the inner court opened by itself (it took 20 men to close it); and in the inner court a strange and ominous voice said, "Let us remove hence." These were terrifying omens, but the most dramatic sign was the ethereal sight of armed soldiers and chariots "running about among the clouds" above the cities of Judea (*Wars*, 6.5.3).

> But all these things are merely the beginning of birth pangs. (Matthew 24:8)

If this was a movie, this could be the script:

Jesus: "With all these wars, famines, and earthquakes going on, you're going to think things are bad. You're going to say '*Vey is mir!* Woe is me!' But it could be worse."

Peter: "Jesus, you've just described the most frightening period in Jewish history. How could it possibly get any worse than this?"

Jesus: "Because I haven't told you what they are going to do to *you*."

Jesus is sharing his heart with his four closest friends, Peter, James, John, and Andrew (see Mark 13:3). He's told them about the grim beginning of birth pangs. Now there's a pause in the conversation. He's not done. There's more to come. It's going to be worse, and it's going to affect his friends personally.

---

[1] J. Jacobs and M. Buttenwieser (1906), "Messiah," *Jewish Encyclopedia*, website: http://jewish-encyclopedia.com/articles/10729-messiah, accessed June 29, 2016.

[2] The story of Theudas is recorded in *Antiquities*, 20.5.1. The imposters listed in Acts include: Simon Magus, a Samaritan sorcerer whose stage name was "the Great Power of God," (Acts 8:10); Theudas, not the one who lost his head but another fraudster, and Judas of Galilee, who led a revolt, are both mentioned in Acts 5:36–37.

[3] For New Testament references to famine and famine relief, see Acts 11:28, 1 Corinthians 16:1–4, and Romans 15:26–27. Josephus wrote about the great famine that afflicted Jerusalem in *Antiquities*, 20.2. For earthquakes, see Matthew 27:51–52, 28:2, and Acts 16:26. The earthquake on the eve of the Jerusalem siege was recorded by Josephus in *Wars*, 4.4.5. The prevalence of earthquakes in the first century inspired one commentator to write, "Perhaps no period in the world's history has ever been so marked by these convulsions as that which intervenes between the Crucifixion and the destruction of Jerusalem." Source: C. Ellicott (1878), "Matthew 24:7, *Ellicott's Commentary for English Readers*, website: http://biblehub.com/commentaries/matthew/24-7.htm.

[4] Tacitus (109), *The Annals*, "Book XVI," website: http://classics.mit.edu/Tacitus/annals.-12.xvi.html. Josephus writes about Jerusalem's pestilential outbreak in *Wars*, 6.1.1.

3. TRIALS AND TROUBLES

Then they will deliver you to tribulation and will kill you, and you will be hated by all nations because of my name. (Matthew 24:9)

Mr. Futurist: "Finally, some end-times stuff. This is a reference to the great tribulation that will happen when the antichrist seizes control of the United Nations and begins persecuting the church."

Mr. Preterist: "Where do you get this stuff? Hollywood?"

Mr. Futurist: "It's all in Daniel."

Mr. Preterist: "But Jesus is talking to his disciples. He's saying *you* will be hated and *you* will experience tribulation, and they did. You can't deny it."

And I won't since it's recorded in scripture. The early church went through several persecutions or tribulations, and no one suffered more than the very people to whom Jesus was talking. Consider Peter, who was interrogated by the Sanhedrin (Acts 4:5), imprisoned for execution by Herod (Acts 12:1–4), and ultimately crucified by Nero.

Next to Peter was his brother Andrew who, according to tradition, was also crucified. Then there was James, who was put to death with the sword (Acts 12:2). Of the four people Jesus was speaking to, three were killed on account of his name.

"All nations will hate you," said Jesus. Not just the Jews, but the Gentiles too. Up until now the disciples had only been persecuted by their countrymen. But as they carried the gospel beyond the borders of Israel, that would change. Consider Paul, who was flogged by Jews, stoned by Lystrans, beaten with rods by Philippians, sneered at by Athenians, and beheaded by Romans. His body was a United Nations of bruises, breaks, and beatings.

"They will kill you," said Jesus, and they did. Not just those sitting with Jesus on the mount but the other apostles as well, including Paul who was beheaded in Rome.

Paul preaching on the steps of the Antonia Fortress (Acts 21:40)

Why did Jesus tell the disciples about the awful futures facing them? He wanted them prepared.

Persecution was a fact of life for the first-century believer, and persecution remains a fact of life for many Christians today. It may not involve flogging or beheading, but for some, following Jesus incurs a painful cost. We need to settle it in our hearts that Jesus is worth following no matter what.

But there was another reason why Jesus forewarned them.

> These things I have spoken to you so that you may be kept from stumbling. (John 16:1)

The words of Jesus would uphold the disciples in times of trouble. They would provide strength and comfort and keep them from falling.

> But be on your guard; for they will deliver you to the courts, and you will be flogged in the synagogues, and you will stand before governors and kings for my sake, as a testimony to them … When they arrest you and hand you over, do not worry beforehand about what you are to say, but say whatever is given you in that hour; for it is not you who speak, but it is the Holy Spirit. (Mark 13:9, 11)

Left to their own devices, the disciples might have wilted under pressure. But as they waited in holding cells or were strapped to scourging posts, they remembered the words of Jesus and were encouraged. When brought before the authorities, the Holy Spirit told them what to say, and their inspired speeches were recorded in the scriptures for our edification (e.g., Acts 4:8–13).

As the disciples' stories prove, Jesus' words are powerful. To this day his words bring comfort to those facing persecution.

4. LAWLESSNESS AND COLD LOVE

At that time many will fall away and will betray one another and hate one another. Many false prophets will arise and will mislead many. Because lawlessness is increased, most people's love will grow cold. (Matthew 24:10–12)

Mr. Futurist: "We see this prophecy in the lukewarmness of the modern church and the many heretics writing blogs. The increase of wickedness refers to abortion, the banning of prayer in schools, and our present moral decay."

Mr. Preterist: "Jesus is referring to the Judaizers and the Gnostics, two groups that tried to harm the first-century church. The first group tried to put everyone under law, while the second taught that Jesus was a mere man. The result was that people fell from the faith."

Except Jesus says nothing about falling from the faith. (The word faith is not in the original text.) Rather, he says many will be offended or will offend. He's predicting a general outbreak of treachery, hatred, and lawlessness.

Mr. Futurist: "There's betrayal and hatred in the modern church."

Mr. Preterist: "There was betrayal and hatred in the early church."

It is true that the church has experienced dark times throughout its long and checkered history, and it's true that some first-century Christians were forced to betray their brothers and sisters in the Lord. But for the most part, these were isolated events. The early church was attacked but stood firm.

Jesus is talking about something bigger. He says *many* will offend, betray, and hate, and *most* people's love will grow cold. The word for many or most implies a great number.

Jesus is describing the total collapse of civil society such as happened during the fall of Jerusalem.

Many will betray one another

When Jesus spoke of an increase of lawlessness, Judea was relatively peaceful. But within four decades the province had degenerated into a state of anarchy and civil war. Outlaw gangs roamed the countryside while Jerusalem was riven by factional infighting. If the Romans had never marched on the city, it is likely the city would have self-destructed on account of the hatred and distrust among the various Jewish groups. One story will serve to illustrate.

In the winter of 67–68, a group of fanatics known as the Zealots seized control of the temple precinct. They executed members of King Agrippa's family and appointed their own high priest to replace the one picked by the Herodians.

The people of Jerusalem were horrified by the Zealot's murderous ways and their trampling of religious protocol. They turned to a former high priest called Ananus for guidance. Ananus was esteemed as a venerable and just man. If anyone could keep Jerusalem from imploding, it was him.[1]

About this time a man called John Levi arrived in Jerusalem. He befriended prominent citizens and seemed to support Ananus. But John betrayed the old priest by telling the Zealots that he was doing deals with the Romans. The panicked and outnumbered Zealots sent out a call for help, and 20,000 Idumean (or Edomite) soldiers marched on Jerusalem from the south.

The misinformed Idumeans went through Jerusalem like a hot knife through butter. They killed thousands including Ananus, and the city erupted into factional violence. The downward spiral into chaos and tyranny was sudden and spectacular. One man told a lie and Jerusalem imploded.

Brother will betray brother to death. (Mark 13:12)

Some interpret Christ's words as referring to Christians betraying brothers and sisters, but Jesus was in Jerusalem talking about many people who would be betrayed, hated, and misled. These things happened in the very place where he was sitting.

John's betrayal of Ananus marked the beginning of the end of Jerusalem. But John was not the only snake in the camp. Jesus said many would betray one another and many did. The backstabbing that took place among the Jews was Shakespearean in complexity.[2]

The Zealots thought the Herodians were betraying the city; the priests thought the Zealots were betraying their religion; and the Idumeans killed thousands because they thought they had been betrayed by Ananus when, in fact, they had been betrayed by the Zealots who had been betrayed by John.

After he betrayed Ananus, John usurped the leadership of the Zealots and began terrorizing the city. Matthias, the chief priest, asked a warlord called Simon, son of Giora, to defend Jerusalem against John. But Simon proved to be no better than John for he brought new terrors to the city and killed the priest who employed him.

Soon Jerusalem was split three ways between the traitor (John), the Zealot leader he usurped (Eleazar), and the man hired to kill him (Simon). Each of these tyrants controlled fanatical armies who thought nothing of killing those who got in their way.

Betrayal, hatred, and death. These were the three ingredients of the stew brewing in the cauldron of Jerusalem. It was Jew against Jew and brother against brother. Anger that might have been better focused on a common enemy fueled a civil war that was largely confined within the city's impregnable walls.

Because lawlessness is increased, most people's love will grow cold

In the years leading up to the siege, Jerusalem was Dodge City, and Judea was the Wild West. But why? What had happened in the interval since Christ's death and resurrection? There were many steps on the path to anarchy, but a couple of events stand out.

In AD64, Lucceius Albinus, the departing Roman governor, sought to ingratiate himself with the people of Jerusalem, so he decided to clear the prisons. He executed the worst criminals but released the rest for a bribe. In this way he filled the country with outlaws and robbers.

The incoming governor, Gessius Florus, turned out to be the biggest crook of all. He partnered with gangs, seized private property, and pillaged entire cities. His wickedness brought untold misery to the nation and ultimately provoked the Jews to take up arms against the Romans.

The lawlessness of the new governor spread like cancer. Florus was so brazen in his misdeeds that many adopted him as their patron in crime. Disregard for civil and religious law became normal, and law-abiding citizens lived in fear. The depraved Zealots in particular "trampled upon the laws of men, and laughed at the laws of God" (*Wars*, 4.6.3).

Lawlessness reached its nadir in Jerusalem as armed gangs affiliated with John, Eleazar, or Simon preyed upon each other, plundered homes, and murdered innocent citizens. In their unrestrained depravity, they burned each other's food supplies, creating the conditions for a devastating famine.[3]

"Because lawlessness is increased, most people's love will grow cold." The breakdown in law and order combined with the miseries of the siege-induced famine stifled natural affections, even among families:

> Women snatched the food from the very mouths of their husbands and children, from their fathers, and what was most pitiable of all, mothers from their babes. And while their dearest ones were wasting away in their arms, they were not ashamed to take away from them the last drops that supported life.[4]

Many false prophets will mislead many

According to Josephus "a great number of false prophets" were instrumental in the fall of Jerusalem. These false prophets were employed by the tyrants to pacify and manipulate the populace. The tyrants didn't want people escaping to the Romans, so false prophets were paid to urge people to wait for divine intervention.

A dramatic example of this deception occurred on the night the temple fell. As the Romans were pressing in, a false prophet convinced many to take refuge in the temple precinct. God would come to their aid, he promised. It didn't happen. The Romans burned the temple, and 6,000 women and children hiding in the porticoes were consumed.

To sum up what Jesus has said to the disciples: Jerusalem's going to fall, and you will be persecuted. "Well, that's just wonderful," the disciples might have said. "Any suggestions on how we might stay alive?"

And with a smile, Jesus replies, "I was just coming to that."

---

[1] The religious Jews of Jerusalem esteemed Ananus as venerable and just, but we would probably judge him otherwise. Ananus was one of five high priest sons of the Biblical high priest Ananus or Annas. Annas was the one who had Jesus bound and sent to Caiaphas for

judgment (John 18:24). He was also among those who adjured Peter and John to stop preaching about Jesus (Acts 4:6). Like father, like son. Thirty years later Ananus Junior convened an illegal meeting of the Sanhedrin for the express purpose of executing James the brother of Jesus.

2 Why did John betray Ananus and stir up strife? According to Josephus, it was for no other reason except he was "fond of war" (*Wars*, 4.2.1). Josephus records that the death of Ananus marked "the beginning of the destruction of the city ... the overthrow of her wall, and the ruin of her affairs" (*Wars*, 4.5.2).

3 Neither John Levi nor Simon cared for religious or civil authority, but John defiled the temple by turning it into his stronghold. For this reason some have suggested that John was the man of lawlessness that Paul spoke of in 2 Thessalonians 2:3. However, there are several reasons why he might not have been. First, the lawless man would proclaim himself to be God (2 Thessalonians 2:4), and there is no evidence that John ever did. Second, the lawless man would move in counterfeit signs and wonders (2 Thessalonians 2:9), and John did not. Third, the lawless man was being held back, said Paul writing 20 years earlier (2 Thessalonians 2:7), when John was not yet a man. Fourth, the lawless man would be destroyed by the Lord's return (2 Thessalonians 2:8), while John ended his days in a Roman prison.

4 Eusebius (c. 295), *Church History* (a.k.a. *Historia Ecclesiastica* or *Ecclesiastical History*), 3.6.7.

5. ENDURE TO THE END

Jesus has been painting a grim picture for his disciples. "Things will get bad. There will be betrayal, hatred, and lawlessness. You will personally be hated and hounded,

> but the one who endures to the end, he will be saved. (Matthew 24:13)

Jesus is not saying your salvation hinges on how well you hold up under torture and tribulation. He's giving his disciples an important survival tip. "By your endurance you will gain your lives," is Luke's version of these words. "Not a hair of your head will perish" (Luke 21:18–19).

Jesus said something similar when he sent out the twelve to the lost sheep of Israel:

> You will be hated by all for my name's sake. But he who endures to the end will be saved. (Matthew 10:22, NKJV)

Again, this was not a qualifying test for the kingdom. Jesus was not putting the disciples through boot camp to see if they had the Right Stuff. (They didn't. None of us do.) Jesus is giving practical advice. He's telling the disciples (and us) how to stay alive in the face of persecution.

> Whenever they persecute you in one city, flee to the next. (Matthew 10:23)

In Matthew 10 endure to the end means flee persecution, and it means the same thing in Matthew 24. This good advice is timeless. If trouble is coming, whether under a Roman eagle, a Nazi swastika, or some other banner of death, get out. Run for your life.

Jesus did not say, "I expect you to die for the cause." Instead, he said: "If they persecuted me, they'll persecute you. But while I have to go to the cross and die, you don't have to. My death stands alone. Yours adds nothing to it. So don't throw your life away but stay alive, endure. When they persecute you in one city, flee to the next, and keep telling people the good news."

How to endure to the end when people are waiting to kill you (Acts 9:25)

There may be no better case study of how to endure in the face of persecution than the Apostle Paul. Stoned and left for dead in Lystra, he picked himself and went to Derbe (Acts 14:19–20). Beaten with rods and imprisoned in Philippi, he left shortly after (Acts 16:22–40). When hounded by Judaizers in Berea and Ephesus, Paul upped stakes and moved on (Acts 17:13–15, 20:1).

Paul was no coward, but when facing persecution he typically walked away. He endured, stayed alive, and kept preaching.

Imagine if he hadn't. Imagine if Paul had resisted his persecutors. Instead of leaving Lystra he walked back into town, half-dead, giving the religious Jews another chance to smash in his head. If Paul had ignored the Lord's instruction, he would've died young. He would not have written his epistles, and we wouldn't have most of the New Testament.

Christ's words for the apostles apply equally to us. If you are facing a hostile reaction on account of the gospel, don't stick around waiting to die. Follow Paul's example and walk away. Endure, stay alive, and go preach the gospel someplace else.

6. THE GOSPEL WORLDWIDE

This gospel of the kingdom shall be preached in the whole world as a testimony to all the nations, and then the end will come. (Matthew 24:14)

Mr. Preterist: "Jesus is speaking about AD70 and the end of Jerusalem ..."

Mr. Futurist: "Aha! I've been waiting for this. There's no way this prophecy could have been fulfilled in the first century. America didn't exist. Australia didn't exist. This has to be an end-time prophecy. You cannot say the gospel was preached in the whole world in the generation following Christ's death."

Mr. Preterist: "The Apostle Paul did."

Mr. Futurist: "Say what?"

Mr. Preterist: "Paul told the Colossians that the gospel was 'bearing fruit and growing throughout the whole world' (Colossians 1:6). He also said the gospel they had heard had been 'proclaimed to every creature under heaven' (Colossians 1:23). Paul also told the Romans that their faith was being talked about 'throughout the whole world' (Romans 1:8)."

Mr. Futurist: "Obviously he didn't mean the *whole* world. America, remember? He meant the Roman world."

Mr. Preterist: "Well, then so did Jesus. He meant the world they knew at the time."[1]

Mr. Futurist: "But Jesus says, 'then the end will come,' meaning the end of the world."

Mr. Preterist: "No, he means the end of Jerusalem and the temple. He's been talking about stones coming down, remember?"

Again, I lean towards Mr. Preterist on this point. Jesus is still answering the disciples' first question, namely, when is the temple coming down? He is not answering their question about the end of the age. (He'll get to that later.)

"Preached in the whole world," means preached beyond Judea. The gospel of the kingdom is not just for the Jews; it's for all tribes and nations.

The gospel must first be preached to all the nations. (Mark 13:10)

Taking the gospel to the nations

For Jewish disciples raised under racist religion, this was a new and scandalous idea. It would take some getting used to.

"*All* nations, Jesus?"

"Every last one."

"You mean we should preach to Jews who have traveled abroad, right?"

"Nope, nations as in tribes and ethnic groups."

"But when you said many would come from east and west and recline at Abraham's table' (Matthew 8:11), you didn't mean that the kingdom of heaven is for (gulp), dirty Gentiles?"

"You got it. Everybody's welcome! Red and yellow, black and white, they're all precious in my sight."

"Lord, this is going to take some getting used to."

"I know. I'm going to have to tell you this again and again. Peter, I'm going to send you a rooftop vision to show you that you should not call anyone unclean. Even then you guys are going to be reluctant to leave Jerusalem and go into all the world with my gospel."[2]

The apostles were slow to get going, but led by Paul and others it wasn't long before Christ's words came true. As the scriptures record, the gospel was soon bearing fruit all over the known world.

---

[1] Which was obviously the Roman world or empire. Some Bibles promote this interpretation by adding the word Roman to certain scriptures. For instance, when Agabus the prophet spoke of "a great famine all over the world," the NIV has it as a great famine "over the entire *Roman* world" (Acts 11:28). And when Caesar Augustus decreed that a census be taken of "all the world," the NIV translates it as a census of the "entire *Roman* world" (Luke 2:1).

[2] Jesus reminded the disciples about the mandate for the nations after he rose from the dead (Matthew 28:19), and again before he ascended into heaven (Acts 1:8). Peter's vision is recorded in Acts 10:9-16, and the apostles' reluctance to leave Jerusalem is mentioned in Acts 8:1.

7. THE ABOMINATION OF DESOLATION

Therefore when you see the abomination of desolation, which was spoken of through Daniel the prophet, standing in the holy place (let the reader understand), then those who are in Judea must flee to the mountains. (Matthew 24:15–16)

Mr. Futurist: "When he comes, the antichrist will do something awful in Jerusalem. Watch out!"

Mr. Preterist: "This is about Caligula, who wanted to erect a statue to Zeus in the temple in AD40."

We have come to what may be the most mysterious part of the prophecy. What on earth is the abomination of desolation? "Let the reader understand"? How can he when he doesn't have a clue what Jesus is talking about?

Note that Jesus is quoting Daniel (which he does more than once in Matthew 24), and here is the relevant passage:

Forces from him will arise, desecrate the sanctuary fortress, and do away with the regular sacrifice. And they will set up the abomination of desolation. (Daniel 11:31)

Daniel's prophecy was fulfilled around 170BC when Antiochus Epiphanes, the Greek king of the Seleucid Empire (modern-day Syria) captured Jerusalem. Determined to stamp out the Jews' religion, he erected a statue to Zeus in the temple, turned the temple into a brothel, and sacrificed a pig on the altar. Needless to say, the Jews were unhappy about this, and they revolted.

By using Daniel's words and referring to a well-known historical event, Jesus suggests something similarly offensive was going to happen again, but what and when?

Mr. Preterist: "Jesus was probably referring to the heathen Roman armies marching on Jerusalem. What could be more detestable to a religious Jew than to see their holy city 'trampled underfoot by the Gentiles'?"

Mr. Futurist: "That makes no sense. If the abomination of desolation is the Roman armies marching on Jerusalem, why does Jesus say this offensive thing would be standing in the temple?"

Mr. Preterist: "The Romans set up their pagan ensigns in the temple and made sacrifices to them. To the Jewish mind that would've been an abomination."

Abominable Romans marching in the Holy Land

Mr. Futurist: "I'm not convinced."

Mr. Preterist: "You have to appreciate how big a deal this was. Forty years earlier, Pontius Pilate tried to introduce effigies of Caesar, which were on the ensigns, into the temple. The Jews asked him not to. He said, 'I'll kill anyone who tries to stop me,' so the Jews bared their throats and said, 'We'd rather die than see our laws broken.' Pilate was so stunned by their resolve that he backpedaled and erected the ensigns in Caesarea instead. And I already mentioned how Petronius tried and failed to erect statues in the temple a few years later. It wasn't until AD70 that the Romans got their abominable ensigns into the temple."[1]

Mr. Futurist: "That's all quite fascinating, but the story doesn't fit the prophecy. Jesus said, 'When you see the abomination of desolation standing in the holy place, flee to the mountains.' If you waited until the Romans got as far as the temple, it would have been too late to flee."

Mr. Preterist: "The holy place means the Holy Land in general. When the Romans got to Israel, it was time to flee."

Mr. Futurist: "But the Romans had been in Israel for 100 years. Pontius Pilate, remember?"

Mr. Preterist: "So what do you think the abomination of desolation refers to?"

Mr. Futurist: "Like I said, the antichrist is going to do something offensive in the temple in Jerusalem."

Mr. Preterist: "But there is no temple. The Romans destroyed it."

Mr. Futurist: "The Jews will rebuild it."

Mr. Preterist: "They tried that already, in the fourth century. An earthquake knocked it down. If they tried it now it would trigger World War 3."

Mr. Futurist: "It won't because the antichrist will control the one-world government."

We'll leave Mr. Futurist and Mr. Preterist to argue their points. The fact is, no one knows for sure what Jesus was referring to when he made reference to the abomination of desolation. Commentators have some ideas on this mysterious act of sacrilege (angry Zealots camping in the temple, bickering priests), but it's largely speculation.

But Jesus' words in Matthew 24 may be explained by his words in Luke 21:

Matthew 24:15–16:	Luke 21:20–21:
When you see the abomination of desolation (*eremōsis*) ... flee to the mountains.	When you see Jerusalem surrounded by armies, then recognize that her desolation (*eremōsis*) is near ... flee to the mountains.

The common word in both passages suggests that the abomination of desolation refers to the Roman armies. This interpretation makes sense. If the world's only superpower is marching on your city to destroy it, then it's time to run for the hills.

Then those who are in Judea must flee to the mountains. (Matthew 24:16)

If there was a book entitled *How to Survive the Roman Apocalypse*, the first rule of survival would be flee. Or maybe cardio. When you see the Romans coming, it's time to run, get out, and stay alive, which is what the Christians did. What is surprising is that the Jews didn't do it. After all, running and hiding in the mountains had a long and glorious tradition among the Old Testament Jews. Lot was told to do it when destruction was hanging over Sodom, the Israelites did it when Midian invaded, and David did it when Saul's men pursued him.[2]

But all those flights happened before the Jews got their brilliantly fortified city of Jerusalem.

"No need to run this time, boys. See these walls? They're eight feet thick, and the catapult that can break them hasn't been invented yet."

If only they had listened to Jesus.

---

[1] See *Antiquities*, 18.3.1 and *Wars*, 2.9.2.

[2] And certain Jews did it when the Romans were stomping around Galilee in AD66. Cestius Gallus marched on a city called Zabulon only to find it "deserted by its men, the multitude having fled to the mountains" (*Wars*, 2.18.9). The Old Testament flight references are from Genesis 19:17 (Lot), Judges 6:2 (the Midianite invasion), and 1 Samuel 23:26 (David).

8. TIME TO RUN

> Whoever is on the housetop must not go down to get the things out that are in his house. (Matthew 24:17)

In other words, when you see the Romans coming, run, don't walk. Don't waste time packing your bags. Just grab your kids and go.

Was Jesus exaggerating for effect?

As it happened, there were multiple opportunities to flee in the years leading up to the siege of AD70. When the Roman legions arrived in Israel, it took them the better part of two years to march to Jerusalem. It seems there was plenty of time to pack your bags, sell the house, and buy a wagon.

But recall that Jesus was referring to a specific event, namely the abomination of desolation, which was most likely a reference to the armies approaching Jerusalem.

The Romans came at Jerusalem from three directions simultaneously. One legion marched from Emmaus in the east, another came up the hill from Jericho in the west, and the rest approached from Mt. Scopus in the north. The smart folks would have left already, but if you were in Jerusalem when the Romans came, there was still time to slip away. Provided you legged it.

> Whoever is in the field must not turn back to get his cloak. (Matthew 24:18)

Jesus doesn't mince words. "If you're outside the city when you see the Romans coming, don't go back in."

"But my travel cloak is at home."

"Forget your cloak. Run!"

"But it has these convenient pockets."

"What good does it profit a man if he gains his cloak but gets his head chopped off by a legionary?"

Okay, enough fun. It's easy for us who carry credit cards to joke about this, but spare a thought for the Judean laborer working in the hot sun with barely any clothing. This chap is not going to travel well without his cloak. When he's sleeping rough he's going to want that outer garment. Hence his hesitation. Cloak or no cloak? It's a tough decision, but Jesus makes it easy. "Forget the cloak. Run for your life!"

Travel tips

It's the details that make Christ's prophecy so startling in its practicality. Jesus never laid down rules for what clothes you should or should not wear, but on this occasion he does. Forget your cloak. That little tip probably went right over the disciples' heads, yet these words would prove to be the difference between life and death.

> Those who are in the midst of the city must leave, and those who are in the country must not enter the city. (Luke 21:21)

When the Roman general Titus arrived at Jerusalem, it was the Feast of Passover. Pilgrims were flooding into the city and Titus permitted them to do so. But he didn't permit them to leave.

Imagine you were a Jewish laborer working in the field when the Romans came marching over the hill. Common sense would tell you to run, but was there time to fetch your gear?

You: "Can I go into the city to get my coat?"

Romans: "Sure, go ahead, take your time."

Jesus: "No, run for your life!"

Heed the Roman and you'd be trapped. You'd face a painful death from starvation or a brutal one at the edge of a sword. But listen to Jesus and you'd survive. Surely Jesus has the words of life!

> But woe to those who are pregnant and to those who are nursing babies in those days! (Matthew 24:19)

Traveling when you're pregnant or nursing babies is difficult at the best of times. Imagine what it's like when Romans are chasing you and you are fleeing over rocky Judean countryside. It's a mother's worst nightmare.

Well, in truth it's not. A mother's worst nightmare is being trapped inside a besieged city with no food for her children and no hope of escape. We will learn about one such mother later.

But pray that your flight will not be in the winter, or on a Sabbath. (Matthew 24:20)

Winter was not a good time to travel. The roads were muddy and rough, which is why the kings of old waited until spring before going to war (2 Samuel 11:1). Besides, Jesus said, "Flee to the mountains." This is not obvious to those who perceive the Middle East to be monotonously hot, but it gets cold in Israel. They have ski fields. I have been on the Golan Heights in winter and it was miserably cold.

Hard times for young mothers in the flight from Jerusalem

Why not flee on the Sabbath? Because long journeys on the Sabbath were forbidden (Exodus 16:29). Anyone traveling could expect the gates and doors of the towns to be shut (Nehemiah 13:19–22). There would be no place to stay.[1]

When did the Christians flee?

History records that no Christian was present during the siege of Jerusalem. Every one of them heeded Christ's warning and fled the doomed city. But when did they leave?

The escape of the Christians wasn't a dramatic, one-off exodus but was most likely a slow and steady departure that unfolded over several decades. For instance, Luke records that on the day Stephen was martyred, a full-scale persecution broke out against the church in Jerusalem, and all except the apostles were scattered throughout the regions of Judea and Samaria (Acts 8:1). It sounds as though the city was emptied of Christians. However, a few chapters later we find the Jerusalem church very much alive and well (Acts 15:4). Either those who fled returned, or these were brand new Christians.

In the 40 years between Christ's prophecy and the fall of Jerusalem, there were at least ten major crises that might have prompted the Christians to flee Jerusalem:

AD34: A great persecution against the church leads to a mass exodus of Christians out of Jerusalem.

AD40: Following orders from Emperor Caligula, Publius Petronius, the governor of Syria, marches with two legions to erect statues in Jerusalem and to turn the temple into an imperial shrine. The entire country protests and Israel is pushed to the brink of war.

AD48: A Roman soldier guarding the temple engages in an indecent act, triggering a riot. Soldiers are sent in to restore the peace, but a stampede occurs and more than 10,000 people are trampled to death.

AD62: James the Just, the leader of the Jerusalem church, is murdered by the Sanhedrin.

AD66: Gessius Florus, the Roman procurator of Judea, demands silver from the temple treasury. The Jews revolt; Roman soldiers retaliate and kill nearly 4,000 people. Soon after the Roman garrison in Jerusalem is torched by Jewish assassins.

AD66: Cestius Gallus, the Roman procurator of Syria, marches on Jerusalem with a besieging army. However, with the defenders on the verge of surrender, he inexplicably withdraws.

AD67: General Vespasian is sent by Emperor Nero to crush the Jewish uprising. Cruel and brutal sieges of Galilean towns give those in Jerusalem a clear picture of what to expect.

AD68: Jerusalem degenerates into gang warfare after Ananus, a former high priest, is killed. Meanwhile, in Rome, Nero dies, causing Vespasian to halt his advance.

AD69: Vespasian resumes his march on Jerusalem. However, unrest in Rome compels him to leave for Italy. Jerusalem gets another reprieve.

AD70: Vespasian's son Titus marches on Jerusalem with a besieging force of
60,000. By early summer the city is encircled with an embankment,
and no hope of escape remains.

If you were a Christian living in Jerusalem, and you had the warnings of Jesus
drummed into you by the men who heard them, how long would you have
remained in the city? How many crises would it have taken you to decide
enough is enough?

According to tradition, many Christians fled after the short siege of
Cestius Gallus in AD66. Although the Romans had been defeated, it didn't
take a Ph.D. in first-century political science to figure out that they would
return in larger numbers.

Whether they left then or some other time, Eusebius records that by
AD70, "the royal city of the Jews and the whole land of Judea were entirely
destitute of holy men."[2]

Where did the believers go? They went north. Some went to Pella, on
the far side of the Jordan River (about 50 miles away as the crow flies). But
Christian settlements also sprung up all over the Roman Decapolis (modern-
day Jordan and the Golan Heights).

The exodus of the Christians from Jerusalem is one of the great untold
stories of history. Although the details are forgotten, we know that those who
listened to Christ fled to safety. By the time the Romans came, they had all
gone, every last one.

The words of life

We have covered a lot of bad stuff (birth pangs, persecution) and we are now
about to get to some Really Bad Stuff (the great tribulation). But before we
press on, let's take a moment to digest what Jesus has told the disciples. He's
just given them three keys to survival: He's told them when to flee (when you
see Jerusalem surrounded by armies), how to flee (fast, don't even stop to
pack), and where to flee (to the mountains).

This is practical, down-to-earth stuff. When Jesus says flee to the
mountains he means *flee to the mountains*. It's not a metaphor or a mystery.

Yet it would've seemed strange to the disciples. "Why the mountains,
Jesus? I understand why we wouldn't go east to the Dead Sea or south to the
wilderness, but why not go west to the coast? It's downhill the whole way,

and there are harbors and ships that can carry us to safety. Why not flee to the coast?"

Because the Romans will be there.

Romans on the coastal plain

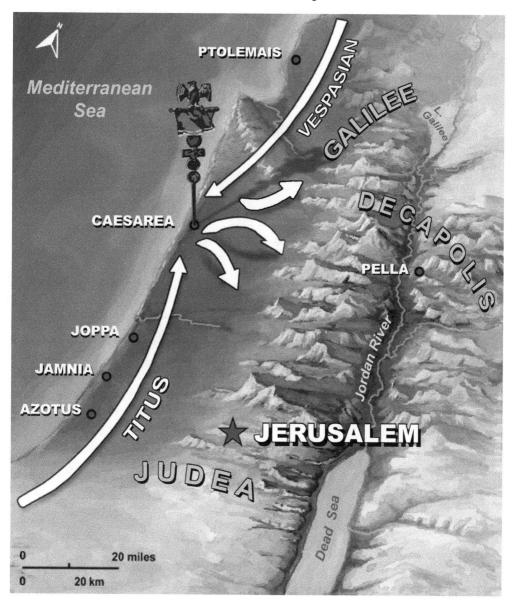

By the late '60s, Israel's coastal plain was crawling with bad guys. Vespasian arrived at Ptolemais on the northern coast, his son marched up from Alexandria far in the south, and together they made their headquarters in Caesarea in the middle. All the coastal towns west of Jerusalem, such as Joppa, Jamnia, and Azotus, were quickly taken by the Romans in AD67. Then all the towns between the coast and Jerusalem were captured in AD68.

If you were trying to flee from the Romans, the coastal route was suicide. Far better to scoot north out of troubled Judea, stay away from occupied Galilee, and find refuge in the hilly but safe towns of the Decapolis. Which is just what the Christians did.

"Flee to the mountains." Jesus' directions would've seemed counter-intuitive to the disciples, like a faulty GPS, but they proved to be pure gold. This is a theme we will return to later in this book: Jesus has the words of life, and those who heed him shall live.

---

[1] Speaking of traveling on the Sabbath: Before he came to Jerusalem, John Levi and his men were entrapped in the Galilean town of Giscala. Titus and 1,000 Roman horsemen had marched on the town, calling for its surrender. John, ever the cunning knave, explained to Titus that would yield, but they could not sign any treaty until the following day on account of it being the Sabbath. Titus was happy to wait until morning and that night John slipped away to Jerusalem.

When he learned of John's duplicity, Titus was furious. But according to Josephus, John's escape was God's doing. The historian wrote that God "preserved this John that he might bring on the destruction of Jerusalem" (*Wars*, 4.2.3). John was possibly the most evil man in Israel. As we have seen, his lies and treachery precipitated the destruction of Jerusalem. Did God help this lying traitor escape the Romans in order to bring about some larger destructive purpose? We'll return to this question in the Chapter 22.

[2] Eusebius, *Church History*, 3.5.3.

9. GREAT TRIBULATION

For then there will be a great tribulation, such as has not occurred since the beginning of the world until now, nor ever will. (Matthew 24:21)

Mr. Futurist: "Okay, I've been listening to all this AD70 nonsense, but a great tribulation unquestionably points to a future time of distress and persecution that will precede the return of Christ."

Mr. Preterist: "No, Jesus is talking about the siege of Jerusalem where as many as a million Jews were starved, tortured, and killed."

Mr. Futurist: "Far more Jews died in the Nazi Holocaust, so how can you say that AD70 was the worst thing that ever happened?"

Mr. Futurist raises a fair question and one that is not easy to answer without quantifying what was truly incalculable suffering. But Mr. Preterist would give two responses: In terms of the atrocities and horrors inflicted upon the Jews, AD70 was a chart-topper, and although more Jews died in the Holocaust, the genocide of AD70 was proportionately greater.[1]

Jesus wept

The destruction of Jerusalem in AD70 was unlike any other disaster that has befallen the city. The tribulation was so great that Jesus wept when he thought about it.

When he approached Jerusalem, he saw the city and wept over it. (Luke 19:41)

In his time on earth only two things made the Son of God cry: the death of his friend Lazarus and the thought of Jerusalem's destruction. For Lazarus he shed tears, but for Jerusalem he wailed and sobbed.[2]

Jesus sobbed because he could see what was coming. He saw the famine with its horrors and the legions with their swords. He saw the streets running with blood and the hills of unburied dead. He saw the end of his people and it wrecked him.

The storm that was coming to Jerusalem was unlike any other. Although the city had been besieged before (by the Assyrians, Babylonians, etc.), the Roman siege of AD70 stands out for a couple of reasons. Inside the city was a larger-than-usual population of locals and pilgrims celebrating the Feast of Passover. Outside the city was the world's most highly trained army. The Jews were fired up by recent victories in their rebellion against the empire, while the Romans were utterly committed to extinguishing their insurrection. It was the perfect storm.

We cannot overstate the Roman resolve in this siege. Past sieges of Jerusalem had been conducted by men with global ambitions. For empire-builders like Sennacherib and Nebuchadnezzar, Jerusalem was but one stop among many. But in AD70 Jerusalem was mission priority number one for Titus and his legions. Suppress Jerusalem and Titus could join his newly crowned father in Rome. But fail and Titus would be the emperor's disgraced son.

Thankfully for Titus, the odds were stacked in his favor. The entire empire, from the emperor to the lowest-ranked legionary, was committed to the success of the siege. Those troublesome Jews had provoked Rome too many times. Assassinations, riots, unpaid taxes, and the annihilation of the Twelfth Legion. (Yes, the Jews actually wiped out a Roman legion. We'll get to that story later.) Such insubordination could not be permitted to spread to the other colonies. The Jews needed to be subdued as an example to others.

Was the siege the great tribulation?

Jesus wept over Jerusalem's imminent demise, but that does not mean the great tribulation he spoke of was fulfilled in AD70. Before we can make that judgment we need to examine the ten signs Jesus listed in connection with the great tribulation:

1. Your enemies will throw up an embankment and surround you (Luke 19:43)
2. False Christs/prophets will arise showing signs and wonders (Matthew 24:24)
3. False leaders will lead people into the desert and inner rooms (Matthew 24:26)
4. There will be great and unprecedented distress (Luke 21:23)

5. People will fall by the sword (Luke 21:24)
6. Nursing mothers will especially suffer (Matthew 24:19, Luke 21:23)
7. The days will be cut short, so not all lives will be lost (Matthew 24:22)
8. Jerusalem will be leveled to the ground, with not one stone left upon another (Luke 19:44)
9. The Jews will be led captive into all the nations (Luke 21:24)
10. Jerusalem will be trampled underfoot by the Gentiles (Luke 21:24)

Were these signs fulfilled in AD70? It's time for us to take a closer look at the events of AD70.

A brief history of the siege of Jerusalem

The siege of Jerusalem was the climax of what became known as the First Jewish–Roman War. According to Josephus, this war was triggered by the greed of the corrupt governor Gessius Florus.[3] Here is the short version. (The full-length movie version can be found in Appendix 1.)

Florus: "I've got two years in this post to feather my nest. You Jews owe me taxes."

Jews: "You greedy governor. You've already robbed us blind. We cannot pay."

Florus: "In that case, I will crucify some of your prominent citizens and help myself to the treasures of your temple."

Jews: "Not the temple! We're going to riot."

The Jews revolted and seized control of the temple. Then they overran the Roman garrison in Jerusalem.

Jews: "This rebellion is going great! Who would've thought such a tiny nation could throw off an empire? God must be with us."

Romans: "We need to put these rebels in their place. Who's nearby? Cestius Gallus is in Syria. Send him in with 30,000 soldiers."

Cestius brought death and terror to Galilee before besieging Jerusalem in late AD66. But after nine days he inexplicably packed up and headed for home. On his way out the Jewish rebels ambushed him at Bethoron and gave his army a real thumping.

Jews: "Haha. In your face Nero!"

Nero: "Oh, that tears it. We are going to teach those Jews a lesson they will be talking about for thousands of years. Send in Vespasian and 60,000 soldiers."

General Vespasian was a seasoned campaigner who had played a prominent role in the invasion of Britain. Vespasian brought such overwhelming force to the north of Israel that many towns practically fainted in fright. Others were brutally suppressed with all their men slaughtered. With Galilee conquered, he turned his attention south, to Judea and Jerusalem.

Around this time Nero committed suicide, triggering turmoil in the capital. Leaving his son Titus to finish the mission, Vespasian returned to Rome to become emperor.

Titus proved to be as capable a military leader as his father. He arrived at Jerusalem with his armies just before the Feast of Passover in AD70. As we have seen, pilgrims from all over were visiting Jerusalem for the feast. Titus

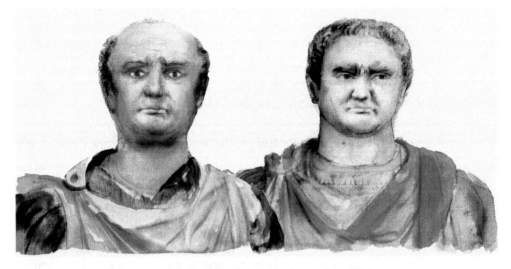

Vespasian and Titus: A father and son demolition team

allowed them to enter the city, but he didn't allow them to leave. As the Roman trap snapped shut, the entire nation was shut up "as in prison."

And what a prison. Right up until the Roman stones and darts came flying, the city was tearing itself apart with factional infighting. With killer Romans outside and murderous gangs inside, the stage was set for a great and terrible tribulation. (Warning: Graphic content ahead.) Jesus said ten things would happen, beginning with this:

Your enemies will build an embankment and surround you (Luke 19:43, 21:20)

"When you see Jerusalem surrounded by armies." It took no less than four Roman legions plus the armies of four client kings to surround Jerusalem, and some of the apostles were alive when it happened. They may not have seen it with their eyes, but they certainly would have heard about it.

When Titus and his legions arrived at Jerusalem, they erected embankments at strategic locations. Later, when it became apparent that the Jews would not surrender, Titus decided to enclose the city. Using rubble taken from Jerusalem's outer wall, the Romans linked their embankments in one unbroken wall.

"Your enemies will build an embankment around you." This was a remarkable prediction: A wall around the entire city of Jerusalem? It was an impossible engineering challenge. No one could do it, yet the Romans pulled it off in three days. As well as cutting off all avenues of escape, the siege wall was meant to shock and awe. Seeing their city sealed off so quickly struck fear into the hearts of the defenders.

The people will fall by the edge of the sword (Luke 21:24)

This is a strange prophecy because embankments and swords don't usually go together. In their earlier siege of the Galilean town of Jotapata, the Romans set up a blockade to starve the city into submission. But for less fortified towns like Gabara and Japha, they went charging in with swords swinging. Different strategies for different conditions. Yet Jesus said both would be adopted, and in AD70 both were.

During the siege of Jerusalem you had a good chance of starving to death or being killed with a sword. Within the city men with swords plundered homes in search of food, while outside the city soldiers slit the bellies of deserters looking for swallowed gold.

When the walls fell, the Romans rushed in, killing everyone they could find. Although they were horrified by the houses full of dead and emaciated bodies, they had no compassion on those who were still alive,

> but they ran every one through whom they met with, and obstructed the very lanes with their dead bodies; and made the whole city run down with blood, to such a degree indeed, that the fire of many of the houses was quenched with these men's blood. (*Wars*, 6.8.5)

The Romans slew those who fought and those who fled. They killed the young and the old, the healthy and the infirm. They killed and killed until they grew "tired with killing men."

There will be great distress upon the land and wrath to this people (Luke 21:23)

The fall of Jerusalem in AD70 was unprecedented in horror and magnitude. By first-century standards, the number of deaths was simply mind-boggling. In a city that was home to around 200,000, more than a million people died.[4]

Allowing Passover pilgrims into the city was a dirty trick because it added pressure to already-limited food supplies. (The tyrants had burned the grain stores just a few weeks earlier.) The resulting famine brought unspeakable misery to those trapped inside. People searched the sewers and dunghills looking for scraps of food, and the houses were full of the dead and dying. More than 600,000 bodies were thrown out of the city gates, and the lanes were filled with bodies. Children with swollen bellies walked among the corpses like shadows until they, too, fell.

In desperation, people ate everything. They ate their shoes and gnawed the leather off their shields. They ate hay and even things animals would not touch.

Starvation drove many Jews over the wall, but those caught by the Romans were crucified atop their embankment. This horrific act was meant to frighten the defenders into surrender. It didn't work. The starving continued to flee because they esteemed death from their enemies, even a brutal death by crucifixion, to be preferable to the slow death of starvation. At one point the Romans were crucifying as many as 500 people per day. There were so many crucifixions that the Romans ran out of wood.

Jesus said, "There will be great and unprecedented distress" and there was. The siege of Jerusalem was genocide on an industrial scale, a first-century holocaust. In words reminiscent of Christ's prophecy, Josephus said the siege of Jerusalem exceeded all "the misfortunes of men from the beginning of the world."[5]

Nursing mothers will especially suffer (Luke 21:23)

To be a mother in Jerusalem during the hellish months of AD70, with no food and with gangs of thieves stealing everything they could eat, was the ultimate nightmare.

> How dreadful it will be in those days for pregnant women and nursing mothers! (Luke 21:23, NIV)

One particularly sad story stands out. During the siege, a once-wealthy woman called Mary was robbed again and again until her cupboards were bare. There was nothing for her or her nursing son to eat, yet every day thieves broke into her house looking for food. The poor woman eventually snapped. Indignant at the repeated home invasions she'd been forced to endure, she killed and cooked her only child. The thieves smelled the roasting meat and broke into her house again. They threatened to cut her throat if she didn't reveal her secret food so she showed them what remained of her son. Aghast, the thieves backed out, trembling and empty-handed. Mary's story spread and soon the whole city was horrified. Even the Romans were shocked.

When you read stories like these you begin to understand why Jesus, on his way to be crucified, stopped to address the women who were weeping for him:

> Daughters of Jerusalem, stop weeping for me, but weep for yourselves and for your children. For behold, the days are coming when they will say, "Blessed are the barren, and the wombs that never bore, and the breasts that never nursed." (Luke 23:28–29)

They will level you to the ground and not leave in you one stone upon another (Luke 19:44)

"Those stones are coming down," said Jesus pointing to the temple. This, too, was a strange prophecy, because why would the Romans, those historic curators of art, want to destroy one of the wonders of the ancient world? The Romans were builders, not Vandals or Goths. Sure, they had to punish the Jews for their insubordination, but why pull down the temple? It would have been an unRomany thing to do.

Indeed, Titus didn't want to damage the temple. But in the heat of battle, a soldier, without waiting for orders and being "hurried on by a divine fury," thrust a burning brand through a temple window. Titus rushed to the temple and tried to stop the fire, but his men had the wind up and were too busy killing Jews. So the temple burned, but did the stones come down? Were the Lord's words fulfilled in AD70, or did the temple come down at a later date?

There's an old tale of how the Roman soldiers pulled the stones apart to get the gold that had melted during the burning of the temple. Although this story has been widely circulated, there is no evidence that it happened. Josephus never mentions it, and since his is the only account we have, we must doubt its veracity.

However, Josephus does record that after the siege Titus ordered the temple's demolition. Although it was a notable landmark, it had been the cause of so much trouble that it had to go.

But was this order carried out? Is there any proof that the temple was demolished?

We can be sure it was because Simon, one of the rebel leaders, went to ground during the last days of the siege only to emerge some time later "in the place where the temple had formerly been" (*Wars*, 7.2.1).

The temple that had stood, in one form or another, for 586 years was no more. Indeed, most of the city was leveled to the ground save for a part of the wall and a few towers that the Romans kept for themselves.[6]

"Recognize that her desolation is near," said Jesus. As a result of the siege, Jerusalem became an unrecognizable pile of rocks and rubble. Much of the surrounding countryside had been deforested, and suburbs once adorned with trees and pleasant gardens no longer existed. Judea had become a wasteland.[7]

They will be led captive into all the nations (Luke 21:24)

After the siege 97,000 Jews were led away to captivity, some to work the mines in Egypt, others to be killed in provincial circuses. The tall and the beautiful were paraded in Rome as part of Vespasian and Titus' joint triumph, while those under the age of seventeen were sold as slaves.

Some of those taken captive did not live long. While being processed in Jerusalem, 11,000 captives died of starvation. Others were slain before the year was out (*Wars*, 6.9.2).

When he returned to Caesarea a few weeks after the siege, Titus celebrated his brother Domitian's birthday by having Jewish captives fight one other. Others were killed by wild beasts or burned. Altogether two and a half thousand Jews died for the entertainment of the victorious general (*Wars*, 7.3.1).

Jerusalem will be trampled underfoot by the Gentiles (Luke 21:24)

When Jesus uttered these words, Jerusalem was very much a Jewish city. But that ended when the Gentile feet of the Romans and their allied armies trampled the city in AD70. From that point on, Jerusalem's history would be shaped by non-Jewish people.

Romans plundering the treasures of Jerusalem

Jerusalem was destroyed twice by Roman legions (in AD70 and 136) and rebuilt twice by Roman Emperors (Hadrian in 130 and Constantine in 335). It was ruled by more than a dozen Gentile nations including the Byzantines, Persians, Ottomans, Crusaders, Mamluks, along with various Arab Caliphates. In the last century, the city was ruled by the British (1917–1948) and partly ruled by Arabs (1948–1967).

Today Jerusalem is once again a predominantly Jewish city, but one that is divided along religious and ethnic lines. The city's population is a little over 800,000 of which one-third are Muslim, and a small percentage are Christian.

For nearly two millennia Jerusalem has been home to Gentiles, or non-Jewish people. If one were to pick a date when the Gentiles first trampled the city with their heathen feet, there would be no better candidate than the summer of AD70.

We have looked at seven of the ten tribulation signs and seen that all were fulfilled in AD70. The remaining three signs are listed in Matthew 24:22–26.

---

[1] The 150-day siege of Jerusalem was the world's deadliest successful siege. I say successful, because the "unsuccessful" 900-day German siege of Leningrad in WWII killed more. Source: "10 of the deadliest sieges in history," Listverse, website: http://listverse.com/2014/01/21/-10-of-the-deadliest-sieges-in-history/

[2] Jesus wept for Lazarus (John 11:35) and the word is *dakruo*̄ (1145), which means to shed tears. Jesus wept over Jerusalem (Luke 19:41) and the word is *klaio*̄ (2799), which means to sob and wail aloud.

[3] What would prompt a small nation to take up arms against an empire? According to Josephus, "it was this Florus who necessitated us to take up arms against the Romans, while we thought it better to be destroyed at once, than by little and little." Florus did everything he could to inflame a Jewish revolt because he believed war would conceal his atrocities from Caesar. The war began in the second year of Florus' tenure as governor (*Antiquities*, 20.1.1 and *Wars*, 2.14.3).

[4] The numbers are so shocking that many historians can't accept them. How did Josephus come up with such incredible figures? By his reckoning, the population of Jerusalem at the time of the siege had swollen to about three million people on account of the pilgrims visiting for Passover. It's a huge number but Josephus has evidence to support it. When Cestius Gallus visited the city four years earlier, he asked the high priests if there was a way to determine the city's population during Passover. "Count the sacrifices," said the high priest. "Every year we do 256,500 sacrifices and one sacrificial lamb will serve for ten people and sometimes as many as twenty." (Thirteen people shared one Passover lamb at the Last Supper (Luke 22:7–8).) Multiply one number by the other and you get about three million people. And this figure excludes the ritually unclean as well as foreigners who did not participate in the Feast (*Wars*,

6.9.3). Incidentally, no one knows what the residential population of Jerusalem was at the time and credible estimates range from 80,000 to 600,000.

[5] *Wars*, preface, 4.

[6] Herod's Temple was only 60 years old or so, but it had been built on the site of an earlier, smaller temple built by Zerubbabel in the sixth century BC. The construction of Zerubbabel's Temple is recorded in the Book of Ezra.

[7] The devastation of the city was so extensive that Josephus said travelers familiar with Jerusalem would no longer recognize it (*Wars*, 6.1.1).

10. SHORTENED DAYS

> Unless those days had been cut short, no life would have been saved; but for the sake of the elect those days will be cut short. (Matthew 24:22)

Sieges could last years and Jerusalem was a tough nut to crack. When he erected his barricade around the city, Titus could have expected to be camped outside Jerusalem for years. As it was, he penetrated the outer walls in a matter of weeks and was all done and dusted in a little over five months. This was a mercy, for it meant the deaths attributable to starvation were limited, as Christ had prophesied.

But how did Titus succeed so quickly? How did he manage to penetrate Jerusalem's solid defenses? According to Josephus, his loyal chronicler, Titus attributed his victory to God:

> We have certainly had God for our assistant in this war, and it was no other than God who ejected the Jews out of these fortifications; for what could the hands of men, or any machines, do towards overthrowing these towers? (*Wars*, 6.9.1)

Did God give Jerusalem to the Romans? Was he an "assistant" to the enemy forces? We can take these words with a pinch of salt because Josephus was hardly an unbiased writer. When he wrote them Titus was Caesar and Josephus was hardly likely to portray his patron as a genocidal war criminal responsible for the deaths of a million noncombatants. No, Titus was a pawn in the hands of an angry God, an innocent agent of heaven's divine vengeance.[1]

Which just goes to show you that you shouldn't believe everything you read in history books.

There are three prosaic reasons why the siege of Jerusalem ended sooner than expected. The first was the might of the Romans. The invaders were organized, mechanized, and led by an ambitious young man in a hurry. They were also battle-hardened and well-trained by their experience subduing Galilee.

The second reason was the city's defenders were weakened by starvation. The famine was so severe that hundreds of thousands perished while many of those who lived longed for death.

The Roman assault on Jerusalem in AD70

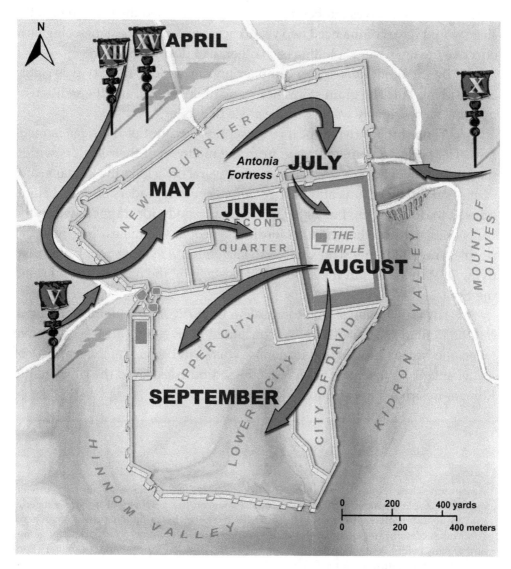

But the biggest reason why Jerusalem fell so quickly was the city was defended by people who spent half their time killing each other.

The politics were complicated and fluid, but when the siege began there were two groups fighting for control of Jerusalem. On one side were the Zealots, a group of 6,000 angry young men led by John Levi, and on the other was Simon the warlord with his army of 10,000. (Eleazar had little influence at this point.)

The fighting between these two groups was so fierce it's a marvel they didn't wipe themselves out before the Romans breached the wall. In fact, the siege would have commenced two years earlier except Vespasian, seeing how effective the Jews were at killing each other, had decided to wait.

By the time Titus set up camp around Jerusalem, the city was rotten and ready to fall. The grain stores had gone up in smoke, and the sedition or uprising had seriously weakened the city's defenses.

A word that often appears in Josephus' account of the siege is madness. The populace suffered more from the madness of their leaders within than the might of the Romans without. On several occasions, the Romans said, "Let's end this siege amicably and go home," but the leaders of the rebellion refused to do anything but fight. This was a tragedy for trapped within the walls were tens of thousands of ordinary people – families, pilgrims, old people, and children – who wanted to surrender. Anything was better than dying of starvation. But they were held hostage by the mad men who ruled the city.

The Babylonian siege of Jerusalem of 587BC lasted eighteen months, but the Roman siege of AD70 was concluded in five. Jerusalem would have fallen one way or another, but its demise was swift because of the madness of its defenders. As Josephus observed, "the sedition destroyed the city, and the Romans destroyed the sedition" (*Wars*, 5.6.1).

---

[1] Apparently Titus refused to accept a wreath of victory because he saw "no merit in vanquishing people forsaken by their own God." However, these noble words Titus allegedly said are at odds with what Titus actually did, which was celebrate like a big-dog Roman hero. After his successful siege, Titus went on a multi-country celebration tour marked by games and crowns before being awarded a triumph – a kind of ticker tape parade for military conquerors – on his return to Rome (*Wars*, 7.5.5–6).

11. COUNTERFEIT CHRISTS

Then if anyone says to you, "Behold, here is the Christ," or "There he is," do not believe him. For false Christs and false prophets will arise and will show great signs and wonders, so as to mislead, if possible, even the elect. Behold, I have told you in advance. So if they say to you, "Behold, he is in the wilderness," do not go out, or, "Behold, he is in the inner rooms," do not believe them. (Matthew 24:23–26)

Mr. Futurist: "This has to be about these last days in which we live, for we are bombarded with false teachers and false prophets. Take these hyper-grace preachers, for instance ..."

Mr. Preterist: "If you knew anything about history you would know that after Christ's death many false men promised deliverance from the Romans."

Jesus is not repeating his earlier and more general warnings of verses 4–5 and verse 12, for this warning is specific to the great tribulation. "When things are at their worst, if someone stands up and says, 'I'm the Messiah, here to save you,' don't believe him." False leaders exploit the fears of the day by promising deliverance, but their phony pledges only make things worse.

As usual, Jesus is very specific, noting that false prophets will draw people to two sorts of places; the wilderness or the inner rooms. Not long after Jesus ascended into heaven, an Egyptian false prophet led 4,000 followers out into the wilderness (Acts 21:38). If this was the same Egyptian false prophet that Josephus wrote about, hundreds of his followers were killed by the Romans. Despite this tragic outcome the Jews didn't seem to learn, and the pattern of deception and death repeated itself again and again.[1]

The inner rooms or chambers may be a reference to the temple where the crazy Zealots holed up for three years in their struggle against the rest of the world. (The Romans torched these rooms and everything in them.) Or it could be a reference to the fortress of Masada where the Zealots were later besieged by the Romans. (Those inside committed mass suicide.) It doesn't matter where the inner rooms were, the lesson is plain enough: Listen to Jesus and live, or follow false prophets and die.

For just as the lightning comes from the east and flashes even to the west, so will the coming of the Son of Man be. (Matthew 24:27)

Mr. Futurist: "Let me guess – you think this is about Jesus coming back in AD70."

Mr. Preterist: "The Romans marched from east to west, and when they did the Son of Man came on Jerusalem in judgment. Lightning is a picture of the Lord's terrifying wrath."[2]

Mr. Futurist: "You gotta be kidding. Surely Jesus is talking about his future return to earth, his Second Coming."

So far I have leaned towards Mr. Preterist, but I'm with Mr. Futurist on this one. Jesus is not changing the subject; he's giving us the authentic so that we won't be fooled by the counterfeit. "Don't fall for false messiahs who mislead people with their signs and wonders. The signature of my return will be like this."

One characteristic of false messiahs and false prophets is they draw their followers away to secret places. They set up compounds in the wilderness and hold covert meetings in hidden chambers. Secrecy and seclusion are their trademarks, but the return of the true King will be no secret event. It will be glorious, public, and known from east to west. Jesus will say more about his return later in Matthew 24.

---

[1] The fate of the Egyptian and his followers is recorded in *Antiquities*, 20.8.6. On another occasion a group of imposters persuaded the multitudes to follow them into the wilderness. Signs and wonders were promised, but most of those who fell for it were killed by cavalry and infantry sent by Felix, the governor of Judea (*Wars*, 2.13.4). Sadly, the Jews did not learn from this tragedy because not long after they marched out into the wilderness behind another phony. This group was slaughtered by Porcius Festus, the governor after Felix (*Antiquities*, 20.8.10). Even that wasn't the end of it, for next came Jonathan the weaver who convinced the poor and uneducated to follow him into the desert. Again "signs and apparitions" were promised, and again those who went out were either slaughtered or captured by the Romans (*Wars*, 7.11.1–2).

[2] Mr. Preterist may be thinking of Ezekiel 21:28: "Thus says the Lord God concerning the sons of Ammon and concerning their reproach: 'A sword, a sword is drawn, polished for the slaughter, to cause it to consume, that it may be like lightning'." Incidentally, the Romans didn't march on Jerusalem from east to west. They started out in Caesarea (in the northwest) and approached Jerusalem from three directions simultaneously.

12. THE EAGLES ARE COMING

For wherever the carcass is, there the eagles will be gathered together. (Matthew 24:28, NKJV)

Mr. Preterist: "Easy one. The carcass is Jerusalem and the eagles are on the Roman ensigns."

Mr. Futurist: "Not so fast. Jesus says something similar in Luke 17:37 where he is clearly talking about his Second Coming. The carcass or corpse is his crucified body and the eagles are the saints gathered about him."

Mr. Futurist may be overthinking this. The main thrust of the Olivet Discourse has (so far) been the destruction of Jerusalem. Jesus' words about gathering eagles sound proverbial as much as prophetic: There's a dead body with birds of prey around it. (Some translations say vultures instead of eagles.) In other words, the city is doomed. "Jerusalem, you're going to die and get picked over."

But let's stick with the eagle theme for a moment because there's an interesting temple aspect to it.

When Herod the Great built the temple, he stuck a golden eagle on its gate, perhaps as a nod to Roman benevolence. The religious Jews, while thrilled with their new temple, were unhappy about the shiny bird.

"What blasphemy! Doesn't Herod know we forbid the making of images?"

In a fit of religious fervor, a couple of scholars incited some zealous young men to pull the eagle down. Furious, Herod had the ringleaders burned alive, but that was the end of it. Herod died not long after, and that was the last anyone saw of the offensive eagle.

Jesus was born around the time this happened, and growing up, he no doubt heard stories about the controversial eagle. And this is what makes Christ's prophecy all the more intriguing.

Picture the scene: Jesus is on a hill overlooking a temple that once had an eagle on it. So when Jesus points to this building and mentions gathering eagles, his listeners would have paid particular attention.

Eagles are coming.

Four years before the siege of AD70 an eagle showed up outside the walls of Jerusalem. This eagle was the ensign of the famous Twelfth Legion, the *XII Fulminata* or Thunderbolt Legion originally levied by Julius Caesar. The legion and their eagle had come with Cestius Gallus to besiege Jerusalem, but they didn't stay long.

One legion equals one eagle and one eagle hardly constitutes a gathering. So this was not the fulfillment of Christ's prophecy. Indeed, the only dead bodies at the end of this ill-fated siege were Roman ones. During its withdrawal, the Twelfth Legion was defeated by Jewish forces at Bethoron. The Romans lost most of their men, their siege weapons, and their *aquila* or eagle.

For a Roman legion to lose its eagle standard was a devastating blow. It was like losing its soul. The Romans would move heaven and earth to retrieve a lost eagle.[1]

Less than a year after the defeat at Bethoron the Romans returned to Israel in strength. This time they meant business.

Cestius Gallus had marched on Jerusalem with one legion, but in AD70 Titus returned with four: the Fifth, the Tenth, the Fifteenth, and a reconstituted Twelfth. It was an impressive display of strength, with 60,000 soldiers and auxiliaries in total. With such massive numbers the Romans were confident of success.

One legion or eagle had not been sufficient to do the job, but four eagles were more than enough.

And when Jerusalem fell, an emaciated and dismembered carcass, there the eagles were gathered.

This eagle came to Jerusalem twice

PART A: The Last Prophecy

---

[1] The loss and retrieval of the *Fulminata's aquila* is the subject of a 2012 novel called *The Eagle of the Twelfth*. In it author MC Scott speculates that the legions of Cestius Gallus lost many of their siege weapons in an ambush in Bethoron on their way *to* Jerusalem. (Josephus only records the loss of the beasts of burden.) Significantly, their ram was captured and destroyed. Lacking the weapons needed to crack Jerusalem, a siege seemed pointless. Besides, Cestius Gallus was ill. So the Romans headed back the way they came, only to be slaughtered in the same pass where they had previously been ambushed. In this fictional account, two survivors of the ambush journey into enemy territory to retrieve their lost eagle.

13. SUN AND MOON

But immediately after the tribulation of those days the sun will be darkened, and the moon will not give its light, and the stars will fall from the sky, and the powers of the heavens will be shaken. (Matthew 24:29)

Mr. Futurist: "These cosmic catastrophes refer to the return of Christ. It's the end of the world as prophesied by Joel."[1]

Mr. Preterist: "Nope, these are Jewish idioms. The sun, moon, and stars refer to governing authorities, as in Joseph's dream when they bowed to him. It's the Jewish equivalent of, 'The sky is falling.'"

It's hard to miss the parallel between Christ's words and those of the Old Testament prophets. For instance, when Isaiah foretold of Babylon's destruction, he said:

> For the **stars** of heaven and their constellations will not flash forth their light; the **sun** will be dark when it rises, and the **moon** will not shed its light. (Isaiah 13:10)

And Ezekiel used similar language when he prophesied the downfall of Pharaoh:

> When I extinguish you, I will cover the heavens and darken their **stars**; I will cover the **sun** with a cloud, and the **moon** will not give its light. (Ezekiel 32:7)

The sun and stars did not literally go dark when Babylon and Egypt fell over. The prophets used figurative language and so does Jesus when speaking of Jerusalem. He's not saying the solar system is going to collapse. He's saying, "The lights are about to go out on Jerusalem and the old religious system."

> There will be signs in sun and moon and stars, and on the earth dismay among nations, in perplexity at the roaring of the sea and the waves, men fainting from fear and the expectation of the things which are

coming upon the world; for the powers of the heavens will be shaken. (Luke 21:25–26)

In Luke's account of the prophecy, Jesus mentions the sun, moon, and stars, but also adds the roaring of the sea and the waves and men fainting with fear. Again, this is figurative. Jesus could be referring to the legions of Rome that would sweep tsunami-like across Galilee and the waves of soldiers soon to crash upon Judea.

"Dismay among the nations," describes the bewildered reaction of Rome's client states to the slaughter of the Jews. "They killed a million people? What might they do to us?" Or it could be a reference to the misery of the relocated captives. There's a tragic symmetry here. While the apostles were taking the good news of Jesus worldwide, 97,000 Jewish prisoners were exporting the bad news of Rome.

"The powers of the heavens will be shaken" is likely a reference to the temple (for reasons that will be explained in Chapter 17). This shakeable building can be contrasted with the unshakeable kingdom of heaven (Hebrews 12:26–27). One is manmade and frail; the other is God-made and everlasting.

When will the lights go out in Jerusalem? Not in the distant future when Christ returns, but "immediately after" the tribulation of the Roman siege. This conclusion is plain as day.

As Adam Clarke said, "The sun is the religion of the Church; the moon is the government of the state, and the stars are the judges and doctors of both."[2] After the Romans were done killing and burning, the sun and moon of Jewish society were darkened, the religious stars had fallen, and the power of the heavenly temple had been thoroughly shaken.

Mr. Preterist: "That's what I said. In AD70 the temple was destroyed, and the old covenant came to an end."

Wait, who said anything about the old covenant? We are talking about a building.

As we will see, it is vitally important to the preterist position to have the old covenant continuing until AD70. Everything hangs on it, for the old

Night falls on Israel

covenant gives permission for God to smite the Jews with divine vengeance. The problem, of course, is that Jesus died well before AD70 and there was a new covenant in town.

There is no question that the temple of Jerusalem came crashing down in AD70, ending the ritual sacrifices practiced in that city. But did that mark the end of the old covenant? And, if so, does that mean God played a role in the destruction of Jerusalem? These are profoundly important questions with huge ramifications for us, as we shall see in Chapter 22. But for now, we will continue our verse-by-verse study of the Olivet Discourse.

---

[1] Mr. Futurist is no doubt thinking of Joel 2:30–32: "I will display wonders in the sky and on the earth, blood, fire, and columns of smoke. The sun will be turned into darkness and the moon into blood before the great and awesome day of the Lord comes. And it will come about that whoever calls on the name of the Lord will be delivered." This could be a reference to a future Judgment Day, but since Peter quotes these verses in Acts 2:19–21 in connection with the Day of Pentecost, we should be open to other possibilities.

[2] Adam Clark, Commentary on Matthew 24, website: www.studylight.org/commentaries/-acc/matthew–24.html

14. THE SON OF MAN IN HEAVEN

Then will appear the sign of the Son of Man in heaven. And then all
the peoples of the earth will mourn when they see the Son of Man
coming on the clouds of heaven, with power and great glory.
(Matthew 24:30, NIV)

Mr. Futurist: "This is about Christ returning from heaven and coming back to
earth."

Mr. Preterist: "This is about Christ coming in judgment on Jerusalem."

It's neither. It is Jesus coming into his kingdom with power and glory. Note
that Jesus is quoting Daniel (as he has done before in Matthew 24). Here is the
relevant passage:

> In my vision at night I looked, and there before me was one like **a son
> of man, coming with the clouds** of heaven. He approached the
> Ancient of Days and was led into his presence. He was given auth-
> ority, **glory and sovereign power**; all nations and peoples of every
> language worshiped him. His dominion is an everlasting dominion
> that will not pass away, and his kingdom is one that will never be
> destroyed. (Daniel 7:13–14, NIV)

In Daniel's vision, Jesus is seen to be coming (not going) to heaven because
the prophet is in heaven watching his glorious and triumphant arrival. When
did this happen? Not in AD70 but 40 years earlier when Jesus ascended into
heaven. It happened,

> when (God) raised (Christ) from the dead and seated him at his right
> hand in the heavenly places, far above all rule and authority and
> power and dominion, and every name that is named, not only in this
> age but also in the one to come. (Ephesians 1:20–21)

Verse 30 is probably the most contentious passage in Matthew 24, but let
scripture interpret scripture and Jesus' prophecy is not hard to explain. Has
Christ been raised from the dead? Then the prophecy has been fulfilled. Has

Jesus been given a name above all names? Then the prophecy has been ful-filled. Is he seated at God's right hand in heavenly places above all rule and authority and power and dominion? Then the prophecy has been fulfilled.

We can draw a straight line from Daniel 7 (distant prophecy) through Matthew 24 (near prophecy) to Ephesians 1 (prophecy fulfilled). To say the prophecy remains unfulfilled is like saying Jesus is not crowned and he's not in heaven.

Here's more proof that Jesus is on the throne:

> Being found in appearance as a man, he humbled himself by becoming obedient to the point of death, even death on a cross. For this reason also, God highly exalted him and bestowed on him the name which is above every name. (Philippians 2:8–9)

Apparently, the New Testament Christians sang these words as a hymn, which meant they understood the Son of Man was enthroned in heaven. But how did they know? The apostles told them. The men who witnessed Christ's ascension understood that they had seen Daniel's prophecy had come true.

Table 1: Coming on the clouds

	Coming on clouds	Sitting at right hand	People mourn
Matthew 24:30	●		●
Matthew 26:64	●	●	
Mark 13:26	●		
Mark 14:62	●	●	
Luke 21:27	●		
Revelation 1:7	●		●

Coming on the clouds

The "Son of Man coming on the clouds" phrase comes from Daniel, but it appears six times in the New Testament. Each time it is mentioned in connection with Christ's ascension and exaltation. When we look at these six scriptures side by side, we find they share some common elements, as shown in the table.

When the Son of Man comes on the clouds he ends up sitting at the right hand of God while the people mourn. It sounds cryptic, but it isn't. It's simply a three-legged stool.

"Sitting at right hand" comes from a psalm Jesus liked to quote when talking to the Pharisees and law teachers in the temple.[1]

Jesus would ask, "If the Messiah is the son of David as you say, how is it that David calls him Lord?" The religious leaders didn't know what to say, but Peter did:

> For it was not David who ascended into heaven, but he himself says: "The Lord said to my Lord: 'Sit at my right hand until I make your enemies a footstool for your feet.'" Therefore let all the house of Israel know for certain that God has made him both Lord and Christ – this Jesus whom you crucified. (Acts 2:34–36)

Psalm 110, which is the psalm Jesus was quoting, is about the ascension. Sitting at the right hand refers to Christ's exaltation from servant to supreme ruler of all. "It was not David who ascended," said Peter, "But this Jesus whom you killed."

And how did the Jews respond to this news?

> When they heard this, they were pierced to the heart, and said to Peter and the rest of the apostles, "Brethren, what shall we do?" (Acts 2:37)

They were pierced or upset or deeply troubled, which brings us to the third leg of the stool.

"The peoples (or tribes) of the earth (or land) will mourn." Jesus said the Jews would mourn when they realized they had crucified the Messiah, and six weeks later 3,000 did. Then they repented and got baptized.

But many of the Jerusalem Jews did not mourn, not right away. That would come later.

So far, so good. But what is the *sign* of the Son of Man that appears in the sky? And what does this have to do with the fall of Jerusalem?

What is the sign of the Son of Man in heaven?

Daniel's prophecy is evidently not well-known for some have offered fantastic interpretations of verse 30's heavenly sign. Some say it was a cross that appeared in the sky around the time of the Roman siege. Others say it was Jesus himself returning (a second coming before *the* Second Coming). Mr. Preterist would say the sign was the divine vengeance Jesus unleashed on Jerusalem.

Mr. Preterist: "And what more dramatic sign could there be than Jesus destroying Jerusalem?"

You may be surprised to learn that many eminent theologians would agree with Mr. Preterist. Matthew Henry said AD70 was "when Christ came to destroy the Jewish nation by the Roman armies." John Gill said Matthew 24:30 was about Jesus coming to the Jews to "give the finishing stroke to the destruction of that people." And Albert Barnes said the passage was most likely about the Son of Man "coming to destroy the city of Jerusalem."[2]

It's incredible that Jesus, of all people, would talk about returning to destroy Jerusalem (and I don't believe he did), but there are Old Testament scriptures one could draw on to make this connection. For instance, one might refer to those Old Testament passages that speak of God coming in destructive judgment on some city or nation (e.g., Isaiah 19:1, Joel 2:1–2). Or one might consider those verses that portray God riding on clouds (e.g., Jeremiah 4:13). But Jesus is not quoting those passages; he's quoting Daniel 7, which has nothing to do with judgment.

When did Jesus come into his kingdom? Mr. Preterist would say it happened in AD70 for no other reason than there was a big fire. "Clouds and smoke signify Christ coming to his temple in judgment, power, and glory." But such a conclusion is based on a mishmash of Old Testament prophecies and scriptures about unrelated comings. Jesus did not come into his kingdom in AD70 but 40 years earlier when he ascended into heaven.

So what is the sign to which Jesus is referring? The Interlinear Bible translates his words like this:

Then will appear the sign of the Son of Man in heaven.[3]

Who's in heaven? Not the sign but the Son. And what is the sign? It is Daniel's vision come true. It is Jesus sitting enthroned at the right hand of God. It is heaven's vindication for the One rejected by the Jews.

But how would the unbelieving Jews know that Jesus was sitting at the right hand of God? How would they see, as Daniel had, the Son of Man coming on the clouds of heaven?

They would know because his prophecies were all coming true. Jesus said there would be famines, earthquakes, and great distress, and there were. He said Jerusalem would be surrounded by armies, and it was. He said the temple stones would come down, and they did.

Jesus made no less than 40 specific prophecies about the fall of Jerusalem – they are listed in Chapter 16 – and all of them were fulfilled within 40 years. Each prophecy-come-true was a sign pointing to the One who had come on the clouds and now sat enthroned in heaven.

When did the disciples see the sign?

The tribes mourned, but the disciples rejoiced after they saw the Lord ascend to heaven (Luke 24:52). They rejoiced because Daniel's prophecy was coming true right before their eyes. Jesus was going to receive his crown.

(How awesome would this be in a movie? Picture the disciples on the Mount of Olives watching the Son of Man ascending into heaven and dis-appearing into a cloud (Acts 1:9). Now cutaway to the heavenly throne room where Daniel is watching one like a son of man coming on a cloud. If that doesn't fry your mind, this will: when Daniel saw it, it hadn't happened yet. Christ's glorious promotion was still 600 years in the future. But Daniel saw it, wrote about it, then Jesus quoted his words a few weeks before doing it. It's like something out of *Back to the Future*.)

Now we begin to understand why Jesus told the disciples that some of them would not "taste death until they see the Son of Man coming in his kingdom" (Matthew 16:28). He was saying, "Some of you, but not you, Judas, will see me raised in power and ascend to heaven in glory." And in Acts 2 some of them did.

Incidentally, the "you will not taste death" promise is recorded in all three synoptic gospels, and in each case, the promise precedes the trans-figuration of Christ (Matthew 16:28, Mark 9:1, Luke 9:27). The transfiguration and ascension of Christ are connected, like a movie and a trailer.

On the Mount of Trans-figuration, the disciples got a glimpse of Christ's kingly iden-tity. Up until then, the disciples may have wondered whether

The Son of Man coming (or going) on the clouds to heaven (from earth)

Jesus was the Messiah. Sure he had healed the sick and raised a few dead people, but hadn't the prophets done the same? Who was to say Jesus wasn't just another prophet (Matthew 21:46)?

But Jesus said, "You will see," and on the Mount of Transfiguration they saw the glory cloud and Jesus shining brighter than the sun, and they heard the affirmation of God. They became, as Peter said, eyewitnesses of his majesty.

> For we did not follow cleverly devised tales when we made known to you the power and coming of our Lord Jesus Christ, but we were eye-witnesses of his majesty. For when he received honor and glory from God the Father, such an utterance as this was made to him by the maj-estic glory, "This is my beloved Son with whom I am well-pleased" – and we ourselves heard this utterance made from heaven when we were with him on the holy mountain. (2 Peter 1:16–18)

The transfiguration was the trailer; the ascension was the feature movie. The transfiguration gave the disciples a glimpse of what was to come, but the ascension left them gazing heavenward in slack-jawed awe.

Jesus knew his disciples would see him ascend to heaven, which is why he also said, "You will not finish going through the towns of Israel before the Son of Man comes" (Matthew 10:23). Jesus sent the disciples to the towns of Israel before he died, and he sent them again after he rose (Acts 1:8). Their travels, as recorded in the early chapters of Acts, had not finished before Jesus ascended to heaven.

What about Luke 21?

Then they will see the Son of Man coming in a cloud with power and great glory. But when these things begin to take place, straighten up and lift up your heads, because **your redemption is drawing near**. (Luke 21:27–28)

Luke's version of Christ's words is a little different because he adds a bit about the disciples' redemption drawing near. What was Jesus referring to?

As we have seen, "the Son of Man coming in a cloud with power and great glory" is a reference to Daniel's prophecy. It is about Christ coming into his kingdom, which happened sometime around AD30. Daniel saw it much earlier than this while the religious Jews saw it much later. They didn't realize that Christ was who he said he was until his prophecies started coming true.

In the verse above Jesus says they will see it, meaning the Jerusalem Jews, not you disciples, because by the time *they* saw it the disciples had already seen it. The disciples were there when Christ ascended into heaven, and they already knew that he was the great King. The book of Acts is a record of the apostles walking in the revelation that Christ Jesus is on the throne. And it's also a story about the conflict between those who saw it (the apostles) and those who didn't (the unbelieving Jews).

But eventually even they would see it, and by AD70 they had.

"When these things begin to take place" is a reference to the things Jesus has been talking about – the beginning of birth pangs, the great tribulation, and the destruction of the temple. "When these things happen, lift up your heads because your redemption draws near." In other words, walk by faith and not by sight. Terrors are coming and the temptation will be to cower in fear. "But fear not," Jesus might have said, "for the fulfillment of my prophecies about Jerusalem will be further proof of what I'm telling you now – that I will have come into my kingdom."

Jesus did not come on Jerusalem in judgment, but he came to heaven with power and great glory. Daniel foretold it and the disciples witnessed it. In Matthew 24 Jesus predicted that even the unbelieving Jews would come to see it, and they would mourn when they did.

---

[1] See Matthew 22:43–44, Mark 12:36–37, and Luke 20:42.

[2] Sources: Matthew Henry's commentary on Luke 17, website: http://biblehub.com/commentaries/mhc/luke/17.htm. Gill's Exposition of Matthew 24:30, website: http://biblehub.com/commentaries/gill/matthew/24.htm. Barnes' commentary on Matthew 24, website http://biblehub.com/commentaries/barnes/matthew/24.htm

[3] Some English Bibles say the sign of the Son of Man will appear in the sky rather than heaven. This seems to support the notion that Jesus was referring to portents such as flying crosses and swords. However, the word for sky (*ouranos*) is the same word for heaven. The word can be translated either way, and the best translation is the one that fits the context.

"Then shall appear the sign of the Son of man in heaven," said the man from heaven. Since Jesus is about to return there heaven is on his mind. He wants heaven to be on his disciples' minds so he tells them to look for the sign of the Son who has made it safely home to heaven. Indeed, the disciples will see many such signs from Christ's ascension to the outpouring of the promised Holy Spirit to the fulfillment of his prophecies.

15. ANGELS AND TRUMPETS

And he will send forth his angels with a great trumpet, and they will gather together his elect from the four winds, from one end of the sky to the other. (Matthew 24:31)

Mr. Futurist: "Trumpets? Angels? Okay, this must be the Second Coming, for the Lord shall return with the trumpet of God, and the dead shall rise at the sound of a trumpet (1 Thessalonians 4:16, 1 Corinthians 15:52)."

Mr. Preterist: "But three verses later Jesus says this will take place within one generation. The angels are his messengers – his apostles and preachers – trumpeting the good news that there is a new king in town. Trumpets signify all sorts of things in scripture. Here it means preaching the gospel throughout the world."

Mr. Futurist: "But 'gathering the elect' sounds like the rapture, when the saints are caught up in the air to meet the Lord on his return."[1]

Mr. Preterist: "Or it could mean the ministers of the gospel are gathering out of the world those predestined for salvation. It's God's messengers gathering God's people with God's word."

We must not jump to end-time conclusions at the mere mention of angels and trumpets. We have seen that angels are often connected with Christ coming to earth, but in this passage Jesus is sending angels, not coming with them. And we can't even be certain that he is referring to heavenly angels, for the word for angel means messenger. It's the same word used elsewhere to describe his disciples (Luke 9:52).

So Mr. Preterist could be right in that Jesus may be talking about people (apostles, prophets, evangelists, bloggers, etc.) carrying the message of the gospel. Or Jesus could be talking about actual angels, given all the references to heaven. But Mr. Futurist is unlikely to be right about the Second Coming because it doesn't fit the context. Everything Jesus has said pertains to the imminent destruction of the temple; he's not yet begun to discuss his return.

The most likely interpretation is this: After the Son of Man ascends to heaven, he will send his messengers, angelic or otherwise, to gather his people from the four winds or corners of the earth. Jesus is hinting at the great commission to the very men who are days away from being commissioned.

Jesus wanted to gather the Jews, but they were not willing (Matthew 23:37). So now he will send his apostles to gather all who will be drawn, regardless of color or race.

Jubilee fulfilled

If you're open to it, Jesus is declaring the Year of Jubilee. Under the Law of Moses, every 50th year was to be a year of redemption and freedom from debt (Leviticus 25:10–14). The Jubilee Law foreshadowed the redemption that is ours in Christ (which is why Jesus quoted from Isaiah at the start of his ministry, "The Spirit of the Lord is upon me to proclaim the year of the Lord's favor" (Luke 4:19)).

The Israelites never celebrated the Jubilee year, but if they had been there would have been a goat and a trumpet. A ceremonial scapegoat would have carried the sins of the people away, and a trumpet would have sounded throughout the land (Leviticus 16:22, 25:9). The goat and the trumpet are symbols. The goat represents Jesus who bore our sins and carried them away, but where's the trumpet? It's right here in the Olivet Discourse.

When Jesus said he would send forth his messengers with a great trumpet, he was heralding the long-awaited Year of Jubilee. In a sense, he was sounding the trumpet. He was saying something like this:

> The Jubilee Law was a shadow, but I am the reality. The old law only applied to Israel, but my Jubilee is for everyone.[2] This is the year of the Lord's favor. This is my day of forgiveness and freedom. Gather my elect from the four winds.

The Lamb of God is greater than the scapegoat for Jesus took away the sin of the whole world (John 1:29). This is the good news message that is trumpeted throughout the land. This is the gospel that brings liberty to the captives.

But when was the prophecy fulfilled?

Mr. Preterist: "The prophecy was fulfilled after AD70. The Jewish religion was a hindrance to the spread of the faith, but once the temple fell, that opposition came to an end."

Mr. Preterist wears AD70 glasses, and this sometimes distorts his vision. Verse 31 of Matthew 24 follows verse 30. The Son of Man comes to heaven in power and glory (the ascension) and then, straightaway, he sends his messengers to gather his elect from the four corners of the earth. The prophecy was fulfilled in the book of Acts, and it continues to be fulfilled to this day.

> And they will come from east and west and from north and south, and will recline at the table in the kingdom of God. (Luke 13:29)

Since the time of Christ the nations have been streaming to his church. The great commission to make disciples of all nations did not commence after the destruction of Jerusalem, but 40 years earlier. Two men who responded to the Lord's call to go into all the world were Paul and Barnabas. They said this:

> For this is what the Lord has commanded us: "I have made you a light for the Gentiles, that you may bring salvation to the ends of the earth." (Acts 13:47, NIV)

As we saw in Chapter 6, the gospel was trumpeted around the known world well before AD70. The messengers who carried it did so in response to Christ's command, not Roman slaughters.

But why mention this in the middle of a prophecy about the fall of Jerusalem? What relevance does the great commission have to the disciples' question about the stones coming down?

It's about hope. In the midst of death and destruction, we need to see Jesus on the throne (verse 31). The Romans are going to scatter, but the Lord is going to gather. The Romans will destroy families by sending captive Jews to all parts of their empire, but the Lord is going to build his family by adopting Jewish and Gentile sons and daughters. The Romans are going to leave a dark mark in the pages of history, but the Lord of all will write a glorious ending.

How can this be anything but encouraging? The kings of this world kill and divide, but the King of kings gives life and draws all to himself.

---

[1] Mr. Futurist is probably thinking of 2 Thessalonians 2:1 where Paul writes about our being gathered to the Lord when he comes. This word gathering is hardly unique to the Second Coming. Similar gatherings happened during Christ's ministry (Mark 1:33, Luke 12:1). And they happen today whenever Christians assemble together (Hebrews 10:25).

[2] At the end of 50 years only Israelites were freed, while foreigners were enslaved for life (Leviticus 25:36–46).

16. SIGNS OF THE SEASONS

Now learn the parable from the fig tree: when its branch has already become tender and puts forth its leaves, you know that summer is near; so, you too, when you see all these things, recognize that he is near, right at the door. (Matthew 24:32–33)

Mr. Futurist: "This is about the restoration of Israel as a nation. When that happens Jesus will return within a generation."

Mr. Preterist: "He's late. Israel became a nation in 1948."

As the budding of the tree proves that summer is nigh, so shall the signs Jesus has given prove that the end is nigh. The unfolding of historical events (wars, earthquakes, armies, then destruction), will be as inevitable as the unfolding of natural events.

But who is at the door?

Recognize that he is near, right at the door. (Matthew 24:33)

Some Bibles say "He is at the door" with a capital H leaving you in no doubt that Jesus is at the door, either in imminent judgment or return. But this is a poor translation. There is no He at the door. Here is the same verse in a literal rendering:

When ye may see all these, ye know that it is nigh – at the doors. (Matthew 24:33, YLT)

What is nigh? The very thing Jesus has been speaking about, namely, the destruction of Jerusalem and the temple. Here's the whole passage in the King James Version:

Now learn a parable of the fig tree; When his branch is yet tender, and putteth forth leaves, ye know that summer is nigh: So likewise ye, when ye shall see all these things, know that it is near, even at the doors. (Matthew 24:32–33, KJV)

Jesus is saying, "When you see all the signs I've told you about, you'll know that the end of the city is near."

However, Luke records a different version of Christ's words:

> Then he told them a parable: "Behold the fig tree and all the trees; as soon as they put forth leaves, you see it and know for yourselves that summer is now near. So you also, when you see these things happening, recognize that **the kingdom of God** is near." (Luke 21:29–31)

In Luke's version, it's not *the end is near* but *the kingdom is near*. It's different but the same. It's the good to balance the bad. "When bad things are happening, and the temptation is to curl up and cry, stand tall because God is on the throne."

> So also ye, when ye may see these things happening, ye know that near is the reign of God (Luke 21:31, YLT)

Don't be afraid. "I'm telling you these things in advance so that you will know who's really in charge. And it's not the Romans."

Christ's words should encourage us. In times of great distress, when it seems like the world is going to the dogs, we need to remember that God has not abandoned us. He is near us and with us. In times of upheaval he remains the Rock we can cling to.

> Truly I say to you, this generation will not pass away until all these things take place. (Matthew 24:34)

"Truly," as in listen up and pay attention. This is serious. These things I've been talking about will happen within a generation. And they did. Within 40 years, or one Biblical generation, the city of Jerusalem had been reduced to rubble.

Mr. Futurist: "I disagree. Jesus is referring to the generation that witnesses the unfulfilled signs of the last days. He was referring to our generation."

If so, then Jesus is misleading the disciples, for several times he tells them that they would personally witness the events he was predicting:

> *You* will hear of wars and rumors of wars. See to it that *you* are not frightened. They will deliver *you* to tribulation, and *you* will be hated by all nations because of my name. Pray that *your* flight will not be in the winter. If anyone says to *you*, "Here is the Christ," do not believe him. See to it that no one misleads *you*. Behold, I have told *you* in advance.

In Matthew 23 Jesus warned the crowds, and in Matthew 24 he warned the disciples. To the crowds he said, "Truly, all these things will come upon this generation" (Matthew 23:36), and to the disciples he said the same thing: "Truly I say to you." Jesus is the truth. One truly from him ought to convince us; two trulies should remove any shadow of doubt. "Truly, truly, these things will happen within a generation."

Mr. Futurist walks a slippery slope by suggesting Jesus didn't mean what he said. It is inconceivable that Jesus sought to mislead these people. His heart was to save them from the coming storm.

But what about us? Does Jesus have words for us in Matthew 24?

He does. And are there lessons for us in his warnings to the first-century Jews? There are.

Yet we will miss what is for us if we misappropriate what was meant for others. For instance, if you believe a great tribulation is coming, you will act differently from someone who believes it is in the past.

> But take heed; behold, I have told you everything in advance. (Mark 13:23)

Jesus warned his first-century listeners to prepare for a Roman siege. But you do not need to prepare for a Roman siege. I'm no prophet, but I guarantee you there won't be a Roman siege in your future. So before we start drawing lessons for us, it will help if we pull together all the lessons meant for them.

Marvelously Strange

As we have seen, Jesus made a number of detailed predictions that can be connected to the events of AD70. It's time to pull these together and see how many were fulfilled in the lead up to that eventful year:[1]

Table 2: Forty fulfilled prophecies

	Matthew	Mark	Luke
A: Persecution of Christians			
Apostles hated by all nations	10:22, 24:9	13:13	21:17
Apostles delivered to courts/prisons		13:9	21:12
Apostles flogged in synagogues		13:9	21:12
Apostles stand before kings and governors		13:9	21:12
Apostles betrayed by family and friends			21:16
Some apostles killed	24:9		21:16
B: Birth pangs			
False messiahs will mislead many	24:5	13:6	21:8
Wars – nation vs. nation, kingdom vs. kingdom	24:6	13:7	21:9–10
Rumors of wars	24:6	13:7	
Famines	24:7	13:8	21:11
Earthquakes	24:7	13:8	21:11
Plagues/pestilence			21:11
Terrors and heavenly signs			21:11
C: The beginning of the end			
Many will betray and hate one another	24:10	13:12	
False prophets mislead many	24:11		
Increase in lawlessness and anarchy	24:12		
The love of most grows cold	24:12		
Abomination of desolation standing in holy place	24:15	13:14	
The gospel preached to all nations	24:14	13:10	
D: The great tribulation			
Enemies build embankment and surround Jerusalem			19:43, 21:20
More false Christs/prophets, with signs and wonders	24:24	13:22	
False leaders go into desert and inner rooms	24:26		
Great and unprecedented tribulation/distress	24:21	13:19	21:23
People fall by the sword			21:24
Nursing mothers especially suffer	24:19	13:17	21:23
Days cut short, so not all lives lost	24:22	13:20	
Leveled to the ground, not one stone upon another	24:2	13:2	19:44, 21:6
Jews led captive into all the nations			21:24
Jerusalem trampled underfoot by the Gentiles			21:24
E: The aftermath			
Eagles gathered about the carcass	24:28		17:37
Jerusalem left desolate	23:38		21:20
The sun and moon darkened; the stars fall	24:29	13:24–25	21:25
Dismay among the nations			21:25
Perplexity at the roaring of the sea and the waves			21:25
Men fainting from fear			21:26
The powers of the heavens shaken	24:29	13:25	21:26
The Jews see the sign of the Son of Man in heaven	24:30	13:26	21:27
The tribes mourn	24:30		
Messengers gather the church	24:31	13:27	
All fulfilled in this generation	23:36, 24:34	13:30	11:50, 21:32

In Matthew 24 and the corresponding accounts in the other gospels, we find a collection of no less than 40 prophecies. We have looked at them individually; now it's time to draw them all together. Are these prophecies for us or others? To answer that we must ask three questions pertaining to where, when, and who.

Where?

Which geographical location was the focus of this set of prophecies? The answer must be Jerusalem for Jesus plainly says so on several occasions (see Matthew 23:37–38, 24:1, Mark 13: 2, Luke 19:41–43, 21:6, 20, 24). It is Jerusalem – not Rome, Megiddo, or the United Nations – that will be surrounded by armies and trampled by Gentiles. It was in Jerusalem that the temple was demolished.

When?

To which generation were these prophecies directed? The literal and most plausible answer is the generation to whom the prophecies were uttered, meaning the apostles' generation. To argue that Jesus had some other generation in mind is to imply that he misled his listeners.

"This generation will not pass away until all things take place" (Luke 21:32). The historical fact is that "all these things" did occur during that generation, as Jesus said they would.

Who?

To whom were these prophecies directed? Christ's words were for those who lived in Jerusalem and Judea. "Let those in Judea flee to the mountains" (Luke 21:21).

These weren't secret prophecies. They were in the public domain. The people of Jerusalem heard Christ's warnings from his own mouth (e.g., Matthew 23:36). In the years following his death and resurrection, they would have heard them repeated by the apostles. And if they were literate, they could have read about them in the gospel accounts of Matthew, Mark, and Luke.

So what?

If Christ's 40 prophecies were for them and not for us, why are they in the Bible? What value could they possibly retain 50 generations after their fulfillment? They are incredibly valuable! All scripture is useful for training in righteousness (2 Timothy 3:16), but some scripture, and especially Matthew 24, goes way beyond mere usefulness into the lofty realm of mind-blowing awesomeness.

Here is what Eusebius had to say about the Lord's prophecy:

> If anyone compares the words of our Savior with the other accounts of the historian concerning the whole war, how can one fail to wonder, and to admit that the foreknowledge and the prophecy of our Savior were truly divine and marvelously strange.[2]

As the ancient historian said, the prophecies of our Savior are marvelously strange. They are proof that Jesus is the Son of God who sees the end from the beginning. But more than that they reveal his heart. These prophecies tell us that Jesus cares for us.

Jesus could have said nothing. He could have taken a hands-off approach and let history run its course, but that's not his way. He's a savior, not a spectator.

We're not meant to be spectators either. There's something in these AD70 prophecies for us. (And keep in mind that we are only halfway through Matthew 24 and there is more to come that is directly relevant.) Consider: In first-century Judea, there were two kinds of people: Those who believed Christ's prophecies and those who didn't. Those in the first group escaped the Roman siege, while those in the second either died or became enslaved. Those who died could not blame God. Their deaths had nothing to do with God's punishment or vengeance and everything to do with not heeding Jesus.

And this is how it has always been.

God counseled Adam to choose life, but Adam said, "I don't trust you" and reaped death. Jesus counseled the Judeans to choose life, but some didn't and died.

He who believes in me will live. (John 11:25)

People divide themselves by their response to Jesus. Those who heed him live; those who scorn him die. Again, this has nothing to do with punishment and everything to do with trusting Jesus.

> For God so loved the world, that he gave his only begotten Son, that whoever believes in him shall not perish, but have eternal life. For God did not send the Son into the world to judge the world, but that the world might be saved through him. (John 3:16–17)

Jesus did not come to judge but to rescue, but only those who heed him will be saved. That's the lesson of AD70.

But there's more. Jesus is not done. He has been talking to the disciples about their future; in a few verses he will start talking about ours.

---

[1] You may be wondering about the division of the five time periods in the table and why I listed the birth pangs second when Jesus lists them first in Matthew 24. Two reasons: (1) In Luke's account of the prophecy, Jesus says to the disciples, "Before all these things (i.e., the birth pangs), they will lay their hands on you and will persecute you ..." (Luke 21:12). (2) History records that the persecution of the apostles began during the New Testament period and preceded the wars and other birth pangs. So the order (persecution first, birth pangs second) is scripturally and historically accurate. Events listed under "the beginning of the end" took place prior to the siege, while the events of the great tribulation occurred during the siege and subsequent destruction of the city. Where the placing of events is debatable, I followed the sequence given by Jesus. Thus the abomination of desolation is listed before the great tribulation because Jesus lists it earlier.

[2] Eusebius, *Church History*, 3.7.7.

17. HEAVEN AND EARTH

Heaven and earth will pass away, but my words will not pass away. (Matthew 24:35)

Mr. Futurist: "Jesus is discussing the future destruction of the cosmos and the end of the world."

Mr. Preterist: "Josephus described the temple as having an inaccessible heavenly part (the Holy of Holies) and an accessible earthly part (the Holy Place). Thus 'heaven and earth' is shorthand for the temple. It was God's heavenly seat on earth. Jesus is saying the temple system will pass away."[1]

Mr. Preterist makes a good argument, particularly when we recall Jesus' words in the Sermon on the Mount:

Do not think that I came to abolish the law or the prophets; I did not come to abolish but to fulfill. For truly I say to you, until heaven and earth pass away, not the smallest letter or stroke shall pass from the law until all is accomplished. (Matthew 5:17–18)

The law-loving Jews were worried that Jesus was going to damage or overturn the law, so he reassured them. "I didn't come to abolish the law but to fulfill it." This was a staggering claim. In fourteen centuries no one had perfectly kept the law, but Jesus said he would. Then he gave what may be the first hint that the temple would not endure. "I will do it before heaven and earth (the temple) passes away." In other words, your temple's coming down, but by then it won't matter because we'll have a new covenant, and the old one will be obsolete."

The old and new covenants are fundamentally different. The old was based on our promises to God, while the new is based on God's promises to us. The old fails because our promises are brittle, while the new endures because God's word lasts forever.[2]

So when Jesus, sitting on the Mount of Olives overlooking the temple, says, "Heaven and earth will pass away," he's saying, "*This* will pass away. This temple-based system of trying to approach God through human effort and resolve will pass away. It has no future. It's a bad bet. But the new covenant forged in my blood and based on my words will not pass away."

Mr. Preterist: "Which is why Revelation 21:1–3 speaks of a new heaven and earth. The old heaven and earth was the temple, God's former meeting place with man. But in the new covenant, you are the temple of the Holy Spirit. You are the new heaven and earth."

Mr. Futurist: "But 2 Peter 3:13 says we are still looking for a new heaven and a new earth."

Mr. Preterist: "That's because the temple was still standing when Peter wrote his letter. The old heaven and earth hadn't yet passed away. He was looking forward to that."

Mr. Futurist: "You're twisting his words. And didn't Paul say you *are* the temple of the Holy Spirit? He didn't say, 'We're looking forward to when the Jewish temple comes down so that you can become the temple of the Holy Spirit.'"

Mr. Preterist: "..."

Mr. Futurist: "Why can't the new heaven and earth simply be a *new* heaven and a *new* earth? Why does it have to be metaphorical?"

Mr. Preterist: "Because Revelation 21:2 speaks of the holy city, the New Jerusalem, descending from heaven as a bride. That's a picture of the church. That's the new heaven and earth!"

Mr. Futurist: "Then why is Peter still looking forward to it? He knew what a church was. And why does he say the new heaven and earth would come on 'that day', meaning the day of the Lord (2 Peter 3:10–12)? He must be talking about a literal destruction of heaven and earth."

Mr. Preterist: "You think the earth will be destroyed? How do you account for those scriptures that suggest it will endure? Ecclesiastes 1:4 says, 'Generations come and go, but the earth remains forever.'"

Mr. Futurist: "..."

This argument is generating more heat than light, so we will move on and leave Mr. Preterist and Mr. Futurist to their debate. Either could be right or perhaps both. Or maybe neither. Another possibility is Jesus is employing a figure of speech as in,

> The grass withers, the flower fades, but the word of our God stands forever. (Isaiah 40:8)

Perhaps he is saying, "Heaven and earth are more likely to pass away than my words fail to come true." These prophecies I've just given you, you can take them to the bank.

Either way, Jesus changing the subject. For the past 30 verses his prophecy has been all doom and gloom, death and destruction, and things that pass away. But take a breath because Jesus is about to talk about something else, something infinitely better.

---

[1] *Antiquities*, 3.7.7. The heaven and earth theme was picked up by Spurgeon, who described the old temple system of animal sacrifices as "like the old heavens and earth to the Jewish believers." That religious system has now passed away, said Spurgeon, "and we now live under new heavens and a new earth." Source: C.H. Spurgeon (1891), "God Rejoicing in the New Creation," Sermon no.2211, The Spurgeon Archive, website: www.spurgeon.org/-sermons/2211.php

[2] The old covenant began with the Israelites making promises to God at the foot of Mt. Sinai – "Everything you say we will do" (Exodus 19:8) – but the new covenant is based on God's promises to us (Hebrews 7:18–22). The old covenant, or heaven and earth, passed away because man is incapable of keeping his word, but the new endures forever because God is faithful.

18. THE DAY AND THE HOUR

But of that day and hour no one knows, not even the angels of heaven, nor the Son, but the Father alone. (Matthew 24:36)

The disciples wanted to know when the temple would fall and Christ would return. Jesus has just finished answering their first question (within a generation) and is now answering their second (no one knows). The first event was predictable – Jesus gave them 40 signposts – but the second is a mystery. The former could be anticipated, but the latter will come like a thief in the night (1 Thessalonians 5:2).

Mr. Preterist: "I disagree. Jesus is talking about one and the same day. The fall of Jerusalem was the day when Christ returned in judgment of that sinful city."

Mr. Futurist: "But one day was marked by signposts; the other day is unknown."

Mr. Preterist: "Jesus knew the fall of Jerusalem would happen within a generation, but he didn't know exactly when. This is why he told the disciples to pray that their flight wouldn't fall on a Sabbath or in winter. And Paul said the day of the Lord would come suddenly, like labor pains upon a woman with child (1 Thessalonians 5:3). An expectant mother knows her baby will come in 40 weeks, but she doesn't know the day or the hour. Similarly, the apostles knew the Lord was coming in judgment in 40 years, but they didn't know the day or the hour."

Mr. Futurist: "But Paul was talking about the Second Coming, not AD70."

Mr. Preterist: "Maybe AD70 *was* the Second Coming. Have you considered that? Perhaps Matthew 24 is about one event, not two."

Mr. Futurist: "Sheesh. It sounds like you want to preterize every prophecy in the Bible."

The idea that Jesus came on Jerusalem in fiery judgment in AD70 has been taught for 2,000 years. However, this ancient teaching is contrary to the gospel, as we will see in Chapter 22. Nor does it square with Christ's warnings:

> And he said, "See to it that you are not misled; for many will come in my name, saying, 'I am he,' and, 'The time is near.' Do not go after them. (Luke 21:8)

One characteristic of first-century false prophets is they went around saying, "I'm the Messiah come to deliver Israel." As the conflict between the Jews and the Romans intensified, there was an expectation that the Messiah would come. "Don't believe it," said Jesus. "I will not be coming to deliver you or judge you or do anything in AD70. That's why you need to flee."

Mordor and Pleasantville

The preterist view that Christ returned in AD70 can only be true if Christ is mistaken, which is a fairly serious problem. Preterism, although it does a reasonable job accounting for the fall of Jerusalem, does a poor job of dealing with the return of Christ. According to preterism, the two events are connected. But according to Jesus, the two events are as different as night and day:

Table 3: Mordor and Pleasantville

Night Falls on Jerusalem (Matthew 24:4–35)	The Day of the Lord (Matthew 24:36–41)
- False Christs - Wars and rumors of wars - Famines - Earthquakes - Persecution	- Eating and drinking - Marrying and giving in marriage - Men working in fields - Women grinding at mills

These are strikingly different pictures. One is Mordor; the other is Pleasant-ville. One is marked by calamities; the other is normal life. One is predictable; the other is unexpected. One ends with a tragic disaster (Jerusalem falls), the other climaxes with a glorious triumph (Christ returns).

Since the disciples asked about two different events (the fall of the temple and his return), Jesus gave two prophecies, and they couldn't be more different. Yet both Mr. Preterist and Mr. Futurist treat these two prophecies as one. Mr. Preterist says everything on the right side of the table belongs on the left, while Mr. Futurist says everything on the left belongs on the right. Mr. Preterist says the Lord came in AD70, while Mr. Futurist says the sign-posts for that generation are for the last generation. They are both mistaken.

Jesus said again and again that the disciples would see the first prophecy fulfilled, but the second prophecy was something they would never see:

> And he said to the disciples, "The days will come when you will long to see one of the days of the Son of Man, and you will not see it." (Luke 17:22)

When you see some injustice or evil, you might pray, "Come, Lord Jesus, and put an end to this suffering." It's possible that the disciples prayed this prayer when they saw false messiahs leading people to their deaths, or when they heard about the Roman siege machines smashing Galilean towns. They would have longed to see King Jesus return in power. But Jesus said, "You will not see it."

There were many things the disciples would see – wars, famines, tribulation – but there was one thing they wouldn't. In the coming generation they would see Jerusalem fall, but they wouldn't see Christ return. They would see the temple come down but not the Lord.

That event was for a future generation.

The days of Noah

> For the coming of the Son of Man will be just like the days of Noah. "For as in those days before the flood they were eating and drinking, marrying and giving in marriage, until the day that Noah entered the ark, and they did not understand until the flood came and took them all away; so will the coming of the Son of Man be. (Matthew 24:37–39)

Mr. Preterist: "This is about Christ coming in flood-like judgment on Jerusalem."

Mr. Futurist: "How can that be when the picture he paints is of life-as-usual? There are no famines or earthquakes, no wars or rumors of war. Jesus is describing a time of peace."

Mr. Preterist: "Not peace but a people who won't heed the warnings. They're eating and drinking in spite of the signs."

Mr. Futurist: "Who eats during a famine?"

Mr. Preterist: "Noah tried to warn people that judgment was coming, but they ignored him and carried on with life as usual."

Mr. Futurist: "But the flood of Noah was unlike the fall of Jerusalem. Jesus said those people didn't understand that destruction was hanging over their heads, but the Jews had plenty of warning."[1]

I'm with Mr. Futurist on this one. The day of the Lord will come unexpectedly, but there was nothing unexpected about the siege of Jerusalem. As we saw in Chapter 8, there were at least ten major crises in the years leading up to the siege. Ten opportunities for the Judean Jews to realize their world was falling to pieces. Before Titus marched on the city, Judea had been separately invaded by the legions of Publius Petronius and Cestius Gallus. The siege of Jerusalem was preceded by dress rehearsals.

> For you yourselves know full well that the day of the Lord will come just like a thief in the night. While they are saying, "Peace and safety!" then destruction will come upon them suddenly like labor pains upon a woman with child, and they will not escape. (1 Thessalonians 5:2-3)

Paul reinforces Christ's warning that the Lord's return will be completely unexpected. It will not happen during a time of war but a time of peace and safety. This demolishes the idea that Christ came in AD70. No one was saying peace and safety before the siege of Jerusalem. Israel was a land in turmoil with civil unrest, guerrilla fighting, and Roman legions slaughtering Galilean towns. Jesus said the day of his return would be like the day of Noah's flood. Peter said the same thing:

> The world that then existed perished, being flooded with water. But the heavens and the earth which are now preserved by the same word, are reserved for fire until the day of judgment and perdition of ungodly men. (2 Peter 3:6–7, NKJV)

When Christ returns, people will be eating and drinking, marrying and giving in marriage, as they did in the days of Noah. People don't eat, marry, and start families during famines and times of genocide. It beggars belief that Jesus was describing events connected with AD70. He was talking about his final coming.

Taken and left behind

> Then there will be two men in the field; one will be taken and one will be left. Two women will be grinding at the mill; one will be taken and one will be left. Therefore be on the alert, for you do not know which day your Lord is coming. (Matthew 24:40–42)

Mr. Preterist: "This is about people getting taken captive or killed by the Romans. Or it's about being taken safely away from Roman danger. Either way, Romans."

Mr. Futurist: "No, it's about the Second Coming and how believers will be caught up in the air to meet Jesus when he returns ..."

Mr. Preterist: "Oh, here we go with the rapture nonsense."

Uh-oh. I can see that tempers are starting to rise, which is a pity because the taken and left behind questions are worth a closer look. Why don't we put this verse and the rapture on the back-burner for now? We'll come back to it in Chapter 36.

---

[1] Which begs the question, why did they stay? If the signs of destruction were so obvious, why didn't the Jews flee? Indeed they did flee, but they fled the wrong way. With Judea and Galilee overrun with Romans, they fled to Jerusalem thinking they would be protected by its massive walls. It was the logical thing to do, but ultimately disastrous.

19. KEEP WATCH

But be sure of this, that if the head of the house had known at what time of the night the thief was coming, he would have been on the alert and would not have allowed his house to be broken into. (Matthew 24:43)

Jesus is no thief, but one day he will break into our world in a sudden and dramatic way.

Behold, I am coming like a thief. (Revelation 16:15)

Paul used similar language to describe the Lord's return (1 Thessalonians 5:2), and so did Peter (2 Peter 3:10).

Like a thief in the night

The day of the Lord is unlike the well-signposted fall of Jerusalem. That day was expected, but the Lord's return will be unexpected. In AD70 there was time to flee, but when the Lord returns there won't be time to do anything.

Those who have been robbed know the truth of these words, for thieves give no warning. One moment it's a regular day full of plans and responsibilities; the next moment everything is upended. Your stuff's all over the floor, you're in shock, and your day just took a whole new direction. That's how it will be when the Lord returns. It will be sudden, dramatic, and it will surely mess with your plans.

But the day of the Lord will come like a thief, in which the heavens will pass away with a roar and the elements will be destroyed with intense heat, and the earth and its works will be burned up. (2 Peter 3:10)

Mr. Preterist: "I disagree. This has nothing to do with the Second Coming, but the Lord visiting judgment on Jerusalem. The elements are a reference to the law being destroyed."

Mr. Futurist: "Then why doesn't Peter say so? And how do you destroy the law with heat? Cook it?"

Mr. Preterist: "He's saying all the rituals and observances connected with the law will come to a fiery end in AD70 when the temple burns."

Mr. Futurist: "So no more Jewish religion."

Mr. Preterist: "Precisely."

Mr. Futurist: "So what religion have the Jews been practicing for the past 2,000 years?"

Again, there are problems with Mr. Preterist's insistence that Jesus destroyed Jerusalem. In other scriptures, the elements refer to worldly principles or the ABCs of earthly wisdom that manifests in the religion of self-improvement (Galatians 4:3, 9, Colossians 2:8). Peter is saying those things that are opposed to God will be dissolved or burned up when the Lord returns.

If Peter had been thinking about the fall of Jerusalem, why didn't he say so? The obvious answer is that Peter wasn't thinking about Jerusalem. He was thinking about the day of the Lord (see 2 Peter 3:8–9).[1]

> But when the Day of God's Judgment does come, it will be unannounced, like a thief. The sky will collapse with a thunderous bang, everything disintegrating in a huge conflagration, earth and all its works exposed to the scrutiny of Judgment. (2 Peter 3:10, MSG)

If the universe began with a Big Bang, the Lord's return will be a Bigger Bang.

The second or final coming of Jesus Christ will be the climactic event of history. His glorious arrival will put everything else in the shade. His return will be the end of life as you know it, but it will be the beginning of life as it was always meant to be.

Be alert, be ready

> Take heed, **keep on the alert**; for you do not know when the appointed time will come. It is like a man away on a journey, who upon leaving

his house and putting his slaves in charge, assigning to each one his task, also commanded the doorkeeper to **stay on the alert**. Therefore, **be on the alert** – for you do not know when the master of the house is coming, whether in the evening, at midnight, or when the rooster crows, or in the morning – in case he should come suddenly and find you asleep. What I say to you I say to all, "**Be on the alert!**" (Mark 13:33–37)

You won't find a clearer or more repeated instruction in scripture: be alert! Some translations say keep watch. The implication is that we should be wakeful regarding Christ's return. Don't be fuzzy-headed. Don't be in a spiritual stupor. Don't waste your life on so much booze that you never give a moment's thought to the Lord's return (see 1 Thessalonians 5:6–7).

Therefore **be on the alert,** for you do not know which day your Lord is coming ... For this reason you also must **be ready.** (Matthew 24:42, 44)

"Be alert. Be ready." This is the punchline of the message and the point of the prophecy.

How do we get ready? Not by cloistering ourselves in a monastery, for the ready men and women in Matthew 24:40–42 are working in the fields and grinding in the mill. They are participating in life and providing for their families. Their readiness does not require them to withdraw from society.

Being ready means being prepared. It's having a positive answer to the following question: If Jesus came back today, would you be happy to see him?

Perhaps you are unsure of your answer to this question. Perhaps you have a mixture of fear and anxiety. If so, keep reading! By the end of this book I hope you will be so grounded in what the Bible says about the Lord's Day and so established in God's love for you, that you will have peace instead of fear and excitement instead of dread.

Hastening the day

Since all these things are to be destroyed in this way, what sort of people ought you to be in holy conduct and godliness, looking for and hastening the coming of the day of God, because of which the heavens will be destroyed by burning, and the elements will melt with intense heat! (2 Peter 3:11–12)

Mr. Preterist: "The early church hastened the day of Jerusalem's judgment by crying out to God for justice (see Luke 18:7)."

Which is a bit like asking God to kill people.

Peter has just told us that God is not willing that any perish, so how is praying for old covenant justice consistent with his heart? How will this hasten the Lord's return?

We hasten the Lord's return by living holy and godly lives. A godly life points to God. It reveals the good news of heaven in such a way that lives are transformed and God is praised. A godly life is built on the revelation of Jesus, who died for us and now lives for us. It's living from the persuasion that God loves us unconditionally and that he does not treat us as the Romans treated the Jews.

---

[1] Although we don't know the exact date of Peter's letter, it is certain that he wrote it after Publius Petronius marched on Israel (in AD40). It is likely that Cestius Gallus had invaded the country as well (AD66). If Peter had the fall of Jerusalem on his mind he surely would've pointed to these contemporary events and said, "This is what Jesus was talking about!" Let's not forget that Peter was on the Mount of Olives when the Lord listed the 40 signs preceding the destruction of Jerusalem. If Peter was writing about AD70, why didn't he mention the signs? Why does he say nothing about famines, earthquakes, wars?

20. THE FAITHFUL SERVANT

Who then is the faithful and sensible slave whom his master put in charge of his household to give them their food at the proper time? Blessed is that slave whom his master finds so doing when he comes. Truly I say to you that he will put him in charge of all his possessions. But if that evil slave says in his heart, "My master is not coming for a long time," and begins to beat his fellow slaves and eat and drink with drunkards; the master of that slave will come on a day when he does not expect him and at an hour which he does not know, and will cut him in pieces and assign him a place with the hypocrites; in that place there will be weeping and gnashing of teeth. (Matthew 24:45–51)

Mr. Preterist: "The first-century Christians needed to be vigilant in watching for Jesus lest they become complacent and not flee the doomed city."

Mr. Futurist: "We need to be vigilant because Jesus' return won't be marked by anything as dramatic as Roman legions stomping about the countryside. The parable reinforces Christ's words about returning at an unexpected time."

Matthew 24 begins with a prophecy and ends with a parable. The parable of the faithful servant illustrates the theme Jesus has been developing: be ready.

For this reason you also must be ready. (Matthew 24:44a)

Some take Jesus' words to mean they should be hyper-vigilant and watchful to such a degree that they put life on hold. They obsess over the signs of the times and are tossed and turned by every latest teaching. If there's a book on astronomical omens, they'll read it. If there's a YouTube clip on the Illuminati, they'll watch it. If they can force-fit current events into Daniel's eschatological prophecies, they'll do it. But the wise servant in the story does none of these things.

You do not know when the master of the house is coming, whether in the evening, at midnight, or when the rooster crows, or in the morning. (Mark 13:35)

The faithful and wise servant doesn't waste time trying to figure out what he does not know and what nobody can know. All his watchfulness requires is that he lives ready and eager for his master's return. His master has given him a job to do and he gets on with it. When the master returns he will be happy to find his servant getting on with the business of living. He would not be happy to find his servant fretting over the latest end-times hullabaloo.

What does it mean to be unready?

In the parable neither servant knows when the master will return, but the evil or faithless servant is the one who lives as though he's never coming back. Lacking this hope, this servant abandons whatever job the master had for him and squanders his life on wasteful living. The result is that other people get hurt and he ends up with a world of regret.

"Don't be that person," says Jesus. "Don't lose sight of me and waste your life."

No one sets out to waste their lives, but this is what happens when we live disconnected from the Author of Life. When we try and write our own story, without input from him, we write inferior stories. Even if our lives have the appearance of success, they leave us empty and unfulfilled because we were not made to live alone.

What happens to the unfaithful servant?

It's a mistake to insist that a parable communicates only one message. For instance, if the faithless servant represents the unbeliever who does not expect Jesus return, then the message for such a person is change your unbelieving mind and look to Jesus. However, the unfaithful servant in the story is violent and abusive, which hardly describes the typical unbeliever. In this sense, the unfaithful servant represents the religious leaders and their violent and abusive religion. These men murdered Stephen, and they tried to kill apostles. Jesus charged the Pharisees with flogging his prophets, and they responded by beating him (Matthew 23:34, 26:67).

In the parable, the master cuts the unfaithful servant to pieces and assigns him a place with the hypocrites. This is what Jesus did to the Pharisees when he verbally tore strips off them and accused them of hypocrisy. The religious leaders saw themselves as God's men, but Jesus said, "You are the devil's men" (John 8:44). They thought of themselves as Abraham's sons, but Jesus called them "sons of hell" (Matthew 23:15). Harsh words, but merciful for only a hard truth can crack a hard heart.

Sadly, the religious leaders didn't listen to Jesus, which is why they found themselves on the outside of all God did in the book of Acts. They were spectators when they could have been participants, and this made them angry.

> Now when they heard (Stephen), they were cut to the quick, and they
> began gnashing their teeth at him. (Acts 7:54)

Jesus said the evil servant would be cut and the Sanhedrin were cut by Stephen's words. Jesus said the evil servant would gnash his teeth, and the Sanhedrin gnashed theirs. To gnash one's teeth is to snarl and growl. It's to be murderously angry, as the Sanhedrin were, yelling and shouting at the tops of their voices (Acts 7:57).[1]

Rage is the fruit of religion. Cain's religion made him mad enough to kill his brother, and the religious Jews were mad enough to kill God's Son. They told themselves they were waiting for the Messiah but their actions said otherwise. They weren't expecting Jesus. When their Master showed up they were verbally cut to pieces and assigned a place with the hypocrites. They lived out their days raging and gnashing their teeth.

But not all of them. Some of them repented and were numbered with the ready (Acts 6:7). They might have said, "I nearly missed his first coming. I won't miss his second." This brings us to the question we all must ask.

How do we get ready?

The faithful and wise servant in the parable is not wise because of his extensive learning. He is wise in the same way that the man who builds on the rock is wise.

> Therefore everyone who hears these words of mine and acts on them
> may be compared to a wise man who built his house on the rock.
> (Matthew 7:24)

The wise servant lives in response to what he has heard. This is the essence of faith since faith is a positive response to what God has said or done. Faith is not impressing God with our initiative; faith is responding to God's initiative. Faith is saying yes to Jesus.

In the parable the master provides the food, the faithful servant serves it, and everyone is fed and blessed. It's a picture of how life is meant to be. God gives (that's grace), we receive (that's faith), and others are blessed. Even though the master is not physically present, he is represented by his servant, and those who eat his food praise him.

When the master returns he is delighted to find that the servant has been spending his master's wealth on others. He responds by giving the servant even more to spend. "Take charge of all my possessions!" He is one generous master!

In another story Jesus told, a master going on a long journey gives money to each of his servants and says, "Do business until I come" (Luke 19:13). The message is the same. When the master returns he is happiest with those who have spent or traded their master's wealth. He is not happy with the servant who does nothing.

These parables are pictures of how God deals with us. God has given each of us good gifts, and if we put his gifts to work others are blessed, and the result is praise to our Father.

> Let your light shine before men in such a way that they may see your good works, and glorify your Father who is in heaven. (Matthew 5:16)

You are a one-of-a-kind special. God made you *you* and there is nobody else who can be who he made you to be. Neglect your God-given gifts and the world will be a poorer place. Other people will miss out on the blessing, and you will waste your life.

So what does it mean to be ready? It's living from the hopeful persuasion that no matter how bad things are, Christ is on the throne and he is coming again. It's using the good gifts he's given you to reveal his heart to an orphaned world. It's the adventure of discovering the dream that God has written into your genes. It is shining in a dark world with the good news of heaven.

There's no guarantee that life will be trouble-free, and you may face abuse from those who are frustrated, unfulfilled, and religious. But see Christ as your source of joy and you will thrive. Live in positive response to what he has said and you cannot go wrong.

And on that day when he returns, he will smile and say, "Well done, good and faithful servant. Enter into the joy of the Lord."

---

[1] This wasn't the first time the Sanhedrin had been reduced to a pack of snarling dogs. "But when they heard (Peter and the apostles), they were cut to the quick and intended to kill them" (Acts 5:33). The grumpy old men of the Sanhedrin were madder than hell. Only the intervention of Gamaliel stopped them from harming the apostles. The definition of gnashing as snarling and growling comes from Thayer's Greek Lexicon (http://biblehub.com/greek/-1030.htm).

21. THE BLOOD OF RIGHTEOUS ABEL

We have concluded our verse-by-verse look at Matthew 24. However, Jesus speaks in many other places about AD70 and the end of the world. In the second half of this book, we will look at some of these other scriptures beginning with the woe-filled Matthew 23. Christ's harsh words to the scribes and Pharisees in Matthew 23 provide the context for his prophecies in Matthew 24.

In his last visit to the temple, Jesus pronounced eight woes to the religious leaders. (Some translations omit Matthew 23:14 reducing the total number of woes to seven.) Here is the first woe:

> But woe to you, scribes and Pharisees, hypocrites, because you shut off the kingdom of heaven from people; for you do not enter in yourselves, nor do you allow those who are entering to go in. (Matthew 23:13)

If you have been raised with a picture of God-as-a-judge, it is easy to read these words as though Jesus was a prosecuting attorney pointing an accusing finger at criminals. But the word woe does not mean "God will punish you!" It's an expression of distress or deep sorrow. When Jesus says, "Woe to those who are pregnant and nursing babies in those days" (Matthew 24:19), he's expressing grief.

In pronouncing woe over the scribes and Pharisees, Jesus is lamenting their disastrous choices. "You're not entering the kingdom of heaven." This is bad. "Nor do you allow others to enter." Really bad.

> Woe to you, scribes and Pharisees, hypocrites, because you travel around on sea and land to make one proselyte; and when he becomes one, you make him twice as much a son of hell as yourselves. (Matthew 23:15)

"Alas! You're hell-bound, and you're taking others down with you. This is terrible!"

Keep in mind that Jesus knows these guys. He's been preaching in the courts of their temple and fielding their questions for years. If he doesn't know their names, he surely knows their faces. And he knows they are more lost than the tax collectors he dines with. Their smug superiority is nothing but a mask. Underneath they are real people with aches and needs just like the rest of us. Jesus knows the depths of their lostness, and this is why he is distressed.

> Woe to you, scribes and Pharisees, hypocrites! For you tithe mint and dill and cummin, and have neglected the weightier provisions of the law: justice and mercy and faithfulness. (Matthew 23:23)

"You've got life back to front. You're hung up on the small things – herbs, for pity's sake! – and you've missed the big things."

> Woe to you, blind guides, who say, "Whoever swears by the temple, that is nothing; but whoever swears by the gold of the temple is obligated." You fools and blind men! (Matthew 23:16–17)

"This religion you've invented –it doesn't even make sense! Your folly is breathtaking. Your ignorance is monumental."

Towards the end of Matthew 23, Jesus' grief turns to anger. "You snakes! You brood of vipers!" His anger is justified for their religion is pernicious. It's keeping people from the love of God. Yet despite his righteous wrath Jesus never says, "I will destroy this city and everyone in it!"

"Woe to you, scribes and Pharisees"

The men of Nineveh and the Queen of the South may condemn this generation (Matthew 12:41–42), but the Savior will not. Instead, he pronounces the condemnation they have brought on their own heads. Like a doctor telling a two-pack-a-day smoker that they have lung cancer, Jesus informs them of the fatal consequences of their actions: "And so will come upon you …"[1]

This brings us to the eighth and final woe.

The death sentence

Woe to you, scribes and Pharisees, hypocrites! For you build the tombs of the prophets and adorn the monuments of the righteous … Therefore, behold, I am sending you prophets and wise men and scribes; some of them you will kill and crucify, and some of them you will scourge in your synagogues, and persecute from city to city, so that upon you may fall the guilt of all the righteous blood shed on earth, from the blood of righteous Abel to the blood of Zechariah, the son of Berechiah, whom you murdered between the temple and the altar. Truly I say to you, all these things will come upon this generation. (Matthew 23:29, 34–36)

Both here and in Luke 11:49–51, Jesus pronounces what is effectively a death sentence. "You're going to pay for the blood of Abel and Zechariah." This raises some interesting questions because the first-century Jews didn't kill Abel or Zechariah. Abel was murdered by Cain, thousands of years earlier, while Zechariah was murdered eight centuries back. But Jesus says, "Zechariah *whom you murdered* between the temple and the altar." That's like telling an Englishman, "You killed Braveheart."

The first-century Jews did not kill Abel and Zechariah, but they paid for the crime. Within a generation, Jerusalem was wiped off the face of the earth. From this we can draw one of three conclusions:

1. God punished them as though they did it
2. God punished them for the sins of their fathers
3. They were punished, but not by God

The first conclusion is easy to dismiss for God is gracious. If he won't punish you for the sins you have done (Psalm 103:10), he certainly won't punish you for the sins you haven't. All this is to the glory of Jesus who bore our sins along with the sins of the scribes and Pharisees.[2]

The second conclusion – "Jesus charged them with these sins because their fathers did it" – sounds like it comes out of the old covenant, but it doesn't. The Law of Moses forbade punishing children for their parents' mistakes. According to the law of the day, the scribes and Pharisees could not be held accountable for the sins of their fathers, let alone their distant ancestors.[3]

Insist that Jesus is preaching divine punishment and you will find you don't have a scriptural leg to stand on. This leads us to the third conclusion, that God was not punishing them at all.

So who punished them?

Not God, but sin. By sin, I am referring to that spiritual power that crouched hungrily at Cain's door (Genesis 4:7). Sin as a noun, rather than a verb. In Romans, Paul talks about how sin desires to enslave and dominate us. Sin is a monster that seeks to kill us.[4]

Sin has no power over those who trust in Jesus, but those who serve sin, as the religious leaders did, tread a perilous path.

> What benefit did you reap at that time from the things you are now ashamed of? Those things result in death! … For the wages of sin is death. (Romans 6:21, 23, NIV)

Sin is a killer. Sow sin and you will reap a fatal harvest. This has nothing to do with divine punishment and everything to do with reaping what you sow. When Jesus told the scribes and Pharisees that a day of reckoning was coming, he was saying their chickens were coming home to roost.

> The tombs you build are monuments to your murdering ancestors. (Luke 11:48, MSG)

The scribes and Pharisees tended the tombs of the prophets and martyrs, but Jesus was unimpressed. Their attempts to honor the dead were a sham. In their hearts they had more in common with the killers than the prophets they killed.

For this reason also the wisdom of God (i.e., Jesus himself) said, "I will send to them prophets and apostles, and some of them they will kill and some they will persecute." (Luke 11:49)

Jesus knew these men would kill him and they did it within the week. He also knew that they would kill and persecute his apostles. So much for tomb-tending.

The blood of all the prophets, which was shed from the foundation of the world, may be required of this generation. (Luke 11:50, KJV)

"Required" in the sense that sin has consequences. Sow death, and you'll reap death.

Again, this has nothing to do with God and everything to do with the natural consequences of our actions. Sin is destructive. Text on the freeway and you could crash. Flirt with your coworker and you might destroy your marriage. Slaughter a Roman garrison and you'll invoke the emperor's wrath. And none of it will be God's fault.

Truly I say to you, all these things will come upon this generation. (Matthew 23:36)

Of all the prophecies made against the stubborn Jews, this one was the most specific. "Guys, you've got one Biblical generation, 40 years max. That's how close you are to the edge."[5]

The parable of the fig tree

A man had a fig tree, which had been planted in his vineyard, and he came looking for fruit on it and did not find any. And he said to the vineyard-keeper, "Behold, for three years I have come looking for fruit on this fig tree without finding any. Cut it down! Why does it even use up the ground?" And he answered and said to him, "Let it alone, sir, for this year too, until I dig around it and put in fertilizer; and if it bears fruit next year, fine; but if not, cut it down." (Luke 13:6–9)

John, the last of the old covenant prophets, urged the religious Jews to "Bear the fruit of repentance" (Matthew 3:8), but they didn't listen. "The axe is already at the root of the tree," warned John (Matthew 3:10). Still nothing. Then for three years Jesus searched Israel in vain for the fruit of faith.

When Jesus entered Jerusalem at the start of his final week, the people waved branches without fruit. The next morning, Jesus cursed a fruitless fig tree (Mark 11:14). Oh, the symbolism!

Mr. Preterist: "The parable foreshadowed God cutting down Israel in AD70."

Except the cursed fig tree withered straight away (Matthew 21:19), not 40 years later, and God didn't cut down Israel; the Israelites cut themselves off through unbelief. "God did not reject his people … they were broken off because of unbelief" (Romans 11:2, 20).

Unbelief can kill you. If your neighbor wakes you in the middle of the night shouting, "Your house is on fire," but you don't believe him, you could die. For three years Jesus warned the Jews with tears that they were on course for destruction, yet they didn't listen.

So Jesus cursed a fig tree.

> As they were passing by in the morning, they saw the fig tree withered from the roots up. Being reminded, Peter said to him, "Rabbi, look, the fig tree which you cursed has withered." And Jesus answered saying to them, "Have faith in God." (Mark 11:20–22)

The point of the parable is not produce fruit, but have faith in God. The religious Jews trusted in themselves. Their source was self and their root was their downfall. Just as the fig tree withered from the roots up, the religious Jews rotted from the inside-out.

What should they have done? They should have listened to Jesus. They should have abandoned their quest for self-improvement and put their faith in God. Had they been grafted into the living Vine they would have been saved from sin and Romans.

The lesson of the fig tree is not "God will smite you if you don't perform," but "Jesus is the life." To reject the Author of Life is to reject life itself.

Those who trust in Jesus have nothing to fear. The believer need not fear the axe at the root because Jesus is our Root and the root sustains us (Revelation 22:16). The believer feels no pressure to produce fruit because Jesus is the Vine and it is his fruit we bear. The believer does not strive to become holy, because "as the root is holy, so are the branches" (Romans 11:16).

Speaking of believers, it's time we returned to the blood of righteous Abel.

Why mention Abel?

Abel was the first man of faith in the Bible. His offering was a signpost to Jesus. But righteous Abel was murdered by his self-righteous brother. It was the beginning of a bad pattern. From Abel to Zechariah, faithful men have been killed by the religious.

> Jerusalem, Jerusalem, who kills the prophets and stones those who are sent to her! How often I wanted to gather your children together, the way a hen gathers her chicks under her wings, and you were unwilling. (Matthew 23:37)

Hear the ache in Christ's lament. "I have given everything for you, and in a few days I'll give you my life. But you won't listen." For hundreds of years God had been trying to draw Israel away from their self-destructive course, but they kept the pedal to the metal, and now their end was imminent.

> Behold, your house is being left to you desolate! (Matthew 23:38)

"Your temple, your religion – it's empty. There's nothing there. God has left the building."

> For I say to you, from now on you will not see me until you say, "Blessed is he who comes in the name of the Lord." (Matthew 23:39)

In Luke's account these words come before Palm Sunday (Luke 13:34–35), but in Matthew's gospel they come after. Palm Sunday was the day the crowds welcomed Jesus into Jerusalem shouting:

> Hosanna to the Son of David. Blessed is he who comes in the name of the Lord. (Matthew 21:9)

In the old days, to say a prophet came in the name of the Lord was to recognize him as a true prophet of God (Deuteronomy 18:22). So when the people of Jerusalem hailed Jesus as coming in the name of the Lord, while singing the salvation song of Psalm 118, they were saying, "We recognize you as the true Savior."

The Pharisees didn't like this one bit (Matthew 21:15). They did not recognize Jesus as Savior so they were offended by the singing. So Jesus told them, "You will not see me again until you sing the same tune."

For three years the religious rulers of Jerusalem had seen Jesus up close, yet they did not believe he was who he said he was. So Jesus tells them, "You have seen me and not believed. Now you will not see me unless you believe." They would not see him again except by faith.

After he rose from the dead the Lord revealed himself to hundreds of believers, but not once did he appear to the unbelieving Jews (except Paul). They had had their chance, but now he was gone.

But all was not lost. The religious leaders had rejected Jesus, but he had not rejected them. If they were to cry, "Lord, save us," he would be there. The moment they saw him as a blessing from the Lord, they would be blessed.

There is comfort in these words. For as long as there is life there is hope. You may be the worst sinner on the planet, even a murderer of prophets and apostles, but cry for salvation and the Savior will hear.

---

[1] What about when Jesus tells the scribes and Pharisees, "You will receive greater condemnation" (Matthew 23:14)? What about when he said the high priest had committed the greater sin (John 19:11)? Jesus is not saying there are levels to God's judgment and they will be getting the maximum amount of smiting. Condemnation of any sort is self-inflicted (see John 3:18). "For by your words you will be condemned" (Matthew 12:37). The greater condemnation is that inflicted by the hardened and grace-resistant heart. More here: http://wp.me/pNzdT-2bu

[2] God didn't even punish Abel's murderer for the death of Abel. Since the Son is the exact representation of the Father, we can interpret Christ's reaction to the Pharisees as being similar to God's reaction to Cain. So when Jesus says, "Woe to you" in Matthew 23, it's the same cry of dismay God utters when he says "What have you done?" in Genesis 4:10. Just as God does not smite or threaten to smite Cain, Jesus does not threaten to smite the Pharisees. And just as God acts to ensure Cain's survival, so does Jesus with the Pharisees. He literally spends entire chapters of the Bible warning them and exhorting them to change their self-destructive course.

3 The Law of Moses mandated that "Fathers shall not be put to death for their sons, nor shall sons be put to death for their fathers; everyone shall be put to death for his own sin" (Deuteronomy 24:16). But what about this verse: "You shall not worship them or serve them; for I, the Lord your God, am a jealous God, visiting the iniquity of the fathers on the children, and on the third and the fourth generations of those who hate me" (Deuteronomy 5:9). Under the old covenant, God kept accounts up to the third and fourth generations. If the parents rebelled, the children would wander in the wilderness. If mom and dad worshipped idols, the kids would grow up in captivity. But even here there was a statute of limitations (three to four generations) that fell well short of the eight centuries that had passed since the murder of Zechariah. God is not a grudge-keeper. If the parents excluded themselves through unbelief, he made sure their children eventually entered the Promised Land or the captives returned home. God's heart is always to show kindness, even to the runaway and rebel.

4 There are two Greek words for sin: One is a verb (*hamartano*) and the other is a noun (*hamartia*). In almost every mention of sin in the book of Romans Paul uses the noun instead of the verb. Sin is an enemy with intelligence, personality, and desires (see Romans 6:12, 16, 7:11, 14, 8.3). The good news is that sin has been condemned and disarmed by Jesus.

5 Some say the Jews were punished by the old covenant law, as though that which is "holy, righteous, and good" kills people. This is a misunderstanding of the law's purpose. Although Paul referred to the law as the ministry of death (2 Corinthians 3:7), the law itself doesn't kill anyone. Rather, it stirs up and empowers sin and *sin* kills people (Romans 7:9–12). Speaking of the law Paul asks, "Did that which is good become a cause of death for me? May it never be! Rather it was sin" (Romans 7:13). The law is the X-ray that reveals the cancer of sin. It reveals the disease, mocks our pathetic attempts to cure it, and points us to Jesus.

At the beginning of his ministry, in the Sermon on the Mount, Jesus preached the law so that the mortal danger of sin might be recognized. At the time his warnings fell largely on deaf ears. It is fitting that here, at the other end of his ministry, he should warn one final time of the dangers of sin. It is not the law that requires blood and is crouching at the door. It is sin.

22. WHEN ARE THE DAYS OF VENGEANCE?

When you see Jerusalem surrounded by armies, then recognize that her desolation is near ... because these are days of vengeance so that all things which are written will be fulfilled ... There will be great distress upon the land and wrath to this people. (Luke 21:20–23)

When prophesying about the fall of Jerusalem, Jesus referred to the days of vengeance. But whose vengeance was it? Why was it brought about? And what does it mean for us?

Many theologians say it was *divine* vengeance. Eusebius, the church historian, wrote that the Jews met "with destruction at the hands of divine justice." John Chrysostom, the Archbishop of Constantinople, said the Jews experienced "wrath from God intolerable." It's a shocking tune yet many sing it. Following these two ancient writers, many theologians have added their voices to the chorus of condemnation. "Jerusalem fell because God was punishing the Jews for killing his Son." (See Appendix 2 for a list of commentators who see God's hand in the fall of Jerusalem.)

This notion of divine punishment is now so widely accepted, it even appears in some Bible translations:

This is the time when God will punish Jerusalem (Luke 21:22, NIrV)

According to some theologians and Bible translators, days of vengeance means "days of God's punishment of the Jews." But God did not punish Jerusalem, the Romans did. God good, Romans bad. Sure, Jerusalem had heaped up its sins, but those sins were punished on the cross in AD30 and not in AD70. On the cross the Son of God did away with all sin, including the sins of those who put him there. If God was punishing the Jews this is bad news for you, for it means the Lamb of God did not carry the sins of the whole world. Apparently, he missed some.

But don't panic. As we will see, it is inconceivable that God punished the Jews. They certainly experienced days of vengeance, but it was not divine vengeance any more than the Nazi Holocaust was divine vengeance. To suggest otherwise is appalling, yet many people do. They blame God for the hell unleashed on the first-century Jews.

The problem is those Jews weren't the only Jews slaughtered. In AD135 the Roman general Severus and his legions exterminated half a million Jews. Was this God's punishment too? What about the massacres of the Jews during the Crusades, or in Granada (1066), France (1321), Spain (1391), Morocco (1465), Ukraine (the 1650s), Poland (1768), and Germany (in 1096, 1298 and 1941)?

Many of these massacres were initiated by so-called Christians who believed they were doing the Lord's work or at least following in his vengeful footsteps. But why do so many believe that God was involved in the slaughter of the Jerusalem Jews? Who was the first to attribute this massacre to the Lord?

It was none other than Josephus.

The long shadow of Josephus

Every Bible scholar has read Josephus' firsthand account of the destruction of Jerusalem because it's the only account. How do we know that a million Jews died or that the Romans built a barricade? Because Josephus tells us. It's his version of the story that has been passed down through history, and according to Josephus the destruction of Jerusalem was God's doing.

> It was God who condemned the whole nation and turned every course that was taken for their preservation to their destruction. (*Wars*, 5.13.5)

Why did Josephus point the finger at God? Because he was Jewish. As a Hebrew and a priest, Josephus was well acquainted with Jewish history. He knew all the old stories of how God used the Assyrians and Babylonians to besiege Jerusalem and punish the Jews for their sins. To his Jewish mind, the Romans were just another tool in the hands of an angry God.[1]

Josephus started out fighting against the Romans in Galilee, but after being defeated by Vespasian he switched sides. He came to the conclusion that God had abandoned Israel and was "now settled in Italy" (*Wars*, 5.9.3).

If God was on the side of the Romans, then so was Josephus. He became an interpreter and a mouthpiece for Vespasian and then Titus. When Jerusalem was under siege he would stand outside the city walls encouraging his Jewish brothers to capitulate with words like these:

It is God himself who is bringing on this fire to purge (this) city and temple by means of the Romans; and is going to pluck up this city, which is full of your pollutions. (*Wars*, 6.2.1)

Josephus would groan and weep as he spoke, as though he was a first-century Jeremiah, calling the Jews to repentance. In speeches peppered with references to Egypt's Pharaoh, Sennacherib of Assyria, and Cyrus the Great of Persia, he urged the Jews to confess their faults and cast away their weapons.

Hearken to me, that you may be informed, how you fight, not only against the Romans but against God himself. (*Wars*, 5.9.4)

Needless to say, the Jewish defenders hated Josephus for being a turncoat, and they did their best to drop rocks on his head. Josephus was off his rocker, they thought. He had Stockholm syndrome. The Romans weren't God's agents but his enemies seeking to erect their abominable idols in his temple.

Righteous Romans?

Had some other Jew written about the fall of Jerusalem, Josephus would have been branded a coward and a traitor. But Josephus wrote the story, so it was important for him to convince his readers that he and the Romans were on the side of righteousness. Consequently, the military tactics of the invaders are framed in the language of divine judgments:

Titus … resolved to storm the temple, the next day, early in the morning, with his whole army: and to encamp round about the holy house. But as for that house (the temple), God had, for certain, long ago doomed it to the fire. And now that fatal day was come. (*Wars*, 6.4.5)

The city fell and the temple burned because God was a Roman and he wore a Roman sword. Seditious Jews were dug out of hiding places because they could not hide "either from God or from the Romans" (*Wars*, 6.7.3) Defenders fled from towers because "they were ejected out of them by God himself" (*Wars*, 6.8.5).

With so much aid from the Lord, it's a wonder the siege lasted as long as it did. Titus could have sent his legions home for with God on his side he barely needed them.

Why was God angry?

Ignorant of all Christ accomplished on the cross, Josephus viewed God through an old covenant lens. If the Jews were slaughtered, it was because God was angry with them. But why? Josephus had no answer beyond vague allusions to wickedness, unavenged deaths, and general impiety.

Enter the Christians.

> I ask the Jews, whence came upon them so grievous wrath from heaven more woeful than all that had come upon them before? Plainly it was because of the desperate crime and the denial of the Cross.[2]

According to John Chrysostom, the Archbishop of Constantinople whose words these are, God was mad at the Jews because they killed his Son. And it was the Jews who killed Jesus, not the Romans, for the Apostle Peter said so on no less than three occasions (Acts 2:36, 3:15, 4:10).

Connect the dots and it made perfect sense: Kill the Son and you'll anger the Father. This was the line taken by Eusebius in the third century, Chrysostom in the fourth, and the many who followed their lead. The destruction of Jerusalem was divine vengeance, pure and simple. But although the teaching came from Christians, its root was undeniably Jewish. The vengeful God was more Josephus than Jesus.

Mr. Preterist: "I resent the implication that I got my views from Josephus. Everything I believe is based on the words of Jesus."

Then how about these words of Jesus: "Anyone who has seen me has seen the Father" (John 14:9). Josephus never saw the Son, so he never saw the Father. He did not know that God had punished all sin on the cross, so he concluded that God was punishing sin in Jerusalem. It was the wrong conclusion, but one that made sense to a priest raised on the old covenant. It also makes sense to some preterists.

To be fair, not every preterist believes that God was vindictive in punishing the Jews. Some say it was a straightforward case of crime and punishment. "God was executing the curses of Deuteronomy 28 upon the Jews as a consequence of their sin and idolatry." Which is like saying Jesus did not carry every sin, and God the Father and Son are a house divided.

Others say God's destruction of Jerusalem was never personal. "God's judgment was not against the Jews but an offensive religious system." So a million dead Jews can be dismissed as collateral damage.

Still others insist that God did not punish the Jews at all. "The Jews cut themselves off through unbelief, causing God to remove his hand of protection." Which makes God an accessory to Roman crimes.

None of these arguments is consistent with the gospel. God did not send the Romans to deal with the lost sheep of Israel; he sent Jesus.

Racist theology

Jesus was Jewish and he loved his countrymen. So did the apostles. They didn't care for the Jews' religion, but they certainly cared for the Jews.

"Brothers and fathers," was how Paul addressed the Jews (Acts 22:1). The Jews weren't criminals but kin. Although Paul did say the Jews killed Jesus and the prophets (1 Thessalonians 2:15), there wasn't a vindictive bone in his body. His heart was for reconciliation, not retribution. His countrymen were misguided for scorning grace, but rather than condemn them he wanted to trade places with them.

> I have great sorrow and unceasing anguish in my heart. For I could wish that I myself were cursed and cut off from Christ for the sake of my people, those of my own race, the people of Israel. (Romans 9:2-4, NIV)

Josephus abandoned his tribe and joined the enemy. In contrast, Paul wished he could be accursed so the Jews could be saved. Josephus had a racist theology that viewed the Jews as uniquely deserving of divine punishment, while Paul had a grace-based theology that saw the Jews in desperate need of salvation. Josephus said the Jews had it coming, but Paul said the Jews were never beyond hope:

> Did God reject his people? By no means! ... Did they stumble so as to fall beyond recovery? Not at all! (Romans 11:1, 11, NIV)

The heart of God, as understood by the apostle of grace, was for reconciliation, not judgment. The Lord desires restoration, not punishment.

Brothers and fathers

Read the New Testament epistles and you sense a kinship between Christian and Jew. However, that began to change after AD70. The Christians fled while the Jews stayed and from then on the distance between them only grew. This dissociation was evident in the way certain Christians spoke about the fall of Jerusalem.

"The Jews had it coming."

Only they didn't. True, there had been a few who shouted at Christ's trial, "His blood be on us and our children" (Matthew 27:25). But just because they said it doesn't mean God did it. It is unthinkable that the One who sits on the throne of grace would punish the descendants of Abraham in this way.[3]

Jesus said, "No one takes my life from me, but I lay it down of my own accord." If so, the Jews cannot be charged with the crime of murder. Even if they did kill the author of life, their sin was borne by Jesus.

Any case against the Jews runs smack into the cross. If God condemned all sin on the cross, he would be unjust in condemning the Jews 40 years later. Not only would he be punishing the wrong generation, he would be insulting his own Son.

I realize I am going against 2,000 years of church tradition, not to mention a couple of badly translated Bibles, but I am 100 percent certain about this. The image of a vindictive Jew-killing God is wholly inconsistent with the gospel of Jesus. It's like saying:

- The Lamb of God carried the sin of the world (John 1:29), except for the Jews'
- Jesus is the propitiation for the world's sins (1 John 2:2), except for the Jews'
- The punishment that brought us peace was on him (Isaiah 53:5), except for the Jews'
- God condemned all sin at the cross (Romans 8:3), except for the Jews'
- God keeps no record of sin (2 Corinthians 5:19), except for the Jews'
- The Holy Spirit forgives all sins (Hebrews 10:17), except for the Jews'
- Love your enemies (Matthew 5:44), except for the Jews

"Father, forgive them."

God did not punish the Jews, and he never had any intention of doing so. So why did Jesus ask for their forgiveness as he hung on the cross (Luke 23:34)?

Why did he ask God to do what he already intended to do? He did it for our benefit. Jesus wanted us to know that God loves his enemies and forgives even the worst of us.

Look at those words again: "Father, forgive them." Jesus is not talking about orphaned refugee children; he's talking about self-righteous prigs who murder in the name of God. Men who smashed Stephen's head with rocks and threw Jesus' half-brother off the top of the temple. Men who responded to the woman caught in adultery by reaching for stones. Men who mocked the Son of God even as he bled and died for them.

Father, forgive *them*.

Don't you see? If God can forgive them, he can surely forgive you. Whatever you've done God's grace is greater. Jesus said it because he wants you to know this.

Why aren't we shouting the good news of God's forgiveness from the rooftops? Why are we ignoring Christ's words and perverting his gospel?

The Roman destruction of Israel unleashed a wave of anti-Semitism that has continued for twenty centuries. This evil is fueled, in part, by racist theology from Christians who ought to know better, such as this guy:

> God visited and avenged the innocent blood of Christ upon the Jews, and they continue to be monuments of his displeasure to the present day.[4]

This anti-Semitic nonsense should be vigorously resisted by everyone and especially those who follow Christ. Jesus did not slaughter the Jews. Nor did he slit their bellies looking for swallowed gems. If you must blame someone for these atrocities, blame the Romans.

When Jesus speaks of armies, vengeance, and wrath in Luke 21, he is referring to *Roman* armies, *Roman* vengeance, and *Roman* wrath. It's the "great distress" of a small nation being squashed by a vengeful empire.

> These are days of vengeance so that all **things which are written** will be fulfilled ... (Luke 21:22)

The days of vengeance phrase is a reference to the "things which are written." Jesus is alluding to calamities foretold by the prophets.

Prophecies about Jerusalem's fall

Centuries before it happened, the prophet Isaiah spoke of siege works and battle towers being raised against Jerusalem. Long before some Roman put an eagle on a pole, Moses spoke of a faraway nation coming "as the eagle swoops down." The coming siege would be so dire, said Moses, that parents would eat their children. Asaph said the blood would run like water, while Micah predicted that the city would become a heap of ruins. All these prophecies were fulfilled in AD70.[5]

The Old Testament prophets saw God through an old covenant lens and so portrayed him as vengeful in an old covenant sense of quid pro quo. But the prophets also revealed a God full of grace. Consider this beautiful picture from Isaiah:

> The Spirit of the Lord God is upon me, because the Lord has anointed me to bring good news to the afflicted; He has sent me to bind up the brokenhearted, to proclaim liberty to captives and freedom to prisoners; to proclaim the favorable year of the Lord and **the day of vengeance of our God**. (Isaiah 61:1–2)

Jesus began his ministry in a synagogue by reading these words (Luke 4:18–19). However, Jesus did not quote the entire passage. He left off the bit about the day of God's vengeance.

Mr. Preterist: "Exactly. Jesus began his ministry to the Jews by preaching favor, but he ended in Luke 21 by declaring vengeance."

Except the vengeance of Luke 21 is Roman vengeance, not divine vengeance. Big difference. Roman vengeance involves armies, wrath, and great distress, while the divine vengeance of Luke 4 brings liberty and freedom. One is bad news; the other is good news.

It's difficult to see how these two kinds of vengeance could ever be confused. Yet for 2,000 years, respected scholars and Bible translators have confused Roman vengeance with divine vengeance. They've mixed good news with bad, and the result has been anti-Semitic grace-killing theology.

We'll contrast the *days* of manmade vengeance with the single *day* of divine vengeance further in Chapter 26.

But first, we'll take a brief look at one of the most badly translated scriptures in the English Bible.

---

[1] Josephus seems to have had a spotty grasp of scripture. He understood that God had used the Babylonians to destroy Jerusalem six centuries earlier, but he seems to have missed the bit where God promised he would never do anything like that again (see Ezekiel 5:9).

[2] Source: Chrysostom, quoted in the *Catena Aurea - Gospel of Matthew* by Thomas Aquinas. Website: www.ccel.org/ccel/aquinas/catena1.ii.xxiv.html. According to the Wikipedia entry for "Jewish deicide", Chrysostom is credited with being the first to use the word deicide and the first Christian preacher to apply it to the Jewish nation. Source: https://en.wikipedia.org/wiki/Jewish_deicide, accessed June 29, 2016.

[3] A Jewish reader, commenting on an early draft of this chapter, noted the deeper meaning of the angry cries of those calling for Christ's execution: "His blood be on us and our children." The blood of the Passover Lamb did indeed cover these sinners, just as the Lord intended. "As a Jew, I'm so grateful that his blood was and always will be upon me and my children!"

[4] This theological nugget is from Adam Clarke's commentary on Hebrews 6. Source: www.studylight.org/commentaries/acc/hebrews-6.html, accessed June 29, 2016.

[5] Deuteronomy 28:49-53, Psalm 79:1-4, Isaiah 29:2-4, Micah 3:9-12.

23. WHOSE WRATH HAS COME?

> (The Jews) killed the Lord Jesus and the prophets and also drove us out. They displease God and are hostile to everyone ... they always heap up their sins to the limit. The wrath of God has come upon them at last. (1 Thessalonians 2:15–16, NIV)

This sounds like something you might read in the Old Testament but it's in the New. It's out of place, and it's almost certainly a reference to the siege of Jerusalem. Those troublesome Jews are sowing the wind and are about to reap the whirlwind. The wrath of God has come upon them at last!

Except it hasn't.

Paul never says this.

Instead, he says, "The wrath has come." Not the wrath of God, just *the wrath*. Certainly, the addition of those two little words *of God* fits the vindictive theology many of us have grown up with, but they're not in the Bible. They were added by the translators who wrote the New International Version.[1]

Does this matter?

Well, considering the NIV is arguably the world's most popular Bible, with 450 million copies in print, I think it does. That's nearly half a billion people who have been led to believe that the Bible says the Jews fell under the wrath of God when it doesn't.

The NIV: "God smashed the Jews."

The Apostle Paul: "Wait, what? I never said that."

The NIV: "But that's what you meant. Right?"

The Apostle John: "Oooh. Has someone been adding words to the Bible?"

The NIV: "But doesn't the Bible say elsewhere that there is wrath for those who reject Jesus?"

Yes, but that's a different kind of wrath. It's righteous wrath from a just God as opposed to state-sanctioned massacres dealt out by bloodthirsty legions.

PART B: The End of the World

If there is wrath for the Jew who rejects Jesus, it is the same wrath for the Gentile, and it is not dispensed by Romans, Nazis, or any human agent. More on this in the next chapter.

Mr. Futurist: "Paul wrote his letter to the Thessalonians in AD51. So why does he say the wrath *has* come when the Romans were still fifteen to twenty years away?"

Because he is quoting Jesus. When Paul speaks of persecution, wrath, and killing, he uses the same words Jesus used when prophesying about the days of vengeance.[2]

The Jews had been murdering the prophets for centuries, but Jesus said their time was up. Their sins had heaped up, and *this* generation would reap the wrathful harvest. So when Paul says the wrath has come, he means the same thing. This generation was so hostile and antagonistic to all that there would be terrible consequences. This generation would experience wrath and it did: Roman wrath.

Get your view of God from the Old Testament or badly translated scriptures, and you may think that God punished the Jews for killing his Son. But this is a perversion of the gospel and a distortion of history. The gospel declares that Jesus died for the Jews, not the other way around.

But what about those parables where Jesus spoke of wrathful kings and murderous landowners? I was just coming to that.

---

[1] The words "of God" are not in the best manuscripts used by the major Bible translations, but the NIV is hardly the only translation to include these extra words. Most of the major paraphrase Bibles interpret "the wrath" as wrath or anger from God. This group includes the Bible in Basic English, the Contemporary English Version, the Easy-to-Read Version, the Good News Bible, the Jubilee Bible, the Message Bible, the New International Reader's Version, and the New Living Translation. Somewhat surprisingly, a few word-for-word translations also add these extra words. This group includes the Revised Standard Version and the Amplified Bible. However, most Bible translations, including the American Standard Version, the English Standard Version, the Holman Christian Standard Bible, the International Standard Version, the King James Version, the New King James Version, the New American Standard Bible, as well as the literal translations (such as Berean's, Wuest's, and Young's), do not add these extra words. Here's how the phrase appears in Young's Literal Translation: "the anger did come upon them – to the end!"

[2] Space precludes me from unpacking the fascinating comparison between Jesus and Paul's words here. For more, see my E2R article entitled, "The wrath has come."

24. GOOD NEWS IN THE PARABLES OF JUDGMENT

> But the king was enraged, and he sent his armies and destroyed those
> murderers and set their city on fire. (Matthew 22:7)

In the Parable of the Wedding Banquet, a king sends servants to invite people
to his son's wedding feast (Matthew 22:2–14). However, some of those invited
mistreat and kill the servants, and the king responds by destroying and burning their city. What is this parable about? For some, it is a prophetic picture of
AD70 and God's so-called destruction of Jerusalem.

> This (parable) doubtless refers to the Jews and to Jerusalem. They were
> murderers, having slain the prophets; and God was about to send
> forth the armies of the Romans under his providential direction, and
> to burn up their city.[1]

This commentator may be doubtless, but I have a few reservations. I can't help
but note that his interpretation conflicts with the parable in several ways. In
the parable, the king's wrath is only poured out on the murderers. But in
AD70 Roman wrath resulted in the deaths of countless women, children, and
people who had nothing to do with the murder of anyone.

In the parable, the king completely destroys his enemies. If the Jews
were God's enemies, how come we still have Jews?

In the parable, the armies of the king is a reference to the heavenly
host. Angel armies, not Roman legions.

It should be obvious to anyone acquainted with the gospel of grace
that the Parable of the Wedding Banquet has nothing to do with AD70. As we
saw in Chapter 22, Jesus came to save the Jews, not destroy them. So what
does the parable mean?

The wrath of the king

To interpret the parable, we need to consider three connected words: wrath,
destroyed, and burning. In the story, the wrath of the king leads to the destruction of his enemies and the burning of their city.

The wrath of the king is a reference to the coming day of wrath
(Romans 2:5). We can be sure that day remains in the future because God's

enemies – child trafficking, domestic violence, cancer, rape, Alzheimer's, terrorism, incontinence, tooth decay, etc. – are still with us.[2]

The word for destroy means utterly or fully destroyed. It is the same word that is translated perish in John 3:16: "Whoever believes in him shall not perish, but have eternal life."

God gives love and life, but some reject his gifts. When you reject life, what is left but death and destruction? God doesn't want anyone to perish, which is why he is holding back on the day of wrath.

Which brings us to the mystery of why the king in the story, having destroyed his enemies, would take the apparently unnecessary step of burning their city. What is to be gained by this since they are already dead? And what is the city that is burned?

Mr. Preterist diminishes the wrath of God by saying it was first-century Jerusalem. Others argue that the burning city is Rome, the Catholic Church, or America. It is none of the above. In John's language it is Babylon the Great. It is the City of Man, which stands opposed to Zion, the City of God.

The tale of humanity's fall and redemption is a tale of two cities. After Cain murdered his brother, he went east and founded a city (Genesis 4:16–17). He laid the foundation for a civilization built on violence and vengeance. In contrast, Abraham went west looking for a city whose architect and builder is God (Hebrews 11:8–10). He was looking for a new civilization, a peaceable city, built on the Prince of Peace.

> For here we do not have an enduring city, but we are looking for the city that is to come. (Hebrews 13:14, NIV)

Cain's city, or the City of Man, embodies the murderous spirit of Satan. It is the "dwelling place of demons and a prison of every unclean spirit" (Revelation 18:2). It is Satan's home from where he has exported untold misery and pain.

> And in her was found the blood of prophets and of saints and of all who have been slain on the earth. (Revelation 18:24)

All the murders and massacres that have ever been inflicted on the human race were birthed in Satan's city. All the genocides and homicides and infanticides and fratricides that ever were originated here. This bloodstained town is the home of hurt and the seat of all suffering. But the King of kings shall send his heavenly armies and burn that hellish city (see Revelation 18:18).

> Then a strong angel took up a stone like a great millstone and threw it into the sea, saying, "So will Babylon, the great city, be thrown down with violence, and will not be found any longer." (Revelation 18:21)

Babylon the Great cannot be Jerusalem of old. After the Romans destroyed Jerusalem, the city was rebuilt. Then they destroyed it again and it was rebuilt again. But the City of Man will never recover from God's ultimate destruction. In the end, there shall be only one city, the King's city from heaven, which endures forever.

The wrath of the landowner

In the parable of the vineyard (Matthew 21:33–41), a landlord rents out a vineyard to some tenants then sends his servants to collect his fruit. The tenants refuse to pay so the landlord sends his son. However, the tenants kill the son incurring the wrath of the landlord.

> What, then, will the owner of the vineyard do to them? He will come and destroy these vine-growers and will give the vineyard to others. (Luke 20:15–16)

Mr. Preterist would say this parable is a picture of the destructive judgment God unleashed on those who killed his Son. Again, this interpretation diminishes the wrath of God. The landlord doesn't merely kill the tenants; he utterly destroys them. It's a picture of what will happen to God's enemies on the day of his wrath.

Those who heard Jesus tell this story were shocked. "May it never be!" (Luke 20:16). Jesus looked at them then gave this seemingly cryptic response:

> What then is this that is written: "The stone which the builders rejected, this became the chief cornerstone"? Everyone who falls on that stone will be broken to pieces; but on whomever it falls, it will scatter him like dust. (Luke 20:17–18)

Jesus is talking about himself. He is the chief cornerstone over which the Jews stumbled (1 Corinthians 1:23). The stumbling stone is a picture of Christ's first coming when he was meek and mild, but when Christ returns he will come hurtling like an asteroid, metaphorically speaking. It is a picture of sudden and destructive judgment.

If this is a lot to take in, consider the Old Testament scripture from which these stone metaphors are taken:

> Then the iron, the clay, the bronze, the silver and the gold were crushed all at the same time and became like chaff from the summer threshing floors; and the wind carried them away so that not a trace of them was found. But the stone that struck the statue became a great mountain and filled the whole earth. (Daniel 2:35)

Nebuchadnezzar saw a stone not cut by human hands crushing the feet of a statue made of gold, silver, bronze, and iron. The statue represents the kingdoms of this earth, while the falling stone is the kingdom of heaven come down. It is King Jesus winnowing, threshing, and crushing those things that are opposed to his rule.

> In the days of those kings the God of heaven will set up a kingdom which will never be destroyed, and that kingdom will not be left for another people; it will crush and put an end to all these kingdoms, but it will itself endure forever. (Daniel 2:44)

Just as Babylon the Great is cast down like a stone in John's revelation, the statue of Daniel's prophecy is crushed by a falling stone. In the end, the City of Man and the kingdoms of the earth shall fall, and Jesus shall reign un-challenged and unopposed.

> Then the seventh angel sounded; and there were loud voices in heaven, saying, "The kingdom of the world has become the kingdom of our Lord and of his Christ; and he will reign forever and ever." (Revelation 11:15)

We've covered a lot of ground to say this: The parables of the wedding banquet and vineyard signal something far more destructive and glorious than the Roman destruction of Jerusalem. They are prophetic end-of-the-world pictures of the wrath that comes on those things that oppose God and harm his children.

The parable of the talents

In Matthew 25 Jesus gives three parabolic pictures of faith and unbelief. Faith is looking forward to the Lord's return (the parable of the ten virgins); it's receiving the wealth of his grace (the parable of the talents), and investing it in the lives of others (the parable of the sheep and goats). These parables should not be read as moral lessons as in, "You'd better keep watch, get busy, and serve or else!" They are stories about Jesus and what people do with him.

In the parable of the talents (Matthew 25:14–30), Jesus is the man going on a journey and the wealth given to the servants represents his grace, for grace is a gift and not a wage. In the story, the faithful servants were faithful because they received the master's gift, while the lazy servant was unfaithful because he rejected it. The faithful servants prospered because they allowed room for God's grace to work in their lives. At the end of the story they are promoted to co-rulers with their master. "You were faithful with a few things; I will put you in charge of many things." Grace turns servants into kings.

However, the wicked servant missed out because he didn't trust the master. His contempt was evident in the lame excuses he offered for doing nothing with the master's gift: "Master, I knew you to be a hard man." A hard man?! His master gave him a free bag of gold. This was his golden ticket, a way out of servitude, yet he scorned it.

I knew you to be a hard man, reaping where you did not sow and gathering where you scattered no seed. (Matthew 25:24)

"This was your ticket to freedom, you wicked and lazy slave."

In other words, "You're unreasonable Lord. You don't play by the rules. Who gives bags of gold to servants? You must be nuts. I want nothing to do with your reckless grace, and I feel justified in not playing your silly games. Besides, you gave me a lot of money and I didn't want to be held accountable for it. I was afraid and hid your talent in the ground. See, here is what belongs to you" (Matthew 25:25).

This refusal of a gift makes sense to the self-righteous mind. "If I don't earn it, I don't want it. Take back your bag of grace. I don't need it, and I will not be in your debt."

Needless to say, Jesus is not impressed with the third servant. He calls him wicked, lazy, and worthless and has him thrown into the outer darkness. His reaction to the self-righteous servant echoes his response to the foolish virgins in the preceding parable ("I don't know you", Matthew 25:12), and the goats in the succeeding one ("Depart from me", Matthew 25:41).

In the parable of the talents, all three servants get what they desire, and so do we. Those who hunger for God's grace shall have it, while those who prefer the solitary path of the self-made man, even though it leads to misery and darkness, shall have that too.

So what is the takeaway? Take the Master's bag of gold and spend it, trade it, invest it, do whatever you like with it, but don't hand it back unopened and unused. Grace, like gold, is meant to be used, not left in the ground. But unlike gold, God's grace never runs out. As you draw on his grace to purchase freedom, health, deliverance, and wisdom, his grace grows, and "the one who has will be given more, and they will have an abundance" (Matthew 25:29).

To see his children growing and prospering in grace makes the Lord happy. It will make you happy too.

---

[1] Albert Barnes (1832), "Matthew 22," *Notes on the New Testament: Explanatory and Practical. Vol. I – Matthew and Mark.* Source: www.biblehub.com/commentaries/barnes/matthew/22.htm.

[2] The New Testament talks about two outpourings of divine wrath: (1) The wrath of God that was poured out on all sin at the cross (Romans 8:3), and (2) the coming day of wrath when God will pour out his wrath on all ungodliness and unrighteousness (Romans 1:18–19). On the cross, God dealt with the toxic fruit of sin; at Judgment Day he will deal once for all with the root of unbelief.

25. PAYBACK AND RELIEF

God is just: He will pay back trouble to those who trouble you and give relief to you who are troubled, and to us as well. This will happen when the Lord Jesus is revealed from heaven in blazing fire with his powerful angels. He will punish those who do not know God and do not obey the gospel of our Lord Jesus. (2 Thessalonians 1:6–8, NIV)

Pay back trouble? Punish those who don't obey? This sounds like law-based vengeance, but it's in the new covenant. It seems out of place.

Paul is not talking about punishment but justice. "God is just." The word for punish is translated in other Bibles as vengeance and is based on a word that means to set things right.[1]

When Paul tells the Thessalonians that God will deal out retribution or render vengeance, he's saying God will set things right. There is evil and injustice in the world, God does not like it, and he will deal with it once and for all when Jesus returns. The troublemakers will reap payback because they "do not obey the gospel of our Lord Jesus" (2 Thessalonians 1:8). They "do not know God," and one day Jesus will say, "I don't know you" (Matthew 7:23). Because of their stubborn and unrepentant hearts, these troublemakers are storing up wrath for the day when God will "render to each person according to his deeds" (Romans 2:5–6). Their payback will be the self-inflicted wage one gets for rejecting God's kindness. It's the full-ripened fruit of hard unbelief.[2]

But how is the promise of future payback supposed to bring relief to the troubled Thessalonians now?

Relief to you who are troubled

The Thessalonians faced opposition from religious Jews. Paul said God would give them relief but how?

Mr. Futurist might say that relief comes in the hereafter. But the offer of distant relief in the sweet by and by is little comfort indeed. "You are experiencing hardship now, but one day you will die, and then things will get better." In other words, death is your savior.

Mr. Preterist would say that relief would come when God ended the Jews' religion by destroying their temple in Jerusalem. So God will bring comfort by orchestrating the massacre of a million Jews in a faraway town in about twenty years.

Neither answer is Biblical. Neither offers the prospect of real relief now.

Relief to the troubled does not imply the removal of trouble. Jesus said, "In the world you will have trouble" (John 16:33). It could be religious Jews today or godless Romans tomorrow, but trouble is a fact of life. When Paul was troubled by a thorn in the flesh, God did not remove the thorn. Instead, he gave him the grace to deal with it. He gave him strength for his weakness (2 Corinthians 12:7–9).

> Blessed be the God and Father of our Lord Jesus Christ, the Father of mercies and God of all comfort, who comforts us in all our affliction so that we will be able to comfort those who are in any affliction with the comfort with which we ourselves are comforted by God. (2 Corinthians 1:3–4)

Paul understood that God comforts us and gives us relief *in our afflictions*, and he does this by revealing more of Jesus to us. "Our comfort abounds through Christ" (2 Corinthians 1:5).

> I have said these things to you, that in me you may have peace. In the world you will have tribulation. But take heart; I have overcome the world. (John 16:33, ESV)

If Christianity means anything, it means we can enjoy supernatural peace in times of trouble. An example will help:

> For even when we came into Macedonia our flesh had no rest, but we were afflicted on every side: conflicts without, fears within. (2 Corinthians 7:5)

When Paul was in Macedonia he was beaten with rods in one city then hounded out of two others. He had no rest or relief. How did God give Paul relief during this time of trouble?

But God, who comforts the depressed, comforted us by the coming of Titus; and not only by his coming but also by the comfort with which he was comforted in you, as he reported to us your longing, your mourning, your zeal for me; so that I rejoiced even more. (2 Corinthians 7:6–7)

"God comforted us" when Titus arrived. It is not hard to imagine Paul leaving Macedonia downcast and depressed. He was battered, bruised, and down in the dumps. Then Titus showed up and Paul was comforted. His cheerful presence and good report brought relief, even joy.

Observe that Paul's comfort did not require a Roman slaughter of the troublesome Macedonians. Nor was it postponed to Judgment Day. Paul experienced the Lord's comfort in the coming of Titus, which is astonishing when you think about it. We who carry Christ can release comfort to the hurting simply by showing up.

Meanwhile in Thessalonica

The Christians were experiencing trouble, but Paul said God would give them relief. What form would that relief take?

Finally, brethren, pray for us that the word of the Lord will spread rapidly and be glorified, just as it did also with you; and that we will be rescued from perverse and evil men; for not all have faith. But the Lord is faithful, and he will strengthen and protect you from the evil one. (2 Thessalonians 3:1–3)

Life would be sweet if we could be spared from perverse and evil men, but Paul is wise enough to know it doesn't always happen. Sometimes the thorns remain. But God's grace is sufficient. Haters gonna hate, but "the Lord is faithful."

What happened in Thessalonica? The Bible doesn't say. Perhaps the Lord sent Titus or another letter from Paul. Maybe he intervened directly. We don't know how the promise was fulfilled, but we can be certain that the Thessalonians found the Lord was faithful.

And he remains just as faithful today.

When troubles come we can rest assured that the Lord will strengthen and protect us.

---

[1] Need an example? Think of the zealous Corinthians clearing their names with zeal and vindication (2 Corinthians 7:11, NKJV). Their desire wasn't to punish but to set things right.

[2] Those who reap payback are those who have encountered Jesus and rejected him (John 3:36). Jesus describes unbelievers as evil-*doers* and *workers* of iniquity (Matthew 7:23), which implies an action. In a Biblical sense an unbeliever is someone who denies the Lord (Jude 1:4), turns away from God (Hebrews 12:25), and delights in wickedness (2 Thessalonians 2:12). What about those who never hear the gospel or who die in infancy? Articles addressing these questions can be found on Escape to Reality.

26. HUMAN VERSUS DIVINE VENGEANCE

When Abel was murdered, his blood cried out to God for vengeance. Yet God did not kill Cain the murderer, but he protected him against those who would seek his life. Clearly, God's idea of vengeance was different from Abel's.

By now it should be clear that Roman wrath is unlike divine wrath, and Roman vengeance has nothing in common with the Lord's vengeance. The scriptures contrast human and divine vengeance. One seeks payback and retribution; the other pursues peace and restoration. One is vindictive; the other is vindicating. One punishes wrong; the other makes right.[1]

Human vengeance is codified in the old law of an eye for an eye. Divine vengeance, in contrast, is revealed in the grace that forgives, restores, and makes new. The former is based on your badness, while the latter is based on God's goodness.

In Isaiah 29, the prophet paints a bleak picture of human vengeance, but in Isaiah 61, he describes divine vengeance. See if you can spot the difference:

Human vengeance involves:	*Divine vengeance involves:*
Distress, being brought low, lamenting and mourning, destruction and death (Isaiah 29:2–4)[2]	Good news to the afflicted, healing to the brokenhearted, liberty to the captives, freedom to the prisoners (Isaiah 61:1–2)

The first prophecy points to the Assyrians, Romans, and every nation who ever besieged Jerusalem; the second points to Jesus (which is why Jesus quoted it at the start of his ministry, see Luke 4:18–19). Roman vengeance involved brutal and violent retribution, but divine vengeance is nothing like that. What does divine vengeance look like? We get an idea from studying Isaiah's prophecy:

> … the day of vengeance of our God, to comfort all who mourn, and provide for those who grieve in Zion – to bestow on them a crown of beauty instead of ashes, the oil of joy instead of mourning, and a garment of praise instead of a spirit of despair. They will be called oaks of righteousness, a planting of the Lord for the display of his splendor. They will **rebuild** the ancient ruins and **restore** the places long devastated; they will **renew** the ruined cities that have been devastated for generations. (Isaiah 61:2–4, NIV)

Words associated with human vengeance include revenge, retribution, and punishment, but words associated with divine vengeance include rebuild, restore, and renew. It's true that some Old Testament writers portrayed God as smiting his enemies, but in the New Testament, the Son of God loved his enemies. The Pharisees thought God hated sinners, but Jesus revealed a God who cares for them and forgives the worst of the worst. Josephus imagined God destroying Jerusalem, but Jesus revealed a God who wept over the city. It was a radically different picture.

> You have come ... to Jesus, the mediator of a new covenant, and to the sprinkled blood, that speaks a better word than the blood of Abel. (Hebrews 12:22, 24)

Abel's blood cried out "Vengeance! Vengeance!" and the result was a curse, but Jesus' blood cries out "Forgiveness! Forgiveness!" and those who hear it are blessed.

The Romans came to Jerusalem to kill and enslave, but Jesus came to bring life and set free. He was a walking, talking testimony of divine vengeance. His heart was to restore rather than punish and to rebuild rather than demolish. This desire to make things right rather than punish wrong things can be seen in the extraordinary way Jesus related to the temple that condemned him and the city that killed him.

Jesus for Jerusalem

On the night he rose from the dead, Jesus instructed his disciples to preach a new message of unconditional forgiveness.

> Thus it is written, and thus it was necessary for the Christ to suffer and to rise from the dead the third day, and that repentance and remission of sins should be preached in his name to all nations, beginning at Jerusalem. (Luke 24:46–47, NKJV)

The message of grace and forgiveness was for all nations, but it was particularly for the Jews. "Beginning at Jerusalem," said Jesus, as though he knew there would be some who would deny grace to his killers. "God's grace is for all, but those in Jerusalem get to hear about it first." Then, before he ascended to heaven, he said it again. "Be my witnesses in Jerusalem ..." (Acts 1:8b).

There is a reason why Jerusalem is considered the birthplace of Christianity and it is not just because Christ died there. By the Lord's command Jerusalem was the first place evangelized with the gospel. By the Holy Spirit's direction, Jerusalem was the location of Pentecost. And by the apostles' obedience, Jerusalem was the birthplace of the church.

Jesus did not wash his hands of Jerusalem. Nor did he tell his apostles to give the city a wide berth. Instead, he designated the city Mission Field Number One. The apostles did what he asked, and their teaching spread all over Jerusalem. The result was nothing short of miraculous. The city that had rejected the Lord began to change, and the number of Christians in Jerusalem increased greatly (Acts 5:28, 6:7).

Jerusalem had rejected Jesus, but he never rejected Jerusalem. The Jews had spurned him, but he continued to woo them to himself. Not even death would hinder his relentless love.

As for the city, so for the temple.

The cross and the temple stood in opposition to one another, yet Christ's cross came down while the temple stayed up. That building, so hostile to the Lord, did not tumble during the earthquake that accompanied his death. Nor was it consumed by heavenly fire when he rose from the grave.

When the Lord needed an apostle of grace, he recruited a hate-filled Pharisee. And when he needed a venue for the early church, he chose the courts of the most anti-Christ building in the world (Acts 2:46, 3:11, 5:12, 42).

Where did the apostles perform their first miracle? It was at the gates of the temple (Acts 3:2).

When an angel released the apostles from prison, where did he tell them to preach the gospel? At the temple (Acts 5:20).

And after the apostles were flogged and ordered not to speak in the name of Jesus, where did they daily continue to preach the good news of Jesus Christ? (Acts 5:42). You guessed it.

This is grace, and this is what God does. He redeems and repurposes. He takes those things that are opposed to him and turns them around for good.

That the Lord would choose *this* building and *this* city to demonstrate his goodness and power speaks volumes to the graciousness of a good God who does not treat us as our sins deserve.

---

[1] According to W.E. Vine, the New Testament word for vengeance means "(that which proceeds) out of justice, not, as often with human vengeance, out of a sense of injury or … a
feeling of indignation." To our minds vengeance connotes payback and retribution for harms
done. But divine vengeance is about righteousness. It's making broken things whole and
crooked paths straight. In commenting on how vengeance is used in 2 Thessalonians 1:8,
Vines notes that "in the Divine exercise of judgment there is no element of vindictiveness,
nothing by way of taking revenge." Sources: "Ekdikesis" (G1557), *Vine's Expository Dictionary
of New Testament Words*, website: http://bit.ly/V_avenge

[2] Isaiah 29 is a prophecy about Jerusalem being besieged (probably by Sennacherib and the
Assyrians in 701BC, although Jerusalem was besieged many times, including twice by the
Romans). Isaiah frames this prophecy as a conversation between the Lord and Ariel ("I will
camp against you encircling you"), but the fact is Jerusalem was besieged by foreign tyrants,
not the Lord. If the Lord was besieging Ariel, why would he send an angel to destroy the
besiegers (2 Kings 19:35)? He would be attacking himself.

Isaiah filtered his words through an old covenant mindset where it made sense to envision
God punishing Israel for her sins. But when Isaiah prophesied about the new covenant, he
didn't write like this. Thus the vengeance of Isaiah 61 is unlike that of Isaiah 29. It's not that
God has changed, but his covenantal relationship with Israel has changed.

27. WHY DID JERUSALEM FALL?

Throw a rock into a room full of theologians and chances are you'll hit someone who says Jerusalem fell on account of divine vengeance. It's an idea as popular as it is wrong. The Jews weren't punished or chastised for their sins; Jesus was (Isaiah 53:5).

But if God didn't punish Jerusalem, why did it fall? What answer does the Bible provide? This one:

> If you, even you, had only known on this day what would bring you peace – but now it is hidden from your eyes. The days will come upon you when your enemies … because you did not recognize the time of God's coming to you. (Luke 19:42–44, NIV)

Jerusalem was doomed because the people and their rulers did not recognize the time of God's coming. They didn't recognize Jesus (Acts 13:27). They shut their eyes to the Prince of Peace even as he walked among them. If the Jews had embraced him and his gospel of peace they would not have been crushed by the Romans.

Jesus said, "Love your enemies," but the Jews hated their enemies. Jesus said, "Pray for those who persecute you," but the Jews fought and murdered their oppressors. Jesus "preached peace to you who were far away, and peace to those who were near" (Ephesians 2:17), but the Jews didn't listen. All his talk about turning the other cheek and going the extra mile was lost on them. They were looking for a sword-wielding messiah, not a peace-making Savior.

Jerusalem did not fall because the Jews sinned more than others or because some of their daddies participated in the crucifixion of the Savior. Jerusalem fell because when you reject the things that bring you peace, you end up with no peace. The city that is named "shall see peace" never did.

By persecuting Jesus the religious Jews showed they were more than ready to engage in the politics of violence as practiced by the Romans. They weren't interested in a new kingdom built on love and forgiveness. They were driven by hatred and a lust for power. The idealistic Zealots murdered all who got in their way, while the "law-abiding" Pharisees persecuted the Christians and tried to kill the apostles (Acts 5:33). And these were the comparatively good citizens of first-century Jewish society. We have not mentioned the homicidal Herodians, the lawless gangs, or the bloodthirsty warlords who emerged in the years following Christ's prophecy.

So why did Jerusalem fall?

Short answer: The Jews ticked off the Romans.

The Jews and Romans hated each other with a passion. There are countless stories of their enmity (you can find some in Appendix 1), but one will suffice. In AD66, Jewish assassins attacked the Roman garrison in Jerusalem and slew all the soldiers. War followed. There is nothing mystical about this. In fact, Jesus said it would happen:

> Put your sword back into its place; for all those who take up the sword shall perish by the sword. (Matthew 26:52)

This is not rocket science. Murder Roman soldiers and you can expect Roman retribution. Yank on the tail of the tiger and you will see his teeth.

Mr. Preterist: "If AD70 had nothing to do with divine revenge, and if Jesus was so concerned about Jerusalem that he wept, why didn't God stop all this from happening?"

My goodness, he tried! He sent a string of old covenant prophets to warn them, but the Jews didn't listen. Then he sent John the Baptist, but they still didn't listen.[1]

Then God sent his own Son. The Jews ignored him too, then they killed him.

At this point, most of us would've thrown up our hands in despair. "To hell with you turkeys." But God is not like that. His love never quits. Even after they killed his Son he kept sending apostles and guys with shining faces like Stephen to preach the message of reconciliation.

And the message began to bear fruit. Many Jews, even priests, received the word of grace (see Acts 2:41, 6:7). But those in power remained violently opposed to the Lord. They persecuted and drove out the followers of Christ until there were no Christians left in Jerusalem.

Many have said that the destruction of Jerusalem was God's doing, or that he removed his hand of protection and was indirectly responsible for the events of AD70. But the evidence says otherwise. It was not God's will for the Romans to slaughter a million Jews and he tried to warn them again and again. But the Jews refused to listen. They preferred war to peace and death to life.

The Jews killed the prophets who warned them; they killed the Son of God who loved them; they killed the apostles who healed them; and they killed the Romans who hated them. In the end, as the bad fruit of their hate-filled tree came to full ripeness, they killed themselves.

Jesus saw it all in advance and he wept bitterly. He didn't want the city to be destroyed, but it happened despite his warnings and pleas. Jerusalem's dramatic fall in AD70 has nothing to do with the wrath of God, but it is a towering testimony to the destructive power of sin and selfishness.

---

[1] I imagine John grew weary of preaching to deaf ears. He knew that the religious Jews were headed for destruction. When he saw the Pharisees and Sadducees coming out of the doomed city he said, "Who warned you to flee from the coming wrath?" (Matthew 3:7). But they didn't get the joke.

28. WHAT DID THE HIGH PRIEST SEE?

On the night he was betrayed, there was a dramatic confrontation between the Sanhedrin and Jesus. Picture the scene: Caiaphas, the high priest, is fishing for evidence they can use against the Lord. Many false witnesses come forward, but their lies are transparent and useless. Finally, someone says, "I heard this man say he could destroy the temple and rebuild it in three days." Caiaphas rubs his hands in anticipation.

"This is a serious claim, Jesus. How do you respond?"

Jesus says nothing.

Caiaphas is fed up. He knows they can't make their charges stick. In desperation, he wags his finger and says, "I command you to tell us if you are the Son of God." Jesus finally breaks his silence:

> "You have said so," Jesus replied. "But I say to all of you: From now on you will see the Son of Man sitting at the right hand of the Mighty One and coming on the clouds of heaven." (Matthew 26:64, NIV)

And what happens next can only be described as a self-inflicted wardrobe malfunction. Caiaphas rips his robes, yells "Blasphemy!" and Jesus is as good as dead.

"You will see," said Jesus. But what exactly did Caiaphas see and when did he see it? And why was he so mad to hear about it?

Answer #1: A return

"Jesus was referring to the Second Coming," says Mr. Futurist. "On Judgment Day, when the Son of Man returns in power, men like Caiaphas will look back with regret. On that day the self-righteous will say, 'What fools we were to dismiss Jesus.'"

This isn't a bad interpretation for it captures the situation facing Caiaphas and the Sanhedrin. But it's an imperfect one for Jesus says they will see him *sitting*, not coming, and they will see it "from now on," not in the distant future.

Annas and Caiaphas: High priests and partners in crime

Answer #2: A judgment

"Jesus was referring to the destruction of Jerusalem," says Mr. Preterist. "Having threatened the Pharisees in Matthew 23 and prophesied the fall of the temple in Matthew 24, he's pointing ahead to AD70 when divine vengeance would be dispensed at the hands of the Romans."

There are numerous problems with this interpretation, not the least of which is that it contradicts the gospel, it confuses human vengeance with divine vengeance, and it portrays God as covenantally inconsistent. (More on this in the next chapter.)

In the prophecy Jesus is sitting at the right hand of God; he's not coming in judgment. As we saw in Chapter 14, the phrase "coming on the clouds" is an Old Testament reference to the ascension. So this has nothing to do with either an imminent or future judgment.

But the biggest problem with the AD70 interpretation is that Caiaphas and the old men of the Sanhedrin will be long dead before it happens. They won't be around to see it, yet Jesus said they would. "You will see." So what was Jesus referring to?

Answer #3: A king

Jesus was talking about his imminent coronation.

Jesus told the Sanhedrin that he was the Son of God. They laughed in scorn, but Jesus said, "You will see." This prophecy came to pass almost immediately. Consider what they saw the following day, which was the day of Christ's death.

They saw darkness covering the land, and the temple veil torn from top to bottom. They experienced a rock-splitting earthquake and tombs breaking open (Matthew 27:45, 51). Within 24 hours of Christ saying "you will see," they witnessed a massive demonstration of supernatural power. And that was only the beginning.

On the third morning, there was another earthquake. The stone guarding the tomb was rolled away by an angel, and tough Roman soldiers wilted with fear (Matthew 28:2–4).

The news feeding into the Sanhedrin would have been tough to deal with. Not only were dead saints wandering the streets of Jerusalem (Matthew 27:52), but Jesus himself had been seen in various places. What was going on? Had Jesus risen from the dead? Was this the promised sign of Jonah (Matthew 12:39–40)?[1]

A few weeks later they heard the uproar of Pentecost. Illiterate fishermen were declaring God's wonders in a variety of languages (Acts 2:8). How was this possible? One of the fishermen even said Jesus was sitting at the right hand of God (Acts 2:34).

Was it true, they wondered? Had Jesus' words come to pass?

Then a disabled man was healed on their doorstep. The Sanhedrin summoned the men who did it and realized that Peter and John "had been with Jesus" (Acts 4:13).

You remember Jesus, the guy we crucified last month.

They tried to nip this thing in the bud – this movement, this groundswell, this gnawing sense that they had been wrong – but Jesus wouldn't stay dead.

One of his followers was brought to them and he said, "I see heaven open and the Son of Man standing at the right hand of God" (Acts 7:56).

Mercy! These were the same words Jesus had uttered in the privacy of their court. How could Stephen know this?

Then one of their own, a Pharisee of Pharisees called Saul, encountered the Lord and turned into a completely different person. He wrote letters about Jesus sitting at the right hand of God (Ephesians 1:20, Colossians 3:1, Hebrews 1:13).

The prophecy had been fulfilled. Everything Jesus said had come true.

"You will see," said Jesus, and they did see – numerous tokens of Christ's victory; piles of proof that Jesus was who he said he was.

---

[1] Jesus told the Pharisees and law teachers that they would get no sign except the sign of the prophet Jonah. "For as Jonah was three days and three nights in the belly of a huge fish, so the Son of Man will be three days and three nights in the heart of the earth" (Matthew 12:40, NIV). The sign to look for was Jesus rising from the dead after three days.

There are some interesting parallels between Jesus and Jonah. After Jonah rose from the depths, he said the city of Nineveh would be overthrown or "turned about" in 40 days. The city repented or turned and there was an outbreak of compassion or grace (Jonah 4:11). Similarly, Jesus walked the earth for 40 days after rising from the dead (Acts 1:3), and this was followed by an outbreak of the Holy Spirit, a.k.a. the Spirit of Grace (Acts 2:2). Both Nineveh and Jerusalem experienced the grace of God 40 days after two men rose from the depths.

29. WHEN DID THE OLD COVENANT END?

The Bible is made up of two documents: the Old Testament and the New Testament. These documents roughly equate to two covenants: the old covenant and the new covenant. I say roughly because the old covenant did not begin in Genesis 1 and the new covenant did not begin in Matthew 1.

A covenant is a binding agreement between two parties characterized by promises and obligations. In a Biblical context, a covenant describes how God relates to people. The old covenant, which was based on law, was how God related to the nation of Israel. The new covenant, which is based on grace, is how God relates to everybody, including the Jews. The old covenant came into effect at Mt. Sinai through Moses, Israel's representative, while the new covenant came into effect at Mt. Calvary through Christ, humanity's representative.

The children of Israel broke their covenantal agreement immediately and repeatedly, yet God remained faithful to his end of the deal. Knowing that the Jews would never be able to fulfill the requirements of the law, he sent his Son to fulfill them on their behalf.

On the night before his death, the Son of God announced a "new covenant in my blood" (Luke 22:20). He was declaring his last will and testament, a new covenant that would come into effect when he died (Hebrews 9:16–17).

This new covenant is unlike the old covenant it replaced. The old covenant failed because it hinged on your imperfect obedience, but new covenant endures because it is founded on Christ's perfect obedience unto death. The old covenant says you will be blessed if you do good, but the new declares we are blessed because God is good. The old covenant warns that you will be punished if you do bad, but the new declares that in Christ you are eternally unpunishable.

In every way, the new covenant is superior to the old.

> For if that first covenant had been faultless, there would have been no occasion sought for a second. (Hebrews 8:7)

On the cross the sinless Savior fulfilled all the righteous requirements of the law. The old covenant that had been so shabbily treated by the children of

Israel could now be satisfactorily concluded. With his final breath, Jesus declared, "It is finished" (John 19:30). The old covenant that began when Moses received the law, ended when Christ fulfilled it.

Mr. Preterist: "No, it didn't end, it merely became obsolete. The temple sacrifices continued until God judged Jerusalem in AD70. It was then, 40 years after the cross that God condemned the old covenant, and those aboard that doomed vessel drowned with it."

According to preterism, the old and new covenants coexisted side by side for a generation. This is a convenient syllogism for it means the destruction of Jerusalem can be attributed to a judgmental God fulfilling his old covenant obligations. It gives God a legal window, a 40-year *Kristallnacht*, during which he can exact vengeance on those Jesus-killing Jews.

Needless to say, there are many problems with overlapping covenants, the chief of which is it portrays God as double-minded and double-dealing.

Covenants are like marriages. When one party dies, the other is freed from all covenantal obligations. We died to the law so that we might bear fruit for God through union with Jesus (Romans 7:1–6). But if we run back to our former husband by trying to live under the old ways of the law, we commit spiritual adultery. That's bad, yet according to preterism, God was unfaithful for 40 years. For an entire generation, God had two marriages.

Two kings on the throne?

Those who subscribe to overlapping covenants note that David was anointed king while Saul was on the throne. "The new and the old orders existed side by side, and this parallels what happened in the generation after Christ's death." It's an interesting comparison but it falls down in several respects. David did not ascend to the throne of Israel until after Saul's death. They were never king at the same time. One king followed the other much as the new covenant followed the old.

"David was anointed as a young boy, but it took 40 years for him to take the throne, just as it took 40 years for the old covenant to be replaced by the new." It's a good line, but the numbers don't add up. David was about fifteen when he was anointed by Samuel, and he became king of Judah about fifteen years after that. Fifteen is not 40. Certainly, there were some who considered David to be the rightful king and who urged him to take the throne while Saul lived, but David resisted this temptation vigorously. There was no overlapping kingship and no overlapping covenant.

Mr. Preterist: "What about the children of Israel wandering 40 years in the wilderness before dying from unbelief? Surely that parallels what happened to the generation after Christ."

Well, at least the numbers match, but this hardly demonstrates overlapping covenants.

Mr. Preterist: "But 40 years! Don't you see the parallel?"

The parallel, as explained by the writer of Hebrews, was for the first-century Jews to learn the lesson of those wilderness years and put their faith in God (Hebrews 3:7–19). It's a message that remains relevant today, and it has nothing to do with overlapping covenants.

But long as we're discussing historical parallels, how about this one: The children of Israel were in bondage until they partook of the first Passover, while the first-century Jews were bound to the law right up until the last Passover. The Passover lamb points to Jesus and the cross. When Jesus went to the cross he fulfilled all the righteous requirements of the law so that we might be free in him.

In a manner of speaking, both the first and final Passovers brought freedom to the Jews. Just as the children of Israel lived under one covenant, the first-century Jews of Jerusalem lived under another.

Mr. Preterist: "Okay, what about Ishmael and Isaac? Two sons, one house. One son represented the old covenant; the other represented the new."

Mr. Futurist: "But wasn't Ishmael driven out? (Galatians 4:30)"

Mr. Preterist: "Yes, but only after they had lived side by side for a while, just as the two covenants existed side by side."

Mr. Futurist: "So Ishmael represents the first-century Jews clinging to the old covenant?"

Mr. Preterist: "Precisely."

Mr. Futurist: "But the Jews weren't cast out. They were murdered and burned."

Mr. Preterist: "You're missing the point."

Mr. Futurist: "Which is what – that the Old Testament God took better care of Ishmael and his descendants than the New Testament God took of the Jews?"

Mr. Preterist: "You're being facetious. I'm saying there was a transition from one to the other. Ishmael was the heir and then Isaac was. Similarly, there was a transition from the old covenant to the new."

A transition of covenants

Ishmael was sent away when Isaac was weaned (Genesis 21:8–14). This paralllels the transition between John, the last old covenant prophet (Matthew 11:13), and Jesus, the "messenger of the (new) covenant" (Malachi 3:1).

John famously said of Jesus: "He must increase, but I must decrease" (John 3:30). John wasn't being modest; he was prophesying. He was saying, "The old covenant ministry that I represent must diminish and make way for the new covenant ministry of Jesus." The old covenant had served its purpose, but now Jesus had come it had to go.

When Ishmael left, Isaac would have been three years old. This was roughly the length of time that John shared the stage with Jesus. Before Isaac was born, Ishmael was the heir. But when Isaac came along, Hagar's son had to make way for the son of promise. Similarly, John is the first prophet mentioned in the New Testament. For a brief spell, he was *the* guy. But when Jesus came along John stepped aside. "I'm not the guy. *That's* the guy. I'm not worthy to untie his sandals."

The transition from John to Jesus mirrors the transition from the old to new. Jesus was born under the old law-keeping covenant, but his death marked the start of the new covenant of grace.

We also see the transition from old to new on the Mount of Transfiguration. The Mount of Transfiguration was like a stage play with three characters. On one side stood Moses and Elijah, representing the law and the prophets. The disciples marveled to see these two pillars of the old covenant talking with Jesus. But this was no cast of equals, for the spotlight shone only on one.

> And (Jesus) was transfigured before them, and his face shone like the sun, and his garments became as white as light. (Matthew 17:2)

Initially, all three actors spoke. The old and the new conversed together. Then the Director of the transfiguration play gave his instruction:

> A cloud formed, overshadowing them, and a voice came out of the cloud, "This is my beloved Son, listen to him!" All at once they looked around and saw no one with them anymore, except Jesus alone. (Mark 9:7–8)

What happened to Moses and Elijah? They exited stage left, leaving the Son of promise to stand alone.

The ministries of John, Moses, and Elijah were glorious, but theirs was a fading glory. They could not share the stage with the more glorious ministry of Jesus. By the mandate of heaven, Jesus, the new covenant messenger, speaks alone.

The cross changed everything

The old covenant did not end with John's beheading. Nor did it end with the disappearance of Moses and Elijah on the Mount of Transfiguration. These were dramatic scenes in the final act of the old covenant play, but the curtain did not fall until the climactic sacrifice of God's Lamb.

In the moment Jesus died the temple veil was supernaturally torn from top to bottom signifying that God was done with the old covenant. The law was a shadow, but Christ is the reality. Jesus is the old covenant fulfilled.

> By calling this covenant "new," he has made the first one obsolete; and what is obsolete and outdated will soon disappear. (Hebrews 8:13, NIV)

Mr. Preterist: "The old covenant was passing away, but it hadn't passed away. It was obsolete but still in operation."

The curtain falls on the old covenant

As far as the religious Jews were concerned the old covenant continued to operate as before. But as far as heaven was concerned, it had gone the way of the dinosaurs. Or Windows 95.

The obsolete covenant

Those of us who use PCs occasionally get messages that say, "This program is no longer supported by the developer." This means the program has become obsolete, and we are supposed to download the newer and better replacement. Obsolete does not mean the program has stopped working, but it does mean we will no longer get support from the people who made it.

Some people, like me, resist change. If the old program is still working, we won't replace it. We'll keep using the old email program or the old browser and ignore the persistent reminders to upgrade.

At first this is not a problem. Everything seems to operate as normal. But the end result is invariably heartache and distress. "Where did all my emails go?"

> No one, after drinking old wine wishes for new; for he says, "The old is good enough." (Luke 5:39)

If you're accustomed to Moses, you won't see your need for Jesus. If your liquor is law, you won't guzzle grace. This is why Jesus said sinners were entering the kingdom ahead of the religious (Matthew 21:31). Unacquainted with the old wine of rule-keeping and proper behavior, they were more than ready to imbibe the new wine of unconditional love and acceptance.

> No one puts new wine into old wineskins; otherwise the new wine will burst the skins and it will be spilled out, and the skins will be ruined. But new wine must be put into fresh wineskins. (Luke 5:37–38)

Almost every time Jesus engaged with the priests in the temple, there was conflict and aggravation. The new wine wouldn't go into the old bottle. The new wine needed a new bottle, a new temple of the Holy Spirit.

No doubt many of the priests breathed a sigh of relief when Jesus died. "Finally we can get back to the way we've always done things." The old covenant had been replaced by the new, but they weren't interested in upgrading. "The old is good enough."

Pause for a moment and reflect on the audacity of that statement: The old is good enough. In other words, Jesus died for nothing. Every penitent who brought an animal to the temple and every priest who killed it was saying, "God, your Son's sacrifice means nothing to me." What an offense to heaven. What a slap in the face of the Savior.

But no lightning bolts fell, and the ground did not open up and swallow these blasphemers.

When Aaron's sons brought an unauthorized offering into the tabernacle, fire from God consumed them (Leviticus 10:1–2). Nadab and Abihu died as screaming, burning testimonies to the seriousness of sin. But that was under the old covenant.

Now in the new covenant, priests who brought unauthorized sacrifices went home unharmed. They didn't know it but they were living testimonies of God's grace. Had the old covenant still been in effect, there could have been fire and screaming. There would have been one animal sacrifice and no more. But the old covenant was finished, so unauthorized and blasphemous sacrifices continued for years.

> But he, having offered one sacrifice for sins for all time, sat down at the right hand of God. (Hebrews 10:12)

Jesus sat down but the Jews remained standing for there are no chairs in the temple. For 40 years they carried on with their religious rituals as though nothing had changed when everything had changed. The proof is God never judged them, not in AD30, nor in AD70. How could he when their sin had been borne by the Savior they rejected?

The untorn veil

The old covenant ended at the cross. The finished work finished it. All that was demanded, Christ supplied. All that you need, he has provided.

But many don't see it. In their minds the old covenant continues under the guise of duty and obligation. You see this in the conflicts and confusion of the New Testament church. "Are we under law or aren't we? Does circumcision still matter?" At times, even the leaders seemed to battle with covenant confusion. Consider Peter. One moment he was preaching to Gentiles (Acts 10); the next he was refusing to eat with them (Galatians 2:12).

Mr. Preterist: "This proves that the old covenant was still in existence up until AD70. It took the destruction of the temple to free the early church from its bondage to Jewish law."

Except the church today is not free. Many remain bound by the law. Most of the issues that were debated in the New Testament church are still debated today. Should we observe the law? Do women have a place in leadership? Must I confess my sins? Who can partake of communion? Is grace a license to sin?

How is it that after all this time we are still dealing with these old chestnuts? Surely it is because we have bought into a mixed-up gospel. We are still running the old operating system when we ought to have upgraded to the new. We've put Moses back on the mountain.

> But to this day whenever Moses is read, a veil lies over their heart; but whenever a person turns to the Lord, the veil is taken away. (2 Corinthians 3:15–16)

The old covenant's fulfillment coincided with the tearing of the temple veil, but in the minds of some, the veil remains. It endures whenever Moses is read and people are put under law.

"The law shows me how to live; it teaches me how to please the Lord." Such a lie veils the heart and cheapens the gospel. To read Moses – to put your trust in your law-keeping in light of what Christ has done – is spiritual adultery. It's approaching the Lord with an unauthorized sacrifice. It's bringing your own sandwiches to his table of abundance.

The veil is removed when we abandon Moses for Jesus. It is taken away when we give up trusting in our performance and rely wholly on his. Only Jesus frees us from the yoke of the law (Galatians 5:1). Where the Spirit of the Lord is, there is freedom. But learning to walk in the liberty of the spirit isn't easy. There will be conflicts and misunderstandings. These struggles are recorded in the Bible to encourage us as we learn to walk in grace.

Jesus is the end or culmination of the law for all who believe (Romans 10:4). His cross is the exclamation mark at the end of the old covenant.

30. WHEN IS THE GREAT TRIBULATION?

When I was a boy in Sunday School, I came across an end-times comic that portrayed believers being executed in something called a great tribulation. It was like a holocaust for Christians and it was coming soon. Probably in 1984. Or maybe 1988. But definitely by 1999.

It was years before I realized that cartoon was a form of child abuse and that the great tribulation Jesus spoke of did not feature in my future.

As we saw in Chapter 9, Jesus listed ten specific signs in connection with a great tribulation and all of them were fulfilled within a five-month period in AD70. Embankments, swords, captivity, suffering mothers, captive Jews; everything Jesus predicted came to pass, right down to the last detail. When was the great tribulation? It was in the summer of AD70.

So what? Why does this matter?

It matters because those who are worried about a coming tribulation are filling their bunkers with wheat and ammo when they could be telling others the good news of King Jesus. It matters because our children are being told they'll get their heads chopped off if they don't take the mark of the beast, but they'll burn in hell if they do. And it matters because young people are holding out for the rapture lifeboat when they could be shining in a sin-darkened world.

I have to confess that as an adult I didn't think much about the great tribulation. Like a bad doctor's report, I shut it out of my mind and tried to ignore it. It was only as I studied the Lord's words in Matthew 24 that I realized, "Jesus is talking about a great tribulation. Could this be *the* great tribulation?" Of course it was. There's only one.

"This changes everything," I said to myself. "If the great tribulation is past, it cannot be future." And a dark cloud lifted from my mind.

A new hope

If you are concerned about the great tribulation, I've got good news for you. You will never experience it. Trials and regular tribulations? Sure, these are inevitable. Life is often hard. But a *great* tribulation of unprecedented distress and destruction? It's not going to happen. Never again.

Jesus doesn't want you fearful but hopeful. If you are fearful of something that's not going to happen, you are not walking in the will of God. Renew your mind, put your faith in Jesus, and watch those dark clouds lift.

And the next time something bad happens and the tribulation preachers start with their doom and gloom sermons, don't listen to them. Peddling fear is an effective way to sell books, but they are bad books. Don't read them. If the U.S. dollar tanks or the European Union falls apart or bombs explode in Israel that does not mean the world is about to end. We may live in dark days, but we are children of the light. So get out of your bunker and shine for Jesus.

I have heard people say that more than two-thirds of humanity will be wiped out in a future tribulation and that God will be the one doing it. Nonsense. Don't listen to such folk; listen to Jesus. See what he says about the great tribulation and decide for yourself who is right.

Mr. Futurist: "I've noticed you haven't made many references to the Book of Revelation. Are you aware that the great tribulation is also discussed in Revelation?"

This is a book about Jesus' prophecies rather than John's vision, but Mr. Futurist raises a fair point. The great tribulation appears three times in scripture and two of those occasions are in Revelation (2:22, 7:14). However, John says little about it while Jesus (in Matthew 24) gives us a play-by-play account. Jesus is the first and last word on the great tribulation.

Mr. Futurist: "You are also ignoring the many scriptures about the day of trouble (Daniel 12:1, Zephaniah 1:15) and the great and terrible day of the Lord (Malachi 4:5)."

These Old Testament references to the future day of wrath or the final coming of the Lord have nothing to do with the great tribulation. But don't take my word for it. Consider the first-century believers who voted with their feet. Those who believed Christ was predicting a great tribulation within their lifetimes fled and lived. Those who didn't stayed and died.

Once again the evidence of history fully supports the claims of scripture. Christ gave us ten prophecies regarding the great tribulation (as we saw in Chapter 9), and all of them have been fulfilled.

What about the antichrist?

Mr. Futurist: "You have said very little about the antichrist ..."

Well, the Bible says very little. The word antichrist appears only four times in John's epistles. That's it. This may surprise you but the antichrist is not mentioned in the book of Revelation, and Jesus never spoke of him.

Mr. Futurist: "The antichrist will play a major role in these last days."

But John said the antichrist, or many antichrists, were at work in *his* generation:

> Children, it is the last hour; and just as you heard that antichrist is coming, even now many antichrists have appeared. (1 John 2:18)

An antichrist is someone who denies Jesus is the Christ who has come in the flesh from God (1 John 2:22, 2 John 1:7). Given the context, John was most likely addressing the demonic spirit behind Gnosticism, a false teaching that infiltrated the first-century church. This spirit, according to John, was "now already in the world" (1 John 4:3).

Mr. Futurist: "But the antichrist is the little horn of Daniel 7 and the prince of Daniel 9. Daniel's 70th week culminates in a great tribulation brought about by the antichrist."

Daniel's prophecy of the 70 weeks (Daniel 9:24–27) is essentially a Messianic prophecy that predicts the timing and purpose of Christ's death. It is a stretch to speculate that Daniel was speaking about a future antichrist (since this is inconsistent with what the Bible actually says about the antichrist) or a future tribulation (since the great tribulation has taken place in the manner and timing predicted by Jesus).[1]

We have been told that the antichrist is a charismatic 21st-century leader who will co-opt a one-world government for nefarious purposes, but such a description is so far removed from the Bible I am reluctant to spend any more time on it. Even if such a person did emerge, I fail to see why we should fear him. Greater is he that is in you, than he that is a figment of an over-excited eschatological imagination.

Never again

The Bible records two never-to-be-repeated calamities. The first was the great flood and the second was the great tribulation. You are not worried about another flood because God promised there wouldn't be one (Genesis 9:11). Similarly, we ought not to be concerned about a great tribulation, because Jesus said there would be only one:

> For then there will be great tribulation (affliction, distress, and opp-ression) such as has not been from the beginning of the world until now – no, and never will be [again]. (Matthew 24:21, AMP)

If I could travel back in time and visit my younger self, here's what I would say: Don't buy into any end-times message that fills you with fear. If you are worried about tomorrow, you are not walking in the full revelation of Jesus who is on the throne. Renew your mind and take those fearful thoughts captive to the obedience of Christ. Don't base your end-time views on teachings that contradict the words of Jesus, but fortify your mind with the promises of God's word.

That's a good word. I hope I'm smart enough to listen.

---

[1] Much of the debate surrounding Daniel's 70 week prophecy concerns the timing of the final week. Has this happened (a fulfilled interpretation)? Is it yet to happen (a futurist interpret-tation)? Or is it a bit of both?

If one believes the six signs of Daniel 9:24 point to the cross, as I do, then one may conclude that the 70th week has been fulfilled. However, Daniel 9:27 says he (Jesus) will confirm the (new) covenant ending (or making obsolete) all sacrifice in the *middle* of that final week. Thus, the final week has two parts, and the first three and a half days probably refer to the three and a half years of Christ's ministry.

But what happens in the second half of the final week? Mr. Preterist would say those 3.5 days refer to the 3.5 year interval between Titus' arrival in Israel and his destruction of Jerusalem. Mr. Futurist might say they refer to 3.5 years of future tribulation with a rapture thrown in somewhere. Others say they refer to the present or new covenant age which is timeless.

Adding intrigue to the debate is Daniel's prediction of a prince who will come and destroy the city (Daniel 9:26). This is most likely a reference to Titus, the little horn (see Daniel 7:8) or pre-emperor, who destroyed Jerusalem and oppressed the Jews ("the holy people") for three and a half years ("a time, times, and half a time," see Daniel 7:25). These are intriguing but tangential issues: Daniel's 70 week vision is primarily about Jesus ending sin, atoning for wickedness, gifting us with everlasting righteousness, sealing or confirming Old Testament prophecy, and being anointed as the Holy One (Daniel 9:24). All of these prophecies were fulfilled at the cross.

31. THE FIVE COMINGS OF JESUS

When is Jesus coming? Some say it will be soon. Others say it has already happened. Some say Jesus will return to Jerusalem. Others say he already did. Some say Jesus will return with angels and trumpets. Others say those are just metaphors.

Much of the debate about the coming of Jesus stems from confusion about the different comings of the Lord. You may be surprised to learn this, but the Bible speaks of at least five comings of Jesus. They are the first coming of Jesus to earth, the coming of Jesus to the temple, the coming of Jesus to his Father, the coming of Jesus via the Holy Spirit, and the second or final coming of Jesus to earth.[1]

Mr. Preterist: "Interesting list, but did you know the Second Coming is not Biblical?"

Mr. Futurist: "Say what?"

Mr. Preterist: "Do a search. You won't find 'second coming' mentioned anywhere in the Bible."

Mr. Preterist is correct. In the scriptures, the physical return of Jesus to earth is not called the Second Coming but is referred to as the coming of the Lord or the coming of the Son of Man. It is also known as the day of Christ, the day of the Lord, or *that* day when Jesus is revealed from heaven "a second time" (Hebrews 9:28). For the sake of convenience, we will follow tradition and lump all these phrases together under the label the Second Coming.

On the Mount of Olives, the disciples asked the Lord, "What will be the sign of your coming?" Since there are five comings, which coming were they asking about?

Mr. Preterist: "Look at the context. They had just left the temple. Jesus had said it was coming down, so they were asking when he would come to the temple in the manner foretold by the prophet Malachi."

Mr. Futurist: "Huh?"

Mr. Preterist: "Malachi 3 says the Lord will come to the temple with judgment and burning. Christ reinforced this message when he pronounced the woes of Matthew 23, and the prophecy came true when the temple was destroyed by fire in AD70."

Coming to the temple

Mr. Preterist is talking about a prophecy that should be better known than it is:

> "Behold, I am going to send my messenger, and he will clear the way before me. And the Lord, whom you seek, will suddenly come to his temple; and the messenger of the covenant, in whom you delight, behold, he is coming," says the Lord of hosts. (Malachi 3:1)

For the Jewish exiles who had returned to Jerusalem and rebuilt the temple, this would have been an exciting prophecy. "The Lord is coming to his temple!" But when was this prophecy fulfilled?

The messenger who clears the way is John the Baptist (see Matthew 11:10), and the messenger of the covenant or the Lord who comes after him is Jesus. According to the prophet, the latter follows the former suddenly, like a two-punch combination. First one, then the other. And this is what we see in the gospels; first John then Jesus.

Did Jesus go to the temple? Many times. When he was in Jerusalem Jesus made it his habit to teach in the temple courts.

> Now during the day he was teaching in the temple ... and all the people would get up early in the morning to come to him in the temple to listen to him. (Luke 21:37–38)

Jesus, the messenger of the new covenant, wanted the Jews to hear him, so he went to where they congregated:

> I have spoken openly to the world; I always taught in synagogues and in the temple, where all the Jews come together; and I spoke nothing in secret. (John 18:20)

The new covenant messenger comes to the temple

By coming to the temple to preach the message of the covenant, Jesus fulfilled the words of the prophet Malachi.

Mr. Preterist: "That's a peachy picture, but Malachi 3 speaks of Jesus coming to the temple in judgment and fire."

> But who can endure the day of his coming? And who can stand when he appears? For he is like a refiner's fire and like fullers' soap. He will sit as a smelter and purifier of silver, and he will purify the sons of Levi and refine them like gold and silver, so that they may present to the Lord offerings in righteousness. (Malachi 3:2–3)

Some believe this passage refers to the Roman destruction of the temple, but the "Who can stand" phrase comes from the Psalms:

> If you, Lord, kept a record of sins, Lord, who could stand? But with you there is forgiveness, so that we can, with reverence, serve you. (Psalm 130:3–4, NIV)

No one can stand before a holy and righteous God. All of us fall short of the lofty standard, and we all need the forgiveness that Christ freely offers. The problem was, the religious leaders didn't see it. They thought they could stand on their own moral performance, which is why Jesus was so hard on them. He pummeled them with the law so that their boasting mouths might be silenced and they might see their need for grace.

The refiner's fire and fuller's soap is not a reference to murderous Romans, but Jesus dividing the pure from the dross and cleansing the sinner. The prophet said, "He will purify the sons of Levi" and Jesus did this by offering himself on the cross:

> (Jesus) gave himself for us to redeem us from every lawless deed, and to purify for himself a people for his own possession, zealous for good deeds. (Titus 2:14)

Mr. Preterist: "But Malachi 3:5 says the Lord will draw near for judgment."

And judgment is what happened when people encountered the Lord in the temple: Some believed him, others rejected him. That's judgment.

> He who believes in him is not judged; he who does not believe has been judged already. (John 3:18)

Judgment is not merely something that happens in the distant future. Judgment Day is a future manifestation of a present reality.

During his time on earth, Jesus declared, "For judgment I came into this world" (John 9:39). He wasn't saying, "I'm here to judge y'all," for he also said, "I pass judgment on no one" (John 8:15). Judgment is what happens when we respond to the person of Jesus Christ.

Put it all together and we see that Malachi's prophecy of the Lord coming to the temple to refine, cleanse, and judge was fulfilled during his time on earth. Jesus went to the temple because he wanted the sons of Levi or the priests to hear the good news of the kingdom. Sadly, many of them rejected his message, which is why, on his last visit, he pronounced the woeful consequences of their choice, as we saw in Chapter 21.

But his mission to purify the sons of Levi was not a failure by any stretch. We have this idea that the priests all hated Jesus, but the fact is he won many:

> The word of God kept on spreading, and the number of the disciples continued to increase greatly in Jerusalem, and a great many of the priests were becoming obedient to the faith. (Acts 6:7)

As a result of the Lord coming to the temple, many sons of Levi became followers of Christ.[2]

> Then the offering of Judah and Jerusalem will be pleasing to the Lord as in the days of old and as in former years. (Malachi 3:4)

Judah and Jerusalem were not made pleasing to the Lord on account of a Roman massacre. They were made pleasing by Jesus. Before Jesus came along, Jerusalem was the center of self-righteous religion. It was a hotbed of hypocrisy. But after Jesus left it became the birthplace of his church and ground zero for his gospel.

The prophecy about the Lord coming to the temple to do all the things Malachi said was fulfilled minutes before the disciples asked Jesus about the sign of his coming. So either they were slow on the uptake, or they had a different kind of coming in mind.

The coming of the Lord

Which coming of the Lord did the disciples ask about? This question has stirred much debate. However, we don't have to guess what the disciples were thinking. We just need to consider the answer Christ gave them. It starts like this: "See that no one misleads you. For many will come in my name, saying, 'I am the Christ,' and will mislead many ..." (Matthew 24:4–5).

Jesus gave them the counterfeit, and then he gave the authentic. He told them what his coming wouldn't be like, and then he told them what it would be like. And to make sure they fully understood, he provided seven pictures that have become familiar to all Christians.

Jesus said the coming of the Son of Man will be like lightning, visible from east to west. It will be as it was in the days of Noah when people knew nothing until it happened. It will be like a thief coming when you don't expect him, or a master returning to his household, or a bridegroom coming to his wedding. It will be like a man who entrusts his wealth to his servants, goes away, and then returns to see what they did with it. It will be like a shepherd separating his sheep from the goats.

These are seven pictures of the second or final coming of Jesus. They are not pictures of Jesus coming to the temple or to his Father, and they certainly are not pictures of Romans coming to kill. They are pictures of the coming day of the Lord, a day which separates the present age from the age to come. The disciples wanted to know when that day would come. So do we.

---

[1] Here is a sampling of scriptures about the five comings of Jesus: The first coming to earth (John 3:13), the coming to the temple (Malachi 3:1–4), the coming to the Father (John 17:11, 20:17), the coming via the Holy Spirit (John 14:18), and the second or final coming to earth (Matthew 16:27, Acts 1:11).

[2] One of the sons of Levi became instrumental in releasing the Apostle Paul into ministry. His name was Barnabas (Acts 4:36).

32. WHEN IS THE SECOND COMING?

> The Son of Man will come at an hour when you do not expect him …
> The master of that servant will come on a day when he does not expect
> him and at an hour he is not aware of. (Matthew 24:44b, 50, NIV)

Again and again, Jesus says his return will be unexpected. In other words, it's
not like having a baby. When you're expecting a baby, you're *expecting* a baby.
But the coming of Jesus will be unexpected. Unexpected is the opposite of
expected.

If you're pregnant and you try to guess the day of the delivery, you
may be more or less right. But try and guess the day of the Lord and you're
guaranteed to be wrong, for the Lord will come "when you do not expect
him."

If you're pregnant you might buy a book listing things to expect when
you're expecting. But there is no such book for the return of the Lord. Or
rather, there are hundreds of books, but they are all wrong, for the Lord will
come "when you do not expect him."

I'm laboring the point because many have been seduced by claims that
are contrary to the words of Jesus. "I can tell you when Jesus is coming back."
No, you can't.

Like the rest of us, the disciples wanted to know when Jesus would
come, and he told them, "I don't know" (Matthew 24:36). Evidently, the disciples had a hard time accepting this because they asked him again after his
resurrection.

> So when they had come together, they were asking him, saying, "Lord,
> is it at this time you are restoring the kingdom to Israel?" He said to
> them, "It is not for you to know times or epochs which the Father has
> fixed by his own authority." (Acts 1:6–7)

Meaning, "I still don't know, and it's none of your business." The timing of
his coming is the Father's business. It's not our business. So don't listen to
anyone who says they know when the Lord will return. They are wrong.

> But you, brothers and sisters, are not in darkness so that this day
> should surprise you like a thief. (1 Thessalonians 5:4, NIV)

Some interpret Paul's words to mean, "We can figure out when the Lord will return so as not to be surprised." Yet after 2,000 years no one has succeeded, and not for lack of trying. Look up the bestseller lists under prophecies on Amazon and you will find plenty of books offering timelines and predictions regarding the Lord's return. (Consumer tip: They can only be right if Jesus is wrong. Save your money.)

Paul is not saying you can figure this out and mark your calendar. He's saying we ought to be ready for the Lord's return so that day will not overtake us or catch us unawares. The wise and foolish virgins knew the bridegroom was coming, but they didn't know when. The faithful and unfaithful servants expected their master to come home, but they didn't know when. You don't need to know when the Lord is returning to be faithful and ready or watchful and wise.

> I charge you to keep this command without spot or blame until the appearing of our Lord Jesus Christ, which God will bring about in his own time (1 Timothy 6:13–15, NIV)

There are more than 90 scriptures in the New Testament pertaining to the second or final coming, but none of them answers the question of when. God shares many things with his children, but the timing of Christ's return is not one of them. In his wisdom our heavenly Father has decided that we do not need to know.[1]

Will it be soon?

Although Jesus said no one knew the hour or day of his return, some scriptures seem to indicate that he will come back soon. What are we to make of these? Mr. Preterist would say these scriptures refer to Jesus coming in judgment in AD70. Mr. Futurist would say these scriptures were written for the benefit of 21st-century believers. There are problems with both interpretations.

As it turns out there are very few scriptures that suggest Jesus may be coming back soon. In fact, most of those that hint at an imminent coming are referring to his ascension to heaven.[2]

However, James seems to suggest the Lord's return is imminent:

> You too be patient; strengthen your hearts, for the coming of the Lord is near. Do not complain, brethren, against one another, so that you yourselves may not be judged; behold, the Judge is standing right at the door. (James 5:8–9)

It sounds as if Jesus' return and Judgment Day are right around the corner, in which case James was mistaken. But the context is waiting patiently and enduring in the face of persecution. If Jesus was just weeks away, we wouldn't need to wait at all, and there would be little opportunity to endure. So when James says, "The Judge is at the door," or Paul says, "The Lord is at hand" (Philippians 4:5), they are encouraging us to persevere and live with the end in mind.

An imminent return?

Here is another scripture that has been used to suggest an imminent return:

> Now may the God of peace himself sanctify you entirely; and may your spirit and soul and body be preserved complete, without blame at the coming of our Lord Jesus Christ. (1 Thessalonians 5:23)

Mr. Preterist: "The first-century believers expected they would still be in their bodies when Jesus returned in AD70."

Except Jesus didn't come and the first-century believers all died.

Paul's point about blameless bodies is that God doesn't do partial sanctifications. "Do you not know that your body is the temple of the Holy Spirit?" (1 Corinthians 6:19). He's exhorting the Thessalonians to "abstain from every form of evil" (1 Thessalonians 5:22). It's a mistake to think that because our spirits are saved we can treat our bodies like they don't matter. "You have been bought with a price: therefore glorify God in your body" (1 Corinthians 6:20).

Did the first-century Christians expect Jesus to return at any moment? There's no evidence they did. The early church used to greet one another with the word Maranatha, which can be translated, "Lord, come" (see 1 Corinthians 16:22). It was an expression of longing similar to the one uttered by Jews at Passover: "Next year in Jerusalem." Maranatha does not mean, "I expect

Jesus to return by September." It means, "I am looking forward to his coming, and the sooner the better."

Mr. Futurist: "But it's got to be soon, right? I mean, all the signs are there, aren't they?"

If by signs you mean earthquakes, famines, wars, lawlessness, and false messiahs, these are signs that Jesus listed in connection with the fall of Jerusalem. There is no scriptural evidence linking them with the Lord's return.

Mr. Futurist: "But there are other signs mentioned in scripture, like the rise of the antichrist, false prophets, animal extinctions, new diseases, a rebuilt Jerusalem, a third temple ..."

These so-called signs have been falsely connected with the return of the Lord for 2,000 years. They are not new, and they are not signs.

One of history's clearest lessons is the consistent wrongness of eschatological predictions. For example, the turn of the first millennium was marked by fears that the devil would be released after 1,000 years of captivity, as predicted by Revelation 20:7. A few months before the critical date a new pope was installed in Rome. Many believed that Pope Sylvester II was the antichrist in league with the devil, for he had studied with the Saracens. Judgment Day was imminent.[3]

When the new millennium came and Jesus didn't, those who sought to excite the masses with their eschatological predictions simply revised their dates. If Jesus wasn't returning in the year 1000 he would come in the year 1006 (when a supernova was seen in the heavens), or 1033 (the thousandth anniversary of his death), or 1186 (when the planets aligned), or 1284 (it was 666 years after the founding of Islam), or 1346 (the apocalyptic terror of the Black Plague), or 1496 (it was 1500 years after the

**Not the antichrist:
Pope Sylvester II**

birth of Jesus), and so on. The dubious practice of picking dates for the Lord's return continues to this day, as evidenced by our current fascination with ISIS, blood moons, and Russia.

You would think that with such a spectacularly abysmal record, the prognosticators would give up. But there's money to be made in this game. In the old days, fearful Christians anticipating the end of the world gave their possessions to the church. These days they buy books and fund doomsday ministries. The puzzle is not that bad predictions continue to be made; it's that people continue to heed them despite a 2,000-year record of being wrong every single time.

The inability to learn from history or believe what Jesus said remains one of the greatest follies of the church.

Mr. Futurist: "Fair enough. But you have to admit that we are closer to the Lord's return than anyone who lived before us. There will be a last generation and it could well be ours, don't you think?"

I honestly don't know. I'm not privy to God's schedule. I'm not even sure he thinks about time like we do.

> But do not let this one fact escape your notice, beloved, that with the Lord one day is like a thousand years and a thousand years like one day. The Lord is not slow about his promise, as some count slowness, but is patient toward you, not wishing for any to perish but for all to come to repentance. (2 Peter 3:8–9)

The Lord is patient or longsuffering. That means his patience is loooong. In his eschatological parables, Jesus told stories of masters, noblemen, and bridegrooms being gone a long time (Matthew 24:48, 25:5, 25:19). This is why Jesus, Paul, Peter, James, and Jude all spoke of the need to wait patiently for the Lord's return. There are far more scriptures exhorting us to wait than there are suggesting his return will be soon.[4]

Mr. Futurist: "Okay, so we don't know the day of the Lord's return, but surely we are in the final season."

Yet Jesus told the disciples, "It is not for you to know the times or the seasons" (Acts 1:7). This could be the final season; it might not be. We don't know. When it comes to the timing of the Lord's return, we are like Sergeant Schultz. We know nothing.

If someone asks you, "When will the Lord return?" the best answer is the one Christ gave. "No one knows the day or hour, but be ready." If pressed to give more than that, then give the other answer Christ gave: "It's not my business, it's God's business."

Mr. Futurist: "But doesn't the Lord himself say 'I am coming soon' in Revelation 22?"

These words at the end of the Bible have brought comfort to many, and rightly so. We should have a confident expectation of the Lord's return. But soon doesn't necessarily mean tomorrow. In fact, soon doesn't even mean soon. A better translation is swiftly or quickly, which is how Christ's words are translated in most Bibles.

Yes, I am coming quickly. (Revelation 3:11, 22:7, 12, 20)

Mr. Preterist: "Jesus told the apostles he was coming soon to Jerusalem in judgment."

Except he never did. He told them he was going to the Father soon, but he never said he was returning soon. How could he when he did not know the time of his return?

All times are soon to Aslan

Jesus didn't know when he would return but he knew how. "I will come quickly. When my Father gives the word, I will return without delay."

But when this priest (Jesus) had offered for all time one sacrifice for sins, he sat down at the right hand of God, and since that time he waits for his enemies to be made his footstool. (Hebrews 10:12–13, NIV)

Jesus is waiting, not coming, but the wait will not be forever. The moment the Father gives the word, the Son will come quickly.

> In just a little while, he who is coming will come and will not delay. (Hebrews 10:37, NIV)

---

[1] You can find the full list of Second Coming scriptures on my AD70 resources pages: www.-escapetoreality.org/ad70/

[2] For example: Matthew 10:23, 16:28, 26:64, Mark 13:26, 14:62.

[3] Source: Robert Lacey and Danny Danziger (1999), *The Year 1000: What Life Was Like at the Turn of the First Millennium*, Little, Brown: Boston, MA.

[4] A sample of waiting scriptures: Luke 12:36, Romans 8:23, 8:25, 1 Corinthians 1:7, 4:5, 1 Thessalonians 1:10, Philippians 3:20, James 5:7, Jude 1:21.

33. ANGELS, CLOUDS, AND THE COMING OF THE KING

In Matthew 24 the coming of the Son of Man is mentioned five times. On four of those occasions (verses 3, 27, 37, and 39) the original Greek word for coming is *parousía*, an oriental word used to describe "the royal visit of a king, or emperor."[1]

When the disciples and Jesus discussed his Second Coming on the Mount of Olives, they used this word *parousía*. However, in verse 30 Jesus used a different word, *erchomai*. This word means to come or go in the ordinary sense. Put them together and you get an interesting picture:

Coming in glory as a king:
- "Jesus, when are you coming back as a king and what are the signs?" (v.3)
- "My coming will be like lightning." (v.27)
- "As it was in the days of Noah, so shall my coming be." (v.37)
- "As they did not understand until the flood, so will my coming be." (v.39)

Coming in the everyday sense:
- They will see the Son of Man coming on the clouds (v.30)

As you can see, verse 30 is the odd one out because Jesus describes his coming without using the kingly word. But verse 30 is about a different kind of coming. Jesus is not talking about his return but his coming to the Ancient of Days to receive a kingdom (as we saw in Chapter 14). He doesn't use the kingly word because he is not yet a king. He's still the Son of Man.

The prophecy of verse 30 was fulfilled 2,000 years ago when Jesus ascended to heaven and was given a Name above all names. When Jesus returns to earth he will come as the King of kings, which is why every reference to the Second Coming in Matthew 24 uses the kingly word *parousia*.[2]

Both Mr. Preterist and Mr. Futurist stumble over Matthew 24:30. Mr. Preterist reads verse 30 and concludes that Christ comes back to earth twice; once to demolish Jerusalem and a second time as a conquering king. But there aren't two Second Comings, just one, and it is yet to happen.

Mr. Futurist interprets verse 30 as the Second Coming, which makes it sound as though he is unfamiliar with Daniel's prophecy. Daniel saw the Son of Man coming to the Ancient of Days. He wasn't coming to earth.

Jesus never said he would come in judgment on Jerusalem, but he did come on the clouds when he returned to heaven. Then he was the Son of Man, but when he returns to earth he will come as the King of kings.

The comings of the Son of Man

All this talk of comings can get a little confusing. As we saw in Chapter 31, there are at least five different comings of Jesus, and all of them are mentioned in Matthew.

Table 4: The Five Comings of Jesus

Which coming of Jesus?	Matthew
His first coming to earth	2:6, 3:11, 5:17, **9:6**, 13, 10:34–35, **11:19**, **18:11**, **20:28**, 21:5, 9
His coming to his temple	12:6, 21:12–15, 21:23, 23:1–39, 26:55
His coming to heaven	9:15, **10:23**, **16:28**, 21:42, **24:30**, **26:64**
His coming via the Holy Spirit	3:11
His second coming to earth	**13:41**, **16:27**, **19:28**, **24:27**, **37**, **39**, 42, 43, **44**, 46, 48, 50, 25:6, 10, 19, 27, **31**

Note: Verses in bold refer to the coming of the "Son of Man."

From this table we can see that Matthew refers many times to the different comings of Jesus. On no less than sixteen occasions he specifically refers to the coming of the Son of Man.

With so many comings and goings, it's easy to see how people can get confused. One scripture says the Son of Man has come to earth, another says the Son of Man is coming to heaven, and then another says he is coming back to earth again. On one occasion two different comings are mentioned side-by-side. In Matthew 16:27 the Son of Man is coming to earth with his angels (i.e., the Second Coming), but in the next verse he is coming into his kingdom (i.e., his exaltation and ascension). It's as though Jesus never sits still. No wonder "the Son of Man has nowhere to lay his head" (Matthew 8:20).

It looks confusing but it isn't, not when you understand the different destinations. And two destinations are mentioned in Matthew 24: heaven and earth. In verse 30 the Son of Man is coming to heaven; in other verses he's coming to earth with *parousia* glory.

Angels and clouds

There are a couple of other ways to distinguish the different comings of Jesus. As we saw in Chapter 14, whenever Christ is mentioned as "coming on the clouds" that is invariably a reference to his exaltation (his resurrection and ascension). If the Son of Man is coming on the clouds, he is coming to heaven. The clouds are the key.

Another key involves angels. Whenever Christ is described as coming with angels, he is on his way to earth. When Christ came the first time there was a heavenly host (Luke 2:13). When he comes a second time there will be more angels.

> For the Son of Man is going to come in the glory of his Father with his angels … But when the Son of Man comes in his glory, and all the angels with him, then he will sit on his glorious throne. (Matthew 16:27, 25:31)

When Christ travels from heaven to earth, angels come with him (see also Mark 8:38, Luke 9:26, 2 Thessalonians 1:7). Just as the president travels with the Secret Service, King Jesus travels with an angelic entourage.

Clouds and angels. These are literary keys that the Holy Spirit has embedded into the scriptures to help us make sense of the many prophecies about the different comings of the Lord. If you can tell the difference between an angel and a cloud, you can determine which sort of coming is being described. Coming on the clouds means the Lord is going up (or coming to heaven); coming with angels means he is coming down (to earth).

---

[1] *Parousia* (http://biblehub.com/greek/3952.htm).

[2] In the Olivet Discourse *parousia* is consistently used in connection with the Second Coming of King Jesus. It is not used when Jesus is talking his other comings. However, in other scriptures *parousia* is sometimes used to describe the ordinary coming of a man (e.g., Paul in Philippians 1:26 or Titus in 2 Corinthians 7:6).

34. WHEN ARE THE LAST DAYS?

Here's a question that has been the subject of much debate but needn't be: When are the last days?

Mr. Futurist: "We're living in them! Study the signs and you will see that we are the last generation."

Mr. Preterist: "The last days are the final days of the temple and AD70."

As you can see, the last day's question is a contentious one. Are the last days now? Are they in the future? Or the past? The Bible provides an unequivocal answer.

Altogether there are about a dozen last-days scriptures. Half of them are in the Old Testament and half of them are in the New. Here's one:

> In the past God spoke to our ancestors through the prophets at many times and in various ways, but in these last days he has spoken to us by his Son. (Hebrews 1:1–2, NIV)

When did God begin speaking through his Son? It wasn't recently and it wasn't in AD70. This passage is referring to the days when Jesus walked the earth.

> This is what was spoken of through the prophet Joel: "And it shall be in the last days," God says, "That I will pour forth of my Spirit on all mankind ..." (Acts 2:16–17)

God poured out his Spirit on the Day of Pentecost. Again, this did not happen recently or in AD70, but it happened in the last days.

The most famous last days' scripture may be this one:

> Now it will come about that in the last days the mountain of the house of the Lord will be established as the chief of the mountains, and will be raised above the hills, and all the nations will stream to it. (Isaiah 2:2)

Isaiah gives us three signs of the last days. First, the house of the Lord (i.e., the church) will become the "chief of mountains," meaning it will exceed the religion of the hilltop temple. The glory of the latter house (the church) will be greater than the former (Haggai 2:9).

Second, the church will be established, meaning it will endure forever. The Jerusalem temple was built and demolished by men, but the church is built by Jesus (Ephesians 2:20). Since the house of the Lord was not built by human hands (Mark 14:58), nothing can knock it over. Not Romans, death, or anything (Matthew 16:18).

Third, the Gentile nations will come streaming to the church, in contrast with the temple, which was reserved for the Jews.

All three signs have been fulfilled: the church has outgrown its Jewish roots, it has endured persecution, and the nations have been streaming to it since the time of Jesus. From this we can conclude that the last days are the days of the church.

Isaiah's mountain is Mount Zion a.k.a. the New Jerusalem or the church (see Revelation 21:10). The last days began with Christ's first coming and will climax with his last. Like the apostles of old, we are living in the last days or the gospel age of the church.

What about Micah's prophecy of judgment?

Mr. Preterist: "Isaiah's prophecy is repeated in Micah 4. Since Micah 3 ends with the destruction of the temple, this proves that the last days are connected to the events of AD70."

Mr. Preterist is partly right. Micah 3 is a prophecy of judgment against the rulers of Israel who trade in violence and injustice. The brutal words of Micah 3:9–11 describe the treatment dished out to Jesus and the apostles by the Sanhedrin. During the time of Christ's ministry and the following years, the religious rulers built their empire with bloodshed and iniquity. Then this happened:

> Therefore, on account of you Zion will be plowed as a field, Jerusalem will become a heap of ruins, and the mountain of the temple will become high places of a forest. (Micah 3:12)

Jerusalem became a heap of ruins in AD70 when the Romans destroyed the city and the temple.

Mr. Preterist: "Keep reading!"

> And it will come about in the last days that the mountain of the house of the Lord will be established as the chief of the mountains. It will be raised above the hills, and the peoples will stream to it. Many nations will come and say, "Come and let us go up to the mountain of the Lord and to the house of the God of Jacob, that he may teach us about his ways and that we may walk in his paths." (Micah 4:1–2)

Mr. Preterist: "You see? One follows the other. The temple comes down at the end of chapter 3 and the new temple arrives in chapter 4. The 'last days' are the last days of the Jerusalem temple."

Yet Micah says the house of the Lord will be established in the last days, and by AD70 this prophecy had been well and truly fulfilled. The church was established, the gospel was bearing fruit all over the world, and the Gentile nations were already streaming in. The book of Acts is a record of the fulfillment of Micah 4.

What about the approaching day?

Mr. Preterist: "Hebrews talks about not forsaking our assembling together but encouraging one another 'all the more as you see the day approaching' (Hebrews 10:24–25). What day? It cannot be Judgment Day because they could see it coming. He must have been talking about the fall of Jerusalem. The approaching day is the last day of the temple."

Then why does the writer of Hebrews encourage his readers to assemble together? Why doesn't he say, "Forget about meeting together and get out of Jerusalem as fast as you can"? Why doesn't he remind them of the words of Jesus? "Flee to the mountains."

There is not the slightest hint that the approaching day is connected with the calamitous events of AD70. The context of this passage is the last day or the final coming of Jesus:

And inasmuch as it is appointed for men to die once and after this comes judgment, so Christ also, having been offered once to bear the sins of many, will appear a second time for salvation without reference to sin, to those who eagerly await him. (Hebrews 9:27–28)

Jesus and judgment are coming. These chapters of Hebrews are full of warnings connected with Judgment Day. "If we go on sinning no sacrifice remains but a terrifying expectation of judgment. What do you think happens to those who spit on the Son of God and insult the Spirit of grace?" (Hebrews 10:26–29). This is dramatic end-of-the-world stuff.

We can be certain the writer is not thinking of AD70 because he has a different takeaway. Instead of "flee Jerusalem", he writes about obtaining a better resurrection and not missing out on the grace of God. Instead of watching for the signs, he has a chapter on faith and being certain of what we don't see. Instead of focusing on doomed Jerusalem, he encourages his readers to follow Abraham's example in looking for the heavenly Jerusalem "whose builder and maker is God" (Hebrews 11:10).

Mr. Preterist: "What about the 'last hour' of 1 John 2:18? Surely that's a reference to AD70?"

John's last hour may be analogous to the last days and latter times of other scriptures. If John is thinking of an ending it is Christ's final coming (see 1 John 2:28), which is marked by the transformation of the saints (1 John 3:2), and judgment (1 John 4:17). He says nothing about the temple or Jerusalem.

The restoration of Israel

Mr. Futurist: "I don't buy this idea that the apostles were living in the last days. Maybe they thought they were, but they were mistaken. Israel is the key. Hosea prophesied that the restoration of Israel would take place in the last days and that hasn't happened. The last days are still in the future."

Mr. Futurist is referring to this last days' prophecy:

> Afterward the sons of Israel will return and seek the Lord their God
> and David their king, and they will come trembling to the Lord and to
> his goodness in the last days. (Hosea 3:5)

The Israelites rebelled against the dynasty of David when they rejected his
grandson Rehoboam (1 Kings 12:16). But Hosea predicted they would return
to David their king meaning Jesus, "the son of David" (see Matthew 1:1). Note
that the sons of Israel do not come crawling on their knees begging for forgiveness, but they come trembling in awe of the Lord's goodness. Hosea is describing the new covenant of grace. He's talking about the awesome goodness
of God that leads men to repentance (Romans 2:4).

Mr. Futurist says it hasn't happened, but this prophecy was fulfilled
on the Day of Pentecost when 3,000 scattered sons of Israel heard the good
news, were cut to the heart and came to Jesus (Acts 2). It was further fulfilled
when great numbers of Jerusalem Jews were drawn to the church (Acts 4:4,
5:14, 6:1). And it continues to be fulfilled whenever a lost son of Israel comes
to the Lord.

The apostles weren't mistaken. They understood that they were living
in the last days spoken of by the prophets. The last days foretold by Hosea,
Isaiah, and Micah are the last days of Peter, Paul, and John. They are the days
of the Lord and his church.

What about Paul's perilous portents?

> But realize this, that in the last days difficult times will come. For men
> will be lovers of self, lovers of money, boastful, arrogant, revilers,
> disobedient to parents, ungrateful, unholy, unloving, irreconcilable,
> malicious gossips, without self-control, brutal, haters of good, treach-
> erous, reckless, conceited, lovers of pleasure rather than lovers of God,
> holding to a form of godliness, although they have denied its power.
> Avoid such men as these. (2 Timothy 3:1–5)

In one of the longest and most depressing lists in the Bible, Paul provides
nineteen negative characteristics of the last days. It is tempting for us to read
this list and conclude that Paul is describing our greedy and hedonistic generation. But if Paul is writing about us, why does he warn Timothy to "avoid
such as these"?

Paul's warning makes no sense except that he and Timothy were living in the last days. Sure, people are bad now but they were bad then. Our generation does not have a monopoly on selfishness.

Mr. Futurist: "Are you kidding? The modern world is rotten with moral decay. We live in dark times – abortion, corruption, slavery, war, genocide ..."

And the Roman Empire had all the same evils. The issue is not which generation is darkest – the darker it gets the brighter we shine – but whether Paul was speaking to Timothy, which he was.

As a leader of the Ephesian church, Timothy had to deal with charlatans like Hymenaeus and Philetus, men whose teaching "spread like gangrene" and upset the faith of many (2 Timothy 2:17–18). These jokers would have ticked most of the nineteen boxes on Paul's list. "Timothy, steer clear of them."

Does this mean that Paul's warning is irrelevant for us? Not at all, for we, too, are living in the last days. Like Timothy, we would do well to avoid false teachers who deny the power of the gospel.

Last days' mockers

It is a privilege to live this side of the cross in the last days, but there will be difficult times, said Paul. There will be challenges. One of the issues Paul had to deal with was the muddle-headed idea that Jesus had already returned and the resurrection had already taken place (2 Timothy 2:18). In contrast, Peter had to deal with people who mocked the idea that Jesus was coming back.

> Know this first of all, that in the last days mockers will come with their mocking, following after their own lusts, and saying, "Where is the promise of his coming?" (2 Peter 3:3–4)

The wrong way to read this scripture is to apply it exclusively to our generation. "We have mockers, therefore Jesus is on his way." Peter's warning is for the last days meaning it is for his generation and our generation and every generation in between.

"We can be certain this is the rapture generation because of scoffers who ask, 'Where is the promise of his coming?'" Such a claim is historically ignorant. Last days' mockers are nothing new. In the nineteenth century, a Baptist preacher called William Miller led people to believe that Jesus would return to earth in March 1844. When Jesus didn't return as expected, the date was pushed back to April and then October. When Jesus still didn't return Miller and his followers were mocked and even beaten in the street. Miller described the painful mockery he experienced:

> Some are tauntingly enquiring, "Have you not gone up?" Even little children in the streets are shouting continually to passersby, "Have you a ticket to go up?"[1]

This is not an unusual story. For 2,000 years there have been last days' mockers. Some mock because they don't believe Jesus is coming back. Others mock because people have foolishly tried to pick the date of the Lord's return.[2]

The market for bad predictions

During my lifetime there have been about 100 false predictions regarding the Lord's return, and every one of them was made by someone who sincerely believed they were living in last of the last days. The end times, in other words (although the phrase end times is found nowhere in scripture). Every time Halley's Comet comes around, or the planets align, or there's a solar flare, or the stock market tanks, or Russia flexes its muscles, or Israel sneezes, these prognosticators come out of the woodwork to make their false and unsettling predictions.

Mr. Futurist: "I would never fall for such predictions."

Many do. When I was in college a book came out that was entitled *88 Reasons Why the Rapture Will be in 1988*. Jesus would return in September of that year, said the book's author. He didn't yet the book is still available on Amazon, and I believe there was a sequel. The market for bad predictions knows no bounds.

Where do these bad dates come from? They come from four sources. First, there are the visions or revelations that inspired such people as William Miller (who said the world would end in 1844), John Hinkle (1994), and Nostradamus (1999).

Then there is the *Newsweek* eschatology of current events. Something big happens involving Israel, Russia, or the UN, and it triggers a fresh wave of rapture hysteria. The stock market falls or a new pope is elected and suddenly it's time to go. In 1997 it was Yitzhak Rabin and Yasser Arafat signing their peace accord on the White House lawn. In 2008 it was the Global Financial Crisis, and in 2016 it was Brexit. According to those with their fingers on the pulse of current events, the world was going to end or experience a great shaking in 1982 (Pat Robertson), 1987 (Hal Lindsey), and 2007 (both Pat Robertson and Hal Lindsey again), and 2015 (Jonathan Cahn).

The third source of end-times fodder is natural phenomena such as meteorite showers, passing comets, and solar flares. An earthquake strikes or a harvest fails and you can just about guarantee that some prophet will declare, "These are the birth pangs of Matthew 24:7. Jesus is coming!" A series of lunar eclipses was interpreted by John Hagee as pointing to a world-shaking event that would occur in 2015.

Finally, you have the prophetic and mystical significance of numbers. Hence some have predicted the Lord would return in 1996 (the 2,000th anniversary of his birth), 1998 (it's three times 666), 2000 (Y2K and the millennium), 2017 (it's 50 Jubilee years since Israel retook Jerusalem), or 2018 (Israel's 70th birthday). It doesn't even have to be numbers from the western calendar – the Jewish calendar also works (watch out in 2017!), as do Mayan calendars for some reason (beware 2012!). According to numerologists, the world will implode or the Lord will return in 1994 (according to Harold Camping), 1995 (Camping again), 1998 (Marilyn Agee), 2006 (Michael Drosnin), or 2011 (Camping having one more swing at it).

We need to stop getting worked up over useless dates. Every time we share some end-times prediction that involves a date, we open the door to mockery. We're saying we know more than the Lord himself.

Ever wonder why the New Testament makes no predictions about the date of the Lord's return? It's because the apostles believed Jesus when he said, "Nobody knows the day or hour, not even the Son himself." If we had the same mindset as them, the market for bad predictions would cease to exist.

When are the last days?

Many of us have been raised with the idea that our generation is *the* last-day's generation, but this is not remotely scriptural. The apostles considered themselves privileged to live in the last days. We should feel the same way. Better to live this side of the cross in union with Christ than to hear about him secondhand from Old Testament prophets.

It is a mistake to define the last days in terms of our generation; the last days are defined by Jesus.

Jesus divides history into two parts, the first days and the last days, BC and AD. In the first days of history, people looked forward to the coming of Christ when he would build his house. In these last days, he is building his church, and the nations are streaming in.

The first half of history ended with Christ coming in humility. The second half ends with him returning in glory. The last days are last because they refer to the last half of history. So far, the last days have lasted for 2,000 years. They may last for many more, but ultimately the last days will end on *the* last day when Christ returns to judge the living and the dead (John 6:39–40, 12:48).

This brings us to the question the disciples asked at the beginning.

---

[1] James White (1875), *Sketches of the Christian Life and Public Labors of William Miller*, Steam Press, Battle Creek, MI, p.310.

[2] When Harold Camping's predicted date for the rapture in 2011 proved to be a dud, skeptics and protesters poked fun. They hosted rapture parties where they sold "Tickets to the other side." For laughs, they released human-shaped balloons filled with helium to simulate souls rising to heaven.

35. WHEN IS THE END OF THE AGE?

The disciples asked, "What will be the sign of your coming and the end of the age?" (Matthew 24:3). What did they mean by the end of the age?

A few verses later Jesus said, "The gospel would be preached all over the world then the end will come" (Matthew 24:14). What end? Did he mean the end of the temple, or the end of the age, or both? Was Jesus answering the disciples' question? It will help if we examine the original meaning of their words:

> The disciples: "When is the end (*sunteleia*) of the age?"
> Jesus: "Then the end (*telos*) will come."

When discussing the end of the age, the disciples used a big word that means completion or consummation of a plan. God has a plan, and it comes to completion at the end or consummation of the age. In contrast, when discussing the fall of Jerusalem, Jesus used a smaller word that simply means an ending or conclusion.[1]

Two words for two types of ending and the difference is a plan. If I crash my car, that's the *telos* end of my car. But if I did it as part of a twisted plan to fake my own death, collect the insurance, and move to the Bahamas, that's a *sunteleia* ending. See the difference? In both cases the car came to an end, but the presence of a plan determines what sort of ending it was.

The disciples asked about the grand plan kind of ending, while in verse 14 Jesus spoke about an ordinary kind of ending. (He'll get to the grand plan later in Matthew 24.) His choice of words reveals that the end of Jerusalem has nothing to do with the end of age they were asking about.

What is the end of the age?

Whenever you read about the end of something in the New Testament, it helps to know which sort of ending is being described. Is it the everyday type of ending (*telos*) or is it a God-wrought consummation (*sunteleia*) of a plan? Here are a few examples:

> So just as the tares are gathered up and burned with fire, so shall it be at the end (*sunteleia*) of the age ... So it will be at the end (*sunteleia*) of

the age; the angels will come forth and take out the wicked from among the righteous, (Matthew 13:40, 49)

In the parable of the tares and wheat, Jesus referred to the harvest at the end of the age using the big word that describes the consummation of a plan. Jesus was talking about *the* ending, or Judgment Day when the tares and wheat will be gathered and separated.

> Lo, I am with you always, even to the end (*sunteleia*) of the age. (Matthew 28:20)

Jesus promised the disciples that he would never leave them. He would be with them, and us, to the utter end.

In these examples, the age in question is the new covenant age, also known as the age of grace. When Christ returns *this* age will end, the wheat and tares will be gathered, and the wicked separated from the righteous. But the new covenant age is not the only age mentioned in the Bible.

> Now once at the consummation (*sunteleia*) of the ages he has been manifested to put away sin by the sacrifice of himself. (Hebrews 9:26)

This verse is pointing back to the cross rather than forward to the Second Coming. It describes the cross as the end or consummation of an age. Paul is talking about the age of the old law-keeping covenant, which came to a glorious culmination at the cross.

> Now these things happened to them as an example, and they were written for our instruction, upon whom the ends (*telos*) of the ages have come. (1 Corinthians 10:11)

This verse is the same but different. It's similar because Paul is again talking about the end of an age, but it's a different kind of ending. It's an ordinary *telos* ending.

Paul is not talking about the consummation of the old covenant (which had already happened), nor is he talking about the consummation of the new covenant (which was far in the future). He is talking about the end of the temple-based worship. "Moses is fizzing out because Christ has come." It was the end of an era, nothing more.

> The end (*telos*) of all things is near; therefore, be of sound judgment and sober spirit for the purpose of prayer. (1 Peter 4:7)

Mr. Preterist might say the end here refers to the end of Jerusalem, but this is about Judgment Day and "giving account to him who is ready to judge the living and the dead" (v.5). So why does Peter use the ordinary word for ending? Because the end of all things is a reference to the end of godless living. What is ending is the way of life characterized by "debauchery, lust, drunkenness, orgies, carousing and detestable idolatry" (v.3). The reign of sin is coming to an end.

When is the end of the age?

Scripture tells us that there is more than one age and more than one ending. There was the age of law or the era of the old covenant, which came to a conclusion at Calvary, and there is the present age of grace or the era of the new covenant, which will reach its climax when Christ returns.

However, it would be a mistake to say the new covenant comes to an end. Since it is based on God's unshakeable promises, the new covenant endures forever. What comes to an end is the age of grace or the grace period between Christ's death and Judgment Day. When will this age end? We have examined this question in Chapters 18 and 32, but the short answer is only God knows.

---

[1] *Sunteleia* and *telos* are related. The chief difference is the prefix *sun* which means union or association. *Sunteleia* is an ending where all the parts come together. The definitions for *sunteleia* (G4930) and *telos* (G5056) come from *Vine's Expository Dictionary of New Testament Words*, website: http://bit.ly/V_end

36. WHAT ABOUT THE RAPTURE?

Mr. Preterist: "Did you know the word rapture is not in the Bible?"

Mr. Futurist: "The word Bible is not in the Bible. What's your point?"

Mr. Preterist: "My point is it's silly to suggest the Lord is going to remove the church from a tribulation that's not going to happen."

Mr. Futurist: "Doesn't sound silly to me. I would very much like to avoid the great tribulation."

Mr. Preterist: "Haven't you been paying attention? The tribulation already happened. Jesus said it won't happen again (see Chapter 30). You're not calling the Lord a liar, are you?"

Mr. Futurist: "In Matthew 24 Jesus said there would be two men in the field; one will be taken, and one will be left. Two women will be working at the mill; one will be taken, and one will be left."

Mr. Preterist: "And you think this is a rapture? What are you going to do next? Suggest we watch *Left Behind*?"

Mr. Futurist: "Who said anything about being left behind?"

Mr. Preterist: "Isn't that what happens to unbelievers? The saints get whisked to heaven on the rapture elevator while everyone else is left behind to go through hell on earth?"

Mr. Futurist: "Whoa, slow down. The saints are caught up to meet the Lord on his return. It's like going to the airport to greet a friend. You meet your friend then turn around and come home again."

Mr. Preterist: "Where is that in the Bible?"

Mr. Futurist: "About ten verses away, in the parable of the wise and foolish virgins. At midnight the cry goes out that the bridegroom is coming, the wise virgins go out to meet him, and together they return."

This Mr. Futurist sounds like a sensible man, but he has futurist friends who believe Jesus returns *twice*. Apparently, there are two Second Comings. In the first, Jesus comes to fetch the saints before returning immediately to heaven. Then in the *second* Second Coming (or the first Third Coming?), he returns to earth to stay. So Jesus comes down, goes up, then comes down again.

This yo-yo theology sounds like the plot of a bad movie. Jesus is coming again, but only once.

A parabolic picture of the rapture

> But at midnight there was a shout, "Behold, the bridegroom! Come out to meet him." Then … the bridegroom came, and those who were ready went in with him to the wedding feast, and the door was shut. (Matthew 25:6, 10)

Jesus is the bridegroom, and the wise virgins are those who are watching and ready for his arrival. He comes, they meet him on the way and then come with him to the feast.

> Then we who are alive and remain will be caught up together with them in the clouds to meet the Lord in the air (1 Thessalonians 4:17)

The parable of the wise virgins is a picture of the second or final coming when, "Our Lord Jesus comes with all his saints" (1 Thessalonians 3:13). It's also a picture of the rapture. True, the word rapture doesn't appear in our English Bibles, but it's sort of in the Latin Bible, which was the Bible the church used for about a 1,000 years.[1]

Paul didn't write in Latin, of course, but in Greek, and the word he used means to seize or snatch away. To be raptured is to be taken or caught up.

Mr. Preterist: "Paul was describing the resurrection. We don't need a fancy word for it."

A resurrection is what happens to dead people. Jesus comes and the dead rise. The rapture is for those "who are alive and remain." Think of a raptor coming down and seizing its prey. We'll be snatched or plucked like field mice.

Mr. Preterist: "How horrifying!"

Okay, that may not be the best picture. Think of Philip on the desert road. One moment he was baptizing the Ethiopian; the next he was snatched away by the Spirit (Acts 8:39). It's the same word that Paul used. It means the rapture will be sudden and disruptive. Boom! And you're gone.

When is the rapture?

Before the 2016 U.S. presidential election, I stumbled on a prominent website that predicted the rapture would occur soon. Why? Because the polls said Hillary Clinton was going to win and another godless Democrat in the Oval Office would surely trigger the great tribulation. "With such gloomy prospects, the rapture has to be close! Get ready."

Then Donald Trump won the election, and the outlook became positively bright, at least as far as this website was concerned. A God-fearing Republican would clean out the justices, end the culture war, and bring heaven to America. Surprisingly, the rapture prediction remained unchanged. "When men are saying peace and safety, the rapture will be soon. Get ready."

This website taught me a valuable lesson about how to generate buzz for your blog or book. Whether times are good or bad, tell people that the rapture is imminent. "Things are bad? That's a sign! Things are good? That's a sign! This doesn't make sense? Buy my book!"

It's amusing stuff, but the question is legitimate: When is the rapture? It may surprise you to learn that the Bible provides a straightforward answer to this question, but many don't know it. They've been led to believe that the rapture will occur either before, during, or after a future tribulation. None of these scenarios is particularly attractive or Biblical.

A pre-trib rapture avoids the unpleasantness of the tribulation but creates the yo-yo picture of two Second Comings. A mid- or post-trib rapture means you have to go through bad times, which you may not survive. And any trib-related rapture raises awkward questions about who is left behind and why.

Consider the kids. Are young children going to be left behind? Trib-preachers tie themselves up in knots over this question. Either all kids are going to be raptured (because God is good, right?), or none of them are (because the little brats are natural-born sinners). Or maybe kids with Christian parents get to go. But what if one parent is saved and the other isn't? What if the kids are adopted or orphaned? It seems God is faced with a Sophie's choice.

These frivolous questions highlight the absurdity of a teaching that is not based on scripture. The rapture has nothing to do with the great tribulation. One event is past; the other is yet to happen. The great tribulation took place in AD70; the rapture will probably happen next March. Just kidding. Sorry, I couldn't help myself.[2]

Mr. Futurist: "Seriously, when is the rapture? I really want to know."

The rapture, or the snatching away of the saints, will happen when the Lord descends from heaven with a shout (1 Thessalonians 4:16–17). Just as the virgins go out in response to the shout, so do we. Since we don't know when the Lord will return, we cannot know when the rapture will occur. But we can be ready.

Who is taken and left behind?

Jesus spoke of two men working. "One will be taken, and one will be left" (Matthew 24:40). Who is taken, the believer or unbeliever? And who does the taking? The Lord, his angels, or people? And what exactly is Jesus talking about?

Mr. Futurist: "The rapture."

Mr. Preterist: "Romans."

On these questions scholars have taken every possible position. Preterists believe the taking was done in AD70; futurists believe the taking is yet to happen.

> And just as it happened in the days of Noah, so it will be also in the days of the Son of Man … It was the same as happened in the days of Lot: they were eating, they were drinking, they were buying, they were selling, they were planting, they were building, but on the day that Lot went out from Sodom it rained fire and brimstone from heaven and destroyed them all. It will be just the same on the day that the Son of Man is revealed. (Luke 17:26–30)

The return of the Son of Man will be like the days of Noah and the days of Lot. In both stories the righteous were taken away and saved; Noah by means of an ark and Lot by means of an angel. From these stories we might conclude that the righteous are taken out of danger by the Lord.

But Jesus also told stories where the wicked are taken away from the righteous, the weeds are weeded out of the kingdom (Matthew 13:40), and the bad fish are discarded from the net (Matthew 13:48). From these stories we may surmise that the wicked are removed.

Or it could be both. The righteous are taken or caught up in the clouds to meet the Lord in the air, and then the wicked are removed as per the parables. Either way, when Jesus returns there will be some sort of separation.

> Do not think that I came to bring peace on the earth; I did not come to bring peace, but a sword. For I came to set a man against his father and a daughter against her mother, and a daughter-in-law against her mother-in-law; and a man's enemies will be the members of his own household. (Matthew 10:34–36)

These words seem hard to reconcile with the image of Jesus the Prince of Peace. But the sword he wields is not a Roman sword; it's a sword of truth, and truth is divisive.

> Do you suppose that I came to grant peace on earth? I tell you, no, but rather division; for from now on five members in one household will be divided, three against two and two against three. They will be divided, father against son and son against father, mother against daughter and daughter against mother, mother-in-law against daughter-in-law and daughter-in-law against mother-in-law. (Luke 12:51–53)

As we saw in the story of Jerusalem's fall, people divide themselves by their response to Jesus. Some listened and lived; others ignored him and died.

How we respond to Jesus is the difference between life and death. A Christian is not necessarily more moral than their unbelieving neighbor; a Christian is someone who does what Jesus says. Conversely, an unbeliever is not necessarily immoral; an unbeliever is someone who rejects what Jesus says. Like the hard-hearted leaders of Jerusalem, they "refuse to come to me to have life" (John 5:40).

Jesus is the Life, and those who come to him shall live. This brings me to the reason why I wrote this book.

---

[1] In the Latin Vulgate the Greek word for caught up (*harpazo*) was translated *rapiemur*. This word is related to the Latin verb *rapio*, which means to snatch or seize. Source: http://latin-dictionary.net/search/latin/rapio

[2] Mr. Futurist might ask, "What about when Jesus promises to protect the Philadelphian believers from the hour of testing that was coming upon the whole world (Revelation 3:10)? That sounds like a rapture-tribulation scenario." Sounds like, but isn't. Neither the rapture nor the tribulation is mentioned in Christ's letter to the church at Philadelphia. "Because you have kept the word of my perseverance" in Revelation 3:10 is analogous to "continuing in the faith" in Colossians 1:23. It is an exhortation to keep trusting in Jesus. Keep your eyes on the Lord and you won't be unsettled by trials and hardships.

37. JERUSALEM AND JUDGMENT DAY

Contrary to all outward appearances, this is not a history book. Sure, there's some history in it, but I didn't write this book so that you might become better informed about the dark days of AD70. I wrote it so that you might heed Christ's words: "Be ready."

The Jewish unbelievers of Jerusalem were not ready when the end came, and they suffered as a result. In contrast, the Jewish believers were ready, and they lived.

If we are to live with the end in sight, the parallels are unmissable. We need not fear a Roman siege, but an end is coming. One day the curtain of history will fall and this present age will come to a close.

Jerusalem and Judgment Day: Jesus spoke about both together because the former illuminates the latter. Judgment Day, like the fall of Jerusalem, is something you can prepare for. It is an event for which you can be ready.

> Be on guard, so that your hearts will not be weighted down with dissipation and drunkenness and the worries of life, and **that day** will not come on you suddenly like a trap; for it will come upon all those who dwell on the face of all the earth. But keep on the alert at all times, praying that you may have strength to escape all **these things that are about to take place**, and to **stand before the Son of Man**. (Luke 21:34–36)

In this passage Jesus is talking about two different events, namely, "these things that are about to take place," meaning the destruction of Jerusalem, and "that day" when all who dwell on the earth will "stand before the Son of Man." He's contrasting Jerusalem with Judgment Day.

These things and that day

For the disciples, both events were in the future. But for us, Jerusalem is in the distant past. However, there are three lessons from AD70 that remain relevant today:

1. Back then Jesus longed to gather the Jews to himself, but they weren't willing (Matthew 23:37). Today Jesus draws all to himself, but not all are drawn (John 12:32).
2. Back then those who heeded Christ's words lived. Today those who heed him reap eternal life (John 5:24).
3. Back then those who dismissed Christ died. One day those who reject him will perish (John 3:36).

Matthew 24 is both historical and future-oriented. It's about an event that has happened and one that is yet to take place. Thus Christ's words for the disciples are his words for us: Be ready.

Being ready means living with a positive response to what God has said or done. It's saying yes to Jesus. But in the passage above we see that the worries and cares of life can cause us to be unready. We should not over-spiritualize this. Matthew 24 is full of practical, down-to-earth advice. So what does it mean to be ready in practical everyday terms?

Practical readiness

Imagine you are living in Jerusalem in the years before the Roman siege. You had heard Christ's warnings but were unsure about them. "Jesus could be right; he could be wrong – I'm still thinking about it." Some of your neighbors are packing to leave, others are staying put, but you're on the fence. Those going urge you to follow their example. "Destruction is coming!" While those staying dismiss Jesus as alarmist. "He's a false messiah."

You listen to both sides and take pride in your open-mindedness. You tell yourself that you're undecided, but you're not. Every day you remain in the city is a vote against Jesus. Eventually, the Romans are going to come marching over the hill and you and your children will be lost.

Or perhaps you have decided that Jesus is right. "We should flee." But the kids are in school, your stone-cutting business is getting established, and you've got bills to pay, so you put off leaving.

Next minute, the Romans are at your door. Oops, too late.

We were born to be free and make choices, but you won't choose if your heart is "choked with worries and riches and pleasure" (Luke 8:14). The recurring theme of scripture is choose life, but fail to choose and you choose badly.

"Don't be like that," says Jesus, "But make up your mind today so the day of the Lord doesn't come on you suddenly like a trap."

Judgment Day means decision day and for the Christian that day is in their past. They have already decided. They have made up their mind and have nothing to fear. But you won't decide if you are burdened with the cares of life.

> But take heed to yourselves, lest your hearts be weighed down with carousing, drunkenness, and cares of this life, and that Day comes on you unexpectedly. (Luke 21:34, NKJV)

To take heed means to pay attention to your situation. It's putting first things first and exercising your freedom to choose. It's hearing and acting on what Jesus has said. To put it in Biblical terms, it's repenting (changing your skeptical or undecided mind) and living from the conviction that King Jesus is on the throne.

How do we receive his grace?

Jesus exhorts his disciples (and us) to pray for strength to stand on Judgment Day. Malachi asked, "Who can stand when he appears?" No one can stand except by the grace of God.

Other translations say, "Pray that you may be counted worthy." The bad news is you are not worthy to stand before a Holy Judge; the good news is Christ makes you worthy. He gives you grace to stand (Romans 5:2).

This is fantastically good news! Everything that needs to be done to save you, Jesus has already done. You don't need to clean yourself before coming to his throne of grace. Just come as you are and receive.

How do you do that? Jesus says to pray, which means to make request. To receive his grace all you need to do is ask. "Lord, give me the grace to stand," and he will because that's who he is and that's what he does. Jesus is the face of grace. He's our strength in our hour of need.

> Lord, be gracious to us; we long for you. Be our strength every morning, our salvation in time of distress. (Isaiah 33:2, NIV)

Perhaps you have never prayed before. Rest assured, praying is as easy as talking. Praying is simply giving thanks and telling God what is on your heart.

You may think, "I don't want to bother God with my small stuff." He's the Maker of heaven and earth – it's all small stuff to God. Yet he cares for you. You are his dearly beloved child. If it matters to you, it matters to him.

"But I might pray wrong." Relax, there is no such thing as a bad prayer. An honest prayer from the heart touches the heart of your Father. He really does hear our prayers.

"I don't know how to start." If you need help you could pray something like this:

> Heavenly Father, thank you for loving me. Thank you that you love me no matter what and through thick and thin. Thank you for sending your Son Jesus to save me. Thank you for raising Jesus from the dead. Because he lives I can truly live. Lord, I trust you, and I receive your grace. Please fill me with your Holy Spirit so that I might know you more. Amen.

38. WHAT HAPPENS WHEN CHRIST RETURNS?

Judging by the number of books written on the subject, we ought to be able to predict Christ's return down to the minute, but the fact is nobody knows the hour or day. Jesus could return before you reach the end of this book, or he might return after you have died of old age.

From time to time a wave of paranoia sweeps over social media regarding the imminent end of the world. Y2K. Mayan calendars. Planets aligning and lunar eclipses. The list of omens is endless, but every misguided prophecy regarding the Lord's return has so far proven false.

You should not be troubled by these random outbreaks of hysteria, for the Bible declares that the *when* of Christ's return is a mystery. You don't know when, you don't need to know when, you just need to be ready for when.

But while the Bible is silent about when, it says a lot about what. Here are six things that will happen when Christ returns.

1. Jesus will arrive with a shout

Jesus' first arrival was a largely unheralded birth in a one-horse town. In contrast, his return will be a glorious and loud procession visible to all.

> For the Lord himself will descend from heaven with a shout, with the voice of the archangel and with the trumpet of God (1 Thessalonians 4:16a)

Some have wondered whether the shout is for us or heaven, or whether the shout might be metaphorical. The word for shout implies a call or summons, and the rest of the verse tells us that the dead respond. So it's a shout loud enough to raise the dead.[1]

> For the Son of Man will come like the lightning which flashes across the whole sky from the east to the west. (Matthew 24:27, GNB)

Some interpret these words as though Jesus were coming from the east. Does that mean China will see him first? Or Japan?

Perhaps the point of the picture is that his return will be universally known from east to west. It won't be a secret. You won't miss it. His arrival will be swift, sudden, and destructive, like lightning. But what that means only the Lord knows. Perhaps the sky will erupt, or the stars will explode. We will have to wait and see, but it's a safe bet that the Lord's return will be grander than any Olympic Opening Ceremony or Fourth of July celebration.

If history is a play, then the final scene is where the Author and Hero of the story steps onto the stage to vanquish his foes. Jesus' return is the climax of history. It will be beyond spectacular!

2. The dead will rise

And the dead in Christ will rise first. (1 Thessalonians 4:16b)

The Apostle Paul wrote these words to people who were sad. "Do not grieve," he said, "For those who sleep in death will rise to new life." And to the Corinthians, "all in Christ will be made alive" (1 Corinthians 15:22).

Was Paul preaching a literal resurrection? Extreme preterism says Jesus returned in AD70 and therefore there is no resurrection. It's metaphorical or symbolic. But Paul would disagree. "How can some of you say that there is no resurrection of the dead?" (1 Corinthians 15:12).

The resurrection of the dead was at the heart of Paul's gospel:

For if we believe that Jesus died and rose again, even so God will bring with him those who have fallen asleep in Jesus. (1 Thessalonians 4:14)

When Paul was going through extremely tough times, such that he despaired of life, his hope remained in "God who raises the dead" (2 Corinthians 1:9). Resurrection isn't merely metaphorical. Just as Jesus was raised, we will be raised.

If only for this life we have hope in Christ, we are of all people most to be pitied. But Christ has indeed been raised from the dead, the firstfruits of those who have fallen asleep. (1 Corinthians 15:19–20, NIV)

Resurrection is not just for Christians, for Paul said, "There shall certainly be a resurrection of both the righteous and the wicked" (Acts 24:15).

On the day the Lord returns, I expect to see my father who died when I was a young boy. Parents will meet their miscarried children. You could meet your great-great-great-granddaddy. It will be a day of joyful reunions.

3. We will be transformed

Flesh and blood cannot inherit the kingdom of God; nor does the perishable inherit the imperishable. Behold, I tell you a mystery; we will not all sleep, but we will all be changed, in a moment, in the twinkling of an eye, at the last trumpet; for the trumpet will sound, and the dead will be raised imperishable, and we will be changed. (1 Corinthians 15:50–52)

Not all of us will die – some of us will be alive when the Lord returns – but we shall all be changed. Just as we have worn the earthly image of Adam, we shall bear the heavenly image of Christ. "When Christ appears, we shall be like him" (1 John 3:2).

We're citizens of high heaven! We're waiting the arrival of the Savior, the Master, Jesus Christ, who will transform our earthy bodies into glorious bodies like his own. (Philippians 3:20–21, MSG)

The older I get, the more I look forward to being clothed in my new "suit" (see 2 Corinthians 5:2–4), a glorious and transformed body that will not be subject to death, decay, and dentist visits.

4. We will meet the Lord in the air

Then we who are living at that time will be gathered up along with them in the clouds to meet the Lord in the air (1 Thessalonians 4:17, GNB)

In the parable of the wise and foolish virgins, the virgins go out to meet the groom and then return with him. As we saw in Chapter 36, that's a picture of the second or final coming when we who are still alive are caught up to meet the Lord.

Recall what the disciples heard as they watched Jesus ascending into heaven:

> Men of Galilee, why do you stand looking into the sky? This Jesus, who has been taken up from you into heaven, will come in just the same way as you have watched him go into heaven. (Acts 1:11)

Jesus comes in the manner he left. Back then he went up; on his return he'll come down. Back then he ascended with resurrected saints (Matthew 27:52–53). When he returns he will come with "all his saints" (1 Thessalonians 3:13). Apparently, Jesus will come back down with a crowd of people.

And we're part of the crowd.

5. God will judge the living and the dead

Perhaps you are living in dread of Judgment Day. "That's when God will play tapes showing all the dirty secrets of my life." Don't panic. It's not going to happen. The God who keeps no record of sins keeps no dirty tapes.

On Judgment Day God may surprise us. Look at the story of the sheep and the goats (Matthew 25:31–46). The sheep are surprised by the Lord's unexpected favor. "Lord, when did we do the things you are commending us for?" The goats are surprised, too, but for different reasons.

> For we must all appear before the judgment seat of Christ, so that each one may be recompensed for his deeds in the body, according to what he has done, whether good or bad. (2 Corinthians 5:10)

On the day the Lord returns we will all receive either life or death (John 3:16), righteousness or wrath (Romans 1:17–18). Righteousness is a gift, but death is a wage. Righteousness leads to eternal life, but wrath leads to death.

> Do not be amazed at this, for a time is coming when all who are in their graves will hear his voice and come out – those who have done what is good will rise to live, and those who have done what is evil will rise to be condemned. (John 5:28–29, NIV)

Those who have done good are those who "hear and believe," for those who hearken to the life-giving words of Jesus will live (John 5:24–25). In contrast, those who have done evil jam their fingers in their ears and refuse to hear the good things God says.

What makes a sheep a sheep? A sheep is not someone who does good works, for goats do good works too (see Matthew 7:22). A sheep is someone who heeds the Good Shepherd.

> My sheep hear my voice, and I know them, and they follow me; and I give eternal life to them, and they will never perish, and no one will snatch them out of my hand. (John 10:27–28)

Jesus knows his own. On that day Jesus will say, "This one is mine and I know them. They have heard my voice and responded." And according to the parable, some sheep are going to be surprised, perhaps because they served Jesus without owning a Bible or going to church. Perhaps some of the sheep are those we might have dismissed as sinners because they didn't fit the mold.

Isn't this the story we have been telling all along?

Judgment Day is not bad news for sinners, for Jesus is the Savior of sinners. But Judgment Day is bad news for those who scorn the Savior. Such people "thrust away" the word of God (i.e., Jesus), "suppress the truth" (i.e., Jesus) and "trample the Son of God underfoot" (Acts 13:46, Romans 1:18, Hebrews 10:29).

> It is appointed unto men once to die but after this the judgment. (Hebrews 9:27, KJV)

The word for judgment means decision or verdict. Every one of us makes a decision about Jesus, and in the end, every one of us gets what we want. Those who desire life shall have it and in abundance, for Jesus is the Giver of Life. And those who prefer to have nothing to do with him shall get their wish too.

6. We shall be with the Lord forever

I used to think that the earth was a bus station and that my permanent home was in heaven. I now realize that the earth is God's gift to humanity (Psalm

115:16), and God's gifts are good. This planet is our home. It was made for us and we were made for it.

However, our home is broken and marred by sin. It's a dilapidated shack that's falling to pieces. But just as God has not given up on us, he has not given up on our home. He's not moving us out; he's moving in. He's not sending us to heaven; he's bringing heaven to earth.

While some envision a future where we leave earth to go off and ruin some other planet, God's plan is to heal creation (Romans 8:19–21). Just as the disobedience of the first man cursed the earth, the obedience of the second man from heaven will restore it.

> … Jesus, the Christ appointed for you, whom heaven must receive until the period of restoration of all things about which God spoke by the mouth of his holy prophets from ancient time. (Acts 3:20–21)

One day creation will be free from the curse placed upon it. Death, decay, pollution, extinction – these are the fruits of the fall. Healing, resurrection, immortality – these are the fruits of Christ's obedience. Adam broke it; Jesus is restoring it. Adam's curse brought disconnection and alienation; Christ's blessing brings *koinonia*, true fellowship flowing from the heart of the Father.

God's renovation is well underway and will conclude when the Son of Man who is the Son of God returns to be with us forever.

> And I heard a loud voice from the throne, saying, "Behold, the tabernacle of God is among men, and he will dwell among them, and they shall be his people, and God himself will be among them, and he will wipe away every tear from their eyes; and there will no longer be any death; there will no longer be any mourning, or crying, or pain; the first things have passed away." (Revelation 21:3–4)

Adam cursed the earth with his disobedience, but Christ blessed the earth with his obedience. Now he sits on the throne until his enemies are put under his feet (1 Corinthians 15:25).

Satan, although defeated and disarmed at the cross, still "prowls around like a roaring lion, seeking someone to devour" (1 Peter 5:8). Happily, his time is limited, and his end is coming. When Jesus returns, Satan goes, and that will be a good day.

Jesus healed the sick, but many still suffer. His enemies of cancer, heart disease, depression, diabetes, and Alzheimer's are still with us. But when he returns they will go, and that will be a good day.

Many of us have buried children, parents, or spouses. Families have been torn apart by death. But when Christ returns death will be defeated, and that will be a good day!

And so we will be with the Lord forever. (1 Thessalonians 4:17, NIV)

Now there's a promise to put all others in the shade. We shall be with him, not just in spiritual union, but physically with him. It staggers the mind.

The Second Coming of the Great King is not something to fear but something to long for. All our lives up until then will seem like a waking dream compared to the life we will share with him in eternity.

"Comfort and encourage one another with these words" (1 Thessalonians 4:18).

---

[1] Vines defines the word *keleusma* (G2752), which is translated as shout, as "a call, summons, shout of command." Source: http://bit.ly/V_shout

39. A BETTER STORY

Our lives are shaped by the stories we tell. As a young boy, I heard a dismal story about the end of the world, and it nearly wrecked me. That story has surely wrecked others. Stories matter.

We need to pay attention to the stories we tell ourselves. To paraphrase Paul in 2 Corinthians 10:5, we ought to demolish stories that contradict the character of God. We should aim to fit our life's stories to the beautiful and life-giving narrative of Jesus Christ.

The story of how God destroyed Jerusalem for killing his Son is a bad story, for it does not mesh with the story of Jesus. It's a twisted piece of fan fiction that doesn't line up with the gospel.

We need a better version of the AD70 story, one that portrays Jesus as a savior instead of a destroyer. The better story would talk about how Jesus came to save the world starting with Jerusalem. He walked its streets and loved its people. He spoke up for the oppressed and stood up to oppressors. Jesus brought heaven to a cold and heartless city by touching the untouchables, befriending the lonely, and forgiving sinners.

Our better story would show Jesus warning the Jews about their fatal choices, and then sobbing over their thick-headed refusal to listen. It would highlight the extraordinary detail of his prophecies and the passion of his cries. The Jews were charging towards the cliffs of destruction while Jesus did all he could to stop them. He was the lone voice of warning on the doomed Titanic.

The religious Jews hated him, of course, but our better story would not emphasize their animosity as much as his inexplicable forgiveness. Even after Christ returned to heaven his grace and love continued to flow through his apostles and their letters. And as the doomsday clock wound down, he made sure that his warnings were recorded and disseminated in the early church teachings that became the Synoptic Gospels.

A better story needs a better ending. In the rotten version of the story, God is scary and capricious. He's Zeus with a rod of lightning or Jupiter with a thunderbolt. He's a deity to fear and run from.

But in the grace-based version of the story, God is exactly like Jesus. He's a champion for the weak and a deliverer for the nations. The God of this story does not stand idly on the sidelines of history. Instead, he steps onto the stage to intervene and guide us toward the path of life.

The bad version of the story shows God with a stick and declares, "Beware the anger of God." But the grace-based version portrays God with open arms and shouts, "God holds nothing against you. Be reconciled to God" (2 Corinthians 5:20).

The theme of the bad story is a frightening: "Deny Jesus and burn." But the theme of our better story captures the heart of Christ: "Choose life."

The bad version of the story generates bad fruit of racism and hatred. "Those Jews got what was coming to them." But the grace-based version produces good fruit of faith and hope. "A God that is good is a God you can trust."

Matthew 24 is nothing less than the history of the world, past and future, as seen from a small hill overlooking a doomed city. It's the story of man's sin and God's grace, our worst and God's best. It reveals what happens to those who reject the peace that God gives, and it gives us hope that there is more to life than suffering and death.

Ignore Christ's prophecies and parables of judgment and you may think that history is a never-ending cycle of violence and hurt. Two thousand years after the fall of Jerusalem and what has changed? The mighty still oppress the weak, and the displaced – the refugees and the stateless – still export their misery to the nations.

But Jesus tells us an end is coming. History is not just "one damn thing after another." History has a destination, a climax, a fulfillment, and he is it. One day the master will return, and the vineyard owner will come.

Life is a choice between two stories. One story is the endless loop of bad news and gossip that fills our screens and social media feeds. The other story is the quiet discovery that all is not what it seems. It's the good news story of heaven invading earth and people being set free. It's the story of a grace that is greater than our hurts and a love that is greater than our worst.

It's the story of a King who has come and is coming again.

40. SUMMARY OF THE MAIN POINTS

Chapter 1: Not one stone (Matthew 24:1–3)

- Matthew 24 contains Christ's answer to questions the disciples asked about the destruction of the temple and the coming of the Lord. The first half of the chapter (verses 4–35) is a prophecy regarding the fall of Jerusalem and the destruction of the temple. This prophecy was fulfilled by the summer of AD70. The second half of the chapter (verses 36–51) contains a prophecy and a prophetic parable about the Lord's future return. This prophecy is yet to be fulfilled.

Chapter 2: Birth pangs (Matthew 24:4–8)

- Jesus told the disciples they would hear of wars and rumors of wars. This was a remarkable prophecy as it was uttered during a time of relative peace. Yet the years following Christ's death were arguably the most violent in Jewish history. King Herod lost his army in a battle with the Nabatean king of Petra; racial conflict with the Greeks resulted in the deaths of tens of thousands of Jews in several cities; and the Jewish-Roman war led to the destruction of many towns and cities, including Jerusalem.
- Jesus told his disciples not to be troubled by rumors of war. Such rumors brought the Judean economy to a standstill in the '40s creating the conditions for food shortages and regional uncertainty.
- Jesus' warning about false messiahs is timeless but had particular relevance in the first century. If Jesus was not the long-awaited Messiah, as many Jews believed, the real Messiah could show up at any moment. This made the unbelieving Jews particularly susceptible to deception.
- In the years between Christ's warning and the fall of Jerusalem, several false messiahs stepped onto the national stage and did immeasurable harm. One of these, John Levi, was instrumental in the downfall of Jerusalem and the deaths of countless Jews.

Chapter 3: Trials and troubles (Matthew 24:9)

- Jesus correctly predicted that the apostles would go through tribulation, they would be hated by Gentiles as well as Jews, and some of them would be martyred.

- Jesus told the apostles in advance so they might be strengthened when trials came. Their Holy Spirit-inspired speeches to the authorities prove that Christ's words came true.

Chapter 4: Lawlessness and cold love (Matthew 24:10–12)
- While some consider Christ's warnings about lawlessness and betrayal as pointing to apostate believers or Judaizers, the general nature of his warning suggests a broader interpretation, namely, the collapse of civil society.
- The lawless prophecy perfectly describes the anarchic years of the late '60s when Israel descended into chaos and civil war. Corrupt Roman governors, religious fanatics, and outlaw gangs sowed the seeds of war and famine. The miseries that followed were so severe that even familial love grew cold.
- Jesus warned that false prophets would mislead many. During the final years of Jerusalem, false prophets were employed by the city's rulers to keep the people in line.

Chapter 5: Endure to the end (Matthew 24:13)
- "Endure to the end and be saved" is not a qualifying test for the kingdom, but practical and timeless instruction on how to survive in the face of persecution.
- "When they persecute you in one city, flee to the next," said Jesus, and the apostles heeded his advice.
- Paul, in particular, responded to persecution by walking away. If he had not done so, much of the New Testament would never have been written.
- Jesus does not expect us to die for the cause. He does not want us to throw our lives away but to live and tell others the good news.

Chapter 6: The gospel worldwide (Matthew 24:14)
- Jesus said the end would come after the gospel had been preached in the whole world. While some believe this prophecy could not have been fulfilled in the first century, the scriptures declare that the gospel had been proclaimed throughout the whole (Roman) world by the time Jerusalem was destroyed.

Chapter 7: The abomination of desolation (Matthew 24:15)

- Although nobody knows for certain what the Lord had in mind when he spoke of the abomination of desolation, one interpretation consistent with scripture is that he was referring to Roman armies surrounding Jerusalem.
- This interpretation is also consistent with Christ's exhortation to flee to the mountains. Sadly, many Jews fled to the fortified city of Jerusalem and died as a result.

Chapter 8: Time to run (Matthew 24:16–20)

- Jesus was specific in his instructions to the disciples. He told them when to flee, how to flee, and where to flee. Those who heeded his instructions lived; those who didn't either died in the siege or were taken captive by the Romans in AD70.
- In the four decades between Christ's warning and the fall of Jerusalem, there were at least ten major crises in Judea that could have prompted people to leave.
- Tradition teaches that the Christians fled Jerusalem in AD66 and escaped to Pella. However, it is likely that the Christians left Jerusalem over many years rather than in one single exodus.

Chapter 9: Great tribulation (Matthew 24:21)

- Jesus listed ten signs in connection with a great tribulation, and all of them came to pass within a five-month period in AD70.
- It is difficult to overstate the horrors visited upon Jerusalem during the Roman siege. Jesus sobbed over the city's imminent destruction. He knew the coming distress of the famine and the slaughter would be an unprecedented disaster that would leave the city in ruins and end the lives of many.
- Some of the prophesied signs regarding the fall of Jerusalem would have made little sense to the disciples, yet they proved to be remarkably accurate. For instance, Christ predicted that Jerusalem would be surrounded by an embankment (suggesting the city would be starved into submission) and that its people would fall by the edge of the sword (suggesting an invasion). Owing to the unusual circumstances of the siege, both prophecies were fulfilled within a matter of weeks.

- Perhaps the most remarkable of the ten tribulation signs was that the Jewish city of Jerusalem would be "trampled underfoot by the Gentiles until the times of the Gentiles are fulfilled." This prophecy was fulfilled in the summer AD70 and remains true to this day.

Chapter 10: Shortened days (Matthew 24:22)
- Contrary to popular belief, Jerusalem did not fall quickly because God set his hand against it. It fell because the Roman attackers were highly motivated, while the Jewish defenders were starving and divided. Owing to factional infighting, the city was rotten and on the verge of imploding before the Romans arrived. The defenders had weakened the city's defenses by killing each other and burning their grain stores.
- From a spiritual perspective, Jerusalem fell because the Jews rejected peace (Luke 19:42–44) while embracing hatred and bloodshed.
- Josephus' claim that the city fell because God was a Roman "assistant" is ludicrous and baseless.

Chapter 11: Counterfeit Christs (Matthew 24:23–27)
- Jesus' warning about false Christs and false prophets is highly specific. He told the disciples that false men would draw people to one of two secret locations. There is ample evidence, both in scripture and history, that this prophecy was fulfilled in the years leading up to the Roman siege.
- "As lightning from the east flashes in the west." Jesus gave the disciples the authentic to help them recognize the counterfeit. While false leaders operate in the shadows, the return of the true Christ will be no secret event.

Chapter 12: The eagles are coming (Matthew 24:28)
- Christ's obscure prophecy about eagles gathering about a carcass is a reference to the Roman ensigns or *aquila*.
- When Herod built the temple, he put an offensive eagle on the gate. That eagle was torn down but Christ said more eagles would come. In AD70 four eagles arrived in the form of four Roman legions. And when the city fell, an emaciated and dismembered carcass, there the eagles were gathered.

Chapter 13: Sun and moon (Matthew 24:29)

- Christ's prophecy about a darkening sun and falling stars is figurative. The sun, moon, and stars are common Biblical metaphors for governing authorities. When Babylon fell, Isaiah said the sun and moon were darkened. Ezekiel said the same thing when Egypt fell, and Jesus used similar language when speaking of the end of Jerusalem. He was not saying that the solar system was about collapse, but that the government of Israel would be shaken and the temple system would end.
- "Dismay among the nations" could be a prophetic reference to the misery of the Jewish exiles. A tragic symmetry: while the apostles were taking the good news of Jesus worldwide, 97,000 Jewish captives were exporting the bad news of Rome.

Chapter 14: The Son of Man in heaven (Matthew 24:30)

- The sign of the Son of Man in heaven was not some mystical sky-sign involving comets or divine retribution. It was Daniel's prophecy come true. Daniel foretold of the Son of Man coming with the clouds of heaven to the Ancient of Days to receive glory and power. This prophecy was fulfilled when Christ ascended into heaven.
- There are six New Testament references to Jesus coming on the clouds, and every one of them pertains to his exaltation and ascension.
- When Jesus said some of the disciples would not taste death until they saw the Son of Man coming into his kingdom, he was not predicting they would live for thousands of years. He was saying they would see him exalted and coming into his kingdom.
- The transfiguration was the trailer; the ascension was the movie. On the Mount of Transfiguration the disciples got a glimpse of Christ's glory. They became "eyewitnesses of his majesty."
- The "peoples of the earth will mourn" is a reference to the tribes of the land realizing that Jesus was who he said he was and that they had missed the timing of God's coming to them. This prophecy was fulfilled in part on the day of Pentecost when 3,000 Jews, cut to the heart, repented and got baptized. It was further fulfilled in the build-up to the Roman siege as the Jews witnessed Christ's prophecies coming true.

Chapter 15: Angels and trumpets (Matthew 24:31)

- Jesus prophecy about sending out angels to gather his elect from the four winds is a reference to the great commission rather than the Second Coming. (Jesus is sending angels, not coming with them.) Jesus is telling the very men who are about to be commissioned that he plans to gather all people, not just the Jews.
- The prophecy heralds the arrival of the long-awaited year of Jubilee. After Christ bore the sins of the world, the gospel messengers went to all corners of the earth to proclaim the day of freedom and forgiveness. The everlasting year of the Lord's favor had finally arrived.
- Earthly kingdoms divide and conquer, but the Lord gathers his people from the ends of the earth. While the Romans were destroying families, the Lord was growing his family.

Chapter 16: Signs of the seasons (Matthew 24:32–34)

- Jesus did not set out to mislead people. When he told the disciples that his prophecies regarding Jerusalem would come to pass within one generation, he meant their generation. His words of warning were direct and personal: "*You* will hear of wars, *you* will be persecuted, *you* will be hated, see to it that *you* are not frightened."
- Jesus made 40 specific prophecies regarding the fall of Jerusalem, and all of them were fulfilled by AD70. Their fulfillment is proof that Jesus is the Son of God, and a savior rather than a spectator on the sidelines of history.

Chapter 17: Heaven and earth (Matthew 24:35)

- Matthew 24:35 is the transition point between two prophecies. Jesus has been speaking of things that pass away (Jerusalem, the temple). He is now about to begin speaking of his glorious return.
- The phrase heaven and earth may be a reference to the temple, the old covenant, or the literal heaven and earth. Alternatively, Jesus is employing an idiom to emphasize the enduring truthfulness of his prophecies.

Chapter 18: The day and the hour (Matthew 24:36–42)

- Jesus said no one knows when he will return.

- Jesus did not return to earth in AD70. The Lord told his disciples they would see (or hear about) the events leading up to the destruction of Jerusalem, but they would not see his return.
- The fall of Jerusalem can be contrasted with the day of the Lord. While the former event followed a predictable timeline, the latter will be unexpected. The former was preceded by war and upheaval; the latter will take place during a time of peace and safety.
- Being ready for Christ's return does not mean withdrawing from society, for the ready men and women in Christ's stories are participating in life and providing for their families.

Chapter 19: Keep watch (Matthew 24:43–44)
- Jesus, Peter, and Paul all described the Lord returning like a thief in the night, meaning it will be unexpected and unlike the well-signposted destruction of Jerusalem.
- The exhortation to be alert and ready should not be interpreted as "sign up to Newsweek and follow political developments carefully." Nor does it mean withdrawing from society in fearful anticipation of the apocalypse. Being ready implies being occupied with the Lord's business and putting his good gifts to work.
- We hasten the Lord's return by living holy and godly lives that reveal the goodness of a good God who does not treat us as our sins deserve.

Chapter 20: The faithful servant (Matthew 24:45–51)
- The prophetic parable at the end of Matthew 24 illustrates the theme of the chapter: be ready. Being ready means being prepared. It's getting on with the business of living in union with the Lord and shining in a dark world.
- In the parable, the faithless servant has no expectation of the master's return. Without this hope, he lives a disconnected and unfulfilled life. In contrast, the faithful servant distributes his master's food and others are blessed. Although the master is not physically present, the servant represents him by giving his stuff away. When the master returns he is so pleased he tells the servant to take charge of all his possessions. This is a story of grace and faith. When we give what God has given us, others are blessed, and God is pleased.

Chapter 21: The blood of righteous Abel

- The word woe denotes distress or deep sorrow. The eight woes Jesus pronounced on the scribes and Pharisees in Matthew 23 can be read as expressions of dismay over their lostness and stubborn refusal to repent.

- Although Christ's anger towards the religious leaders is justified, Jesus never says, "I will destroy this city and everyone in it!" Instead, he pronounces the condemnation they have brought upon their own heads. Like a doctor making a diagnosis, Jesus informs them of the fatal consequences of their actions.

- The parable of the fig tree highlights the dangers of trusting self instead of God. When Jesus cursed the fig tree it withered from the roots up, symbolizing the destructive effects of unbelief. The faithless Jewish nation rotted from within.

- When Jesus charged the religious Jews with "the blood of righteous Abel" (Matthew 23:34–36), he was not saying that God would punish them for sins they never committed. He was saying that sin has consequences. And sin on an industrial scale (such as that practiced by the Jews when they murdered the apostles and the Romans), would lead to catastrophic consequences. Live by the sword and you'll die by the sword.

- However, even murderous hypocrites are not beyond the reach of salvation. Jesus told the religious Jews, "You will not see me until you say 'Blessed is he who comes in the name of the Lord'." He was saying, "You have seen me and not believed. Now you will not see me unless you believe." All who ask for salvation shall have it.

Chapter 22: When are the days of vengeance?

- The long tradition of blaming God for the destruction of Jerusalem has more to do with a Jewish historian schooled in the Old Testament than the gospel of Jesus. Josephus accused God of destroying Jerusalem while early Christian writers came up with a plausible motive: It was divine punishment for killing his Son. However, this graceless and anti-Semitic theology is contrary to the character of God as revealed by Jesus.

- The traditional view of God punishing Jerusalem is partly responsible for the repeated injustices visited upon the Jews in the centuries since AD70.
- Others have said that God judged the old covenant or a corrupt religious system. Alternatively, God did not judge anyone but he removed his hand of protection. Neither view is consistent with the active love and forgiveness demonstrated by Jesus. God did not send the Romans to deal with the lost sheep of Israel; he sent his Son.
- "Father forgive them." The dying words of Christ testify to the riches of God's grace even towards those who sought his death.
- The days of vengeance mentioned by Jesus in Luke 21:20-23 is a reference to manmade calamities foretold by the Old Testament prophets. These days can be contrasted with the coming and singular Day of Vengeance of our God (Isaiah 61:2). Roman vengeance involved armies and great distress. Divine vengeance brings liberty and freedom.

Chapter 23: Whose wrath has come?

- There is nothing in the New Testament to suggest God punished the Jews in AD70. Although a handful of English translations say the "wrath of God" had come upon them in 1 Thessalonians 2:16, the Bible doesn't say this. It simply says, "The wrath has come," meaning the Roman wrath soon to be visited upon Galilee and Judea.
- When Paul said, "The wrath has come" he was quoting the prophecies of Jesus. Even though the Roman invasion was still a few years away, Paul understood from the Lord that the current generation would reap a wrathful harvest.

Chapter 24: Good news in the parables of judgment

- The wrath of the king in the Parable of the Wedding Banquet and the vineyard owner in the Parable of the Tenants points to the coming day of wrath, not the historical destruction of Jerusalem.
- Just as Babylon the Great is cast down like a stone in Revelation 18:21, the statue of Daniel 2:35 is crushed by a falling stone. The stone represents King Jesus (Luke 20:18) and his eternal reign.
- In the end, the City of Man and the kingdoms of earth shall fall and Jesus shall reign unchallenged forever and ever.

- The Parable of the Talents is about the grace of God and what people do with it. The faithful servants receive their master's grace, put it to work, and are ultimately promoted to co-rulers with the king. In contrast, the unfaithful servant contemptuously rejects the gift and is dismissed as wicked and lazy.
- At the end of the parable each servant gets want he wants. The faithful servants enter into their master's joy, while the wicked servant departs down the miserable and dark path of the self-made man.

Chapter 25: Payback and relief
- When Paul said God would pay back trouble and render vengeance to those who do not obey the gospel, he was referring to Judgment Day, not AD70, "when the Lord Jesus is revealed from heaven" (2 Thessalonians 1:7).
- The relief that Paul promised to the troubled Thessalonians was the comfort that abounds to us in Christ. God gives us relief in our troubles. He does not give us relief by removing our troubles or destroying troublesome Jews.
- The scriptures provide a case study of how this works: Paul experienced no rest after his persecution in Macedonia, but God comforted him by sending Titus with a good report.

Chapter 26: Human versus divine vengeance
- Abel's blood cries out for vengeance, but the forgiving blood of Jesus speaks a better message.
- Human vengeance can be contrasted with divine vengeance. One is characterized by retribution; the other is marked by righteousness. One is vindictive and destructive; the other is vindicating and restorative. One describes what happened to Jews at the hands of the Romans; the other foretells what God will bring to a climax on Judgment Day.
- The divine desire to make things right rather than punish wrong things can be seen in the gracious way the Lord related to the temple that condemned him and the city that killed him. Jesus designated Jerusalem as Mission Field Number One, and he chose the temple courts as the venue for the early church.

- Jerusalem rejected Jesus, but Jesus never rejected Jerusalem. The rapid growth on the early church in that city testifies to a love that keeps no record of wrongs.

Chapter 27: Why did Jerusalem fall?
- Israel was invaded and Jerusalem was destroyed because the Jews picked a fight with the powerful Roman Empire. Divine smiting had nothing to do with it.
- Jesus said those who live by the sword, die by the sword. Murder Roman soldiers (as the Jews did in AD66 and on several later occasions), and you can expect Roman retribution (as the Jews experienced in AD70).
- Jerusalem was doomed because the people didn't recognize Jesus (Acts 13:27). Jesus said "Love your enemies and pray for those who persecute you," but the Jews hated and fought their enemies.

Chapter 28: What did the high priest see?
- On the night before he died, Jesus told Caiaphas and the old men of the Sanhedrin that they would see the Son of Man sitting at the right hand of God (Matthew 26:64). This prophecy of exaltation began coming to pass within 24 hours.
- Within weeks Peter and Stephen both declared that Jesus was sitting at the right hand of God. Thus the preterist notion that the prophecy was not fulfilled until AD70 cannot be correct. The prophecy was fulfilled in the manner that Jesus predicted and in the timeframe that he specified.

Chapter 29: When did the old covenant end?
- The Bible is composed of two documents – the Old and New Testaments – that roughly equate to two covenants: the old covenant and the new covenant. The old covenant began on Mt. Sinai while the new covenant came into effect when Christ shed his blood on the cross.
- The old covenant began when Moses received the law and culminated when Christ fulfilled it on the cross.
- Christ's matchless sacrifice made the old system of animal sacrifices instantly obsolete. Nevertheless, religious Jews continued bringing animal sacrifices for as long as the temple stood. This has led some to

conclude that old and new covenants overlapped for 40 years. How-ever, the torn temple curtain signified that God was done with the old covenant. God did not act one way towards the Jews and a different way to everyone else.

- The Passover lamb points to Jesus. Just as the children of Israel were in bondage until they partook of the first Passover, the first-century Jews were bound to the law until Christ was sacrificed in the final Passover.
- The relationship of Ishmael to Isaac parallels the transition of cove-nants from John, the last old covenant prophet, to Jesus, the new cove-nant messenger.
- Similarly, the Mount of Transfiguration reveals a transition from the law and the prophets (represented by Moses and Elijah) to Jesus.
- The old covenant did not end with John's beheading or the Mount of Transfiguration. The curtain did not fall until the sacrifice of God's Lamb.
- The destruction of Jerusalem in AD70 marked the end of the temple but not the end of law-based religion. Moses is still read to this day, and the result is covenant confusion and bondage. Freedom is found in trusting Jesus who is the culmination of the law. His death is the exclamation mark at the end of the old covenant.

Chapter 30: When is the great tribulation?
- The great tribulation is past not future. First-century Christians who believed Christ was predicting a great tribulation within their life-times fled and lived. Those who didn't believe in a first-century trib-ulation stayed and died.
- Although trials and tribulations are normal for the believer, Jesus promised the great tribulation would be a one-off event (Matthew 24:21). Like the great flood, the great tribulation will never be re-peated.
- When John said the antichrist spirit was at work in his generation, he was most likely referring to the spirit behind first-century Gnosticism.
- The antichrist does not appear in the book of Revelation and Jesus never mentioned him. A charismatic 21st-century antichrist in charge of a one-world government has as much basis in scripture as a future great tribulation (i.e., none at all).

Chapter 31: The five comings of Jesus

- The scriptures speak of at least five comings of Jesus: his first and second comings to earth, his coming to the temple, his coming via the Holy Spirit, and his coming to the heavenly throne room.
- The Second Coming is not mentioned directly in scripture but is generally referred to as the day or coming of the Lord or the coming of the Son of Man, when he appears "a second time."
- Malachi's prophecy of the Lord coming to the temple to refine, cleanse, and judge, was fulfilled during Christ's lifetime. Jesus "purified the Sons of Levi" by dying on the cross, and after his death a "great many" priests became Christians.
- Which coming of the Lord did the disciples ask about in Matthew 24? From Christ's response (seven word pictures about his return) we can infer they were asking about his second coming.

Chapter 32: When is the Second Coming?

- Unlike an expectant mother who knows when her baby is coming, Jesus' return will be wholly unexpected.
- Jesus told the disciples that he did not know when he would return and that it was not their business to know.
- There are more than 90 scriptures in the New Testament pertaining to the Second Coming, but none of them answers the question of when.
- Jesus told stories of masters and noblemen being gone "a long time." Jesus never told the disciples he would be back soon. (How could he when he did not know the time of his return?) Jesus and the epistle writers all spoke of the need to wait patiently for the Lord's return.
- Scriptures indicating an imminent coming soon pertain to his coming to heaven (the ascension) rather than his final coming to earth.
- For 2,000 years people have been predicting dates for the Lord's return, and every one of them has proven wrong. The inability to learn from these mistakes combined with the stubborn refusal to heed Christ's words on the subject remains one of the greatest follies of the church.
- Futurists sometimes interpret the fulfilled prophecies of Matthew 24 as signposts of Christ's return. But signs meant for that generation cannot be for ours.

Chapter 33: Angels, clouds, and the coming of the King
- In Matthew's gospel no less than four comings of the Lord are described. Failure to understand these different comings can lead to eschatological confusion.
- In the Olivet Discourse Jesus discussed two sorts of comings: his coming home to heaven and his final coming or return to earth. He used different words to describe each coming.
- Preterists and futurists typically stumble over Matthew 24:30. Preterists interpret this passage as Jesus coming in judgment to destroy Jerusalem, while futurists consider it a reference to the Second Coming. However, several prophetic and literary keys reveal that Jesus was talking about his ascension.
- In scripture, every time the Son of Man is described as coming on the clouds, he is going up (or coming to heaven). Every time he is described as coming with angels, he is coming down (to earth).

Chapter 34: When are the last days?
- Jesus divides history into the first and last days. The first days concluded with him coming in humility; the last days will conclude when he returns in glory.
- The last days foretold by the prophets refer to the gospel age of the church when the mountain of the Lord's house will be established, and the nations will stream to it.
- The phrase "end times" is not Biblical and can lead to the mistaken belief that ours is the last days' generation. However, the apostles believed they were living in the last days.
- Countless false predictions have been made by those who believed they were living in the last of the last days. Typically these false predictions come from four sources: visions/revelations, current events, natural phenomena, and dates which are thought to be of special significance.
- Predictions regarding the timing of the Lord's return can lead to mockery and scorn. The New Testament is free of such predictions. If we had the same mindset as the apostles the market for bad predictions would cease to exist.
- The restoration of Israel does not refer to a 20th-century geopolitical event but an ancient prophecy. Hosea's prophecy about the sons of

Israel returning to David their king (i.e., Jesus, the Son of David), was first fulfilled on the day of Pentecost and continues to be fulfilled whenever a Jew comes to Jesus.

Chapter 35: When is the end of the age?

- The Bible talks about different ages (e.g., the old covenant age, the new covenant age) and different endings (i.e., ordinary endings, the consummation of God's plans).
- The prophecies of Matthew 24 cover at least two kinds of endings: the end of Jerusalem and temple-based worship (historic), and the end of the present age of grace (future). This present age will end when King Jesus returns to earth in glorious triumph.

Chapter 36: What about the rapture?

- The word rapture comes from the Latin Bible and is used to describe the living saints being caught up in the air to meet the Lord on his return. The dead are resurrected; those who are alive and remain are caught up to meet the Lord in the clouds (1 Thessalonians 4:17).
- The parable of the wise virgins is a picture of the rapture: the bridegroom (the Lord) comes with a shout and the wise virgins (the ready saints) go out to meet him and return with him.
- Just as some preterists believe in two second comings (Jesus came in AD70 and will come again), some futurists also believe that Jesus will return twice; first to rescue his church, then later to judge the earth. However, the scriptures describe only one second coming of the Lord.
- The yo-yo picture of Jesus ferrying the saints to heaven to avoid a tribulation is unscriptural. The great tribulation is past; the rapture is future.
- Rapture preachers tend to interpret both good and gloomy outlooks as signs of an imminent rapture. Such speculation is foolish. Since we do not know when the Lord will return, we do not know when the saints will be caught up to meet him.
- When Jesus returns there will be some type of division or separation. When Jesus said he had come to earth with a sword, he meant that fathers and sons, mothers and daughters divide themselves by their response to him.

Chapter 37: Jerusalem and Judgment Day

- Although the fall of Jerusalem and the future return of the Lord are separate events, the former illustrates the latter. Then, as now, those who heeded Christ's words lived, while those who dismissed him perished.
- In Matthew 24 and Luke 21 Jesus told the disciples to prepare for both the fall of Jerusalem and Judgment Day. Jesus exhorted his disciples to pray for strength to stand on Judgment Day. To pray is to make request. It's asking Jesus for the grace to stand. What we require, Jesus provides.

Chapter 38: What happens when Christ returns?

- Although the Bible is silent on when Christ will return, it lists six things that will happen when he does: Jesus will arrive with a shout (meaning his return will be public and spectacular), the dead will rise (it will be a day of joyful reunions), we will be transformed and given new bodies, we will meet the Lord in the air (and return with him to earth), God will judge the living and the dead, and we will be with the Lord forever.
- The Second Coming is not something to fear; it is a glorious day to long for!

Chapter 39: A better story

- The stories we tell ourselves matter. A bad story enslaves and imparts fear; a good story liberates and gives hope.
- The story of how God destroyed Jerusalem for killing his Son is a bad story, for it does not mesh with the story of Jesus. A better version of the AD70 story portrays Jesus as Savior. It reveals a God who is exactly like Jesus.
- The bad version of the story generates bad fruit of racism and fear, but the better version produces hope and faith.
- Matthew 24 is nothing less than the history of the world. It's the story of man's sin and God's greater grace.
- Christ's parables and prophecies of judgment reveal that history has a climax. The master will return, and the vineyard owner will come. A grace-based eschatology reveals a King who has come and is coming again.

LAST DRINKS

The hour is late, and the bartender is wiping down the bar. Mr. Futurist finishes his drink and puts his glass on the counter.

Mr. Futurist: "You almost had me, you know, with all this AD70 talk. Maybe I can accept that famines, earthquakes, and wars all happened in the first century. Maybe I can accept that the fall of Jerusalem was an unprecedented time of distress, even a great tribulation. But there's one thing I can't accept. There's a wrinkle in your argument."

Mr. Preterist: "And that is?"

Mr. Futurist: "The abomination of desolation. It's the critical piece of the puzzle, and it doesn't fit your picture. It's supposed to be this idol that's set up in the temple and then everyone flees. But there was no idol."

Mr. Preterist: "What about the Roman ensigns?"

Mr. Futurist: "*Pfft.* Those weren't idols, and by the time they were put in the temple it was too late to flee.

Mr. Preterist: "Do you believe in dual fulfillment, that one prophecy can be fulfilled twice?"

Mr. Futurist: "What do you mean?"

Mr. Preterist: "Well, some say there was great tribulation in AD70 and there will be another great tribulation at the end of days."

Mr. Futurist: "I'm not buying it. A prophecy points to one thing only. Otherwise we could have a bunch of messiahs."

Mr. Preterist: "Okay, we agree on that. Jesus said the great tribulation would be unrepeated, so there can only be one. It could be AD70 or some future date, but not both."

Mr. Futurist: "Sure. So what?"

Mr. Preterist: "If a prophecy points to only one thing, and Daniel's prophecy pointed to the idol erected by Antiochus Epiphanes in 160BC, then the same prophecy can't point to another idol set up by someone else."

Mr. Futurist: "You lost me."

Mr. Preterist: "I'm saying that the abomination of desolation that Jesus spoke of could be the same thing Daniel had in mind or it could be a completely different thing. Point is, it doesn't have to be an idol. That's not a requirement for the prophecy to be true."

Mr. Futurist: "So it could be an army?"

Mr. Preterist: "It could be anything."

Mr. Futurist: "As long as it's offensive and standing in the holy place."

Mr. Preterist: "Exactly. I sometimes wonder if it wasn't the temple sacrifices themselves. Once the Lamb of God was sacrificed at Calvary, those animal sacrifices served no purpose, yet the religious Jews kept bringing them. God would probably find that offensive."

Mr. Futurist: "Maybe."

Mr. Preterist: "So the abomination could be something we've not considered or that history never recorded."

Mr. Futurist: "Or it could be something yet to happen. Perhaps everything Jesus said about the temple is still in the future."

Mr. Preterist: "Except the temple doesn't exist anymore, which makes it kind of hard to tear down."

Mr. Futurist: "Many Jews believe the temple will be rebuilt. You have to admit it's a possibility."

Mr. Preterist: "But if that were to happen many of Christ's predictions would become untrue. Jesus told the disciples, 'You will see it.' Not us, but them. He said 'these things' would be fulfilled in their generation. Not ours, but theirs."

Bartender: "Forgive me for intruding, gentlemen, but I've been listening to you argue all evening. I wasn't eavesdropping, but you guys shout when you're excited. No, no need to apologize. I just wanted to say there are gaps in both your arguments. Mr. Futurist, Jesus said the stones would come down and they did. He told the Christians to flee and they fled. Now you're convinced that Jesus was not talking about AD70, but if you thought that back then, you would've died in the siege. Now, don't laugh Mr. Preterist because you've missed some things too. It's as plain as the nose on my face that the signs pointing to the fall of Jerusalem are different from the signs pointing to his coming. You couldn't make them more different if you tried."

Mr. Preterist: "What are you saying?"

Bartender: "I'm saying that you're on the money when it comes to the first part of the prophecy, but he's right when it comes to the second. Jesus told the disciples about the fall of Jerusalem because they asked. Then he told them about his coming because they asked about that too. One thing has happened; the other is yet to happen. How is this not obvious?"

Mr. Preterist: "So you're a partial preterist."

Mr. Futurist: "No, he's a partial futurist. Ha-ha!"

Bartender: "No, I'm just a bartender with sore feet, and if you gents are all done, I'd like to be getting home. *Matlock's* on."

Mr. Futurist and Mr. Preterist apologize for staying late and raising their voices. They leave a generous tip on the bar and lift their coats off the rack. Shaking the bartender's hand, they promise to remember him to their father. Outside, the two men scarf up against the cold. "That was fun," says one.

"You gave me a lot to think about," says the other. They look up at the stars for a moment, exhaling gentle puffs of vapor. Then pulling their coats about them, the two brothers turn and head for home.

First-century Palestine

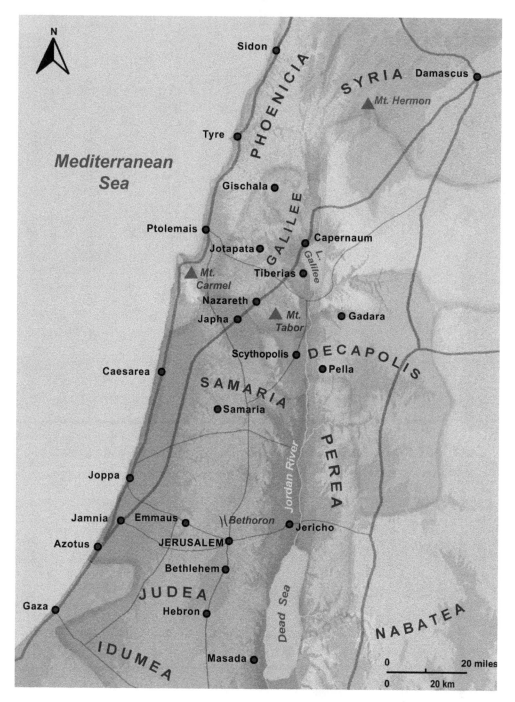

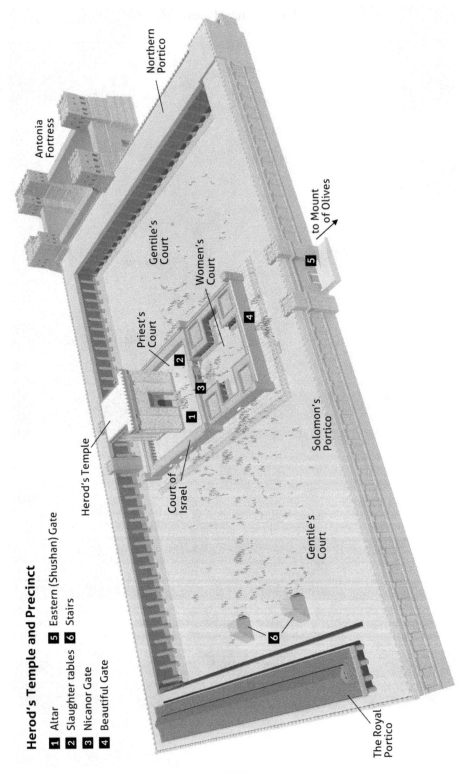

Herod's Temple and Precinct

1 Altar **5** Eastern (Shushan) Gate
2 Slaughter tables **6** Stairs
3 Nicanor Gate
4 Beautiful Gate

Antonia Fortress

Northern Portico

Gentile's Court

Women's Court

Priest's Court

Herod's Temple

Court of Israel

to Mount of Olives

Solomon's Portico

Gentile's Court

The Royal Portico

APPENDIX 1: TIMELINE OF KEY EVENTS PRIOR TO THE FALL OF JERUSALEM

Marginal references below include the date and source. Sources are abbreviated as A for *Antiquities of the Jews* and W for *War of the Jews*, both written by Josephus, followed by book, chapter, and paragraph. Thus A20.2.5 refers to book 20, chapter two, and paragraph 5 of *Antiquities*.

AD34   A great persecution against the church leads to a mass exodus of Christians out of Jerusalem (Acts 8:1).

AD36
A18.5.1   Herod Antipas, the tetrarch who beheaded John the Baptist and asked Jesus to perform a miracle, loses his army in a battle with King Aretas IV of Nabatea.

AD40–41
W2.10   The Roman emperor Caligula sends Publius Petronius and two legions to Israel to erect statues in the temple. The army is met by tens of thousands of protesting Jews. Petronius threatens war, but the unarmed Jews say they are ready to die. Petronius backs down. Furious, Caligula orders Petronius' death, but the emperor is assassinated before the order can be carried out.

On account of the unrest in Judea, the harvest is interrupted, and the resulting food shortage leads to tensions with neighboring Tyre and Sidon (Acts 12:20).

AD46–47
A20.2.5   The severe worldwide famine predicted by Agabus comes to pass (Acts 11:28). Jerusalem suffers and many die.[1]

AD48
W2.12.1   A Roman soldier guarding the temple during the feast of Passover engages in an indecent act triggering a riot. Soldiers are sent in to restore the peace, but the crowds panic and flee down narrow streets. More than 10,000 people are killed in the stampede.[2]

AD54
A20.8.5
W2.13.3   Antonius Felix, the corrupt Roman governor who detained the apostle Paul (Acts 24:26), hires men to murder Jonathan the high priest. The killers approach Jonathan by hiding daggers under their garments and mingling with worshippers in the temple. When they go unpunished for their crime, they begin to attack others on a daily basis. Thus the *Sicarii*, or dagger men, are born. A fanatical group of assassins, the *Sicarii* bring terror to Judea hastening the descent to anarchy and war.[3]

AD62
A20.9.1   James the Just, the leader of the Jerusalem church, is murdered. His death is orchestrated by the newly-appointed high priest Ananus, a

Sadducee. The murder of James offends the citizens, and they complain to Herod Agrippa, the man who appointed the high priest, and Lucceius Albinus, the yet-to-arrive Roman governor. As a result, Ananus is dumped from office after just three months.

AD64
A20.9.5

On the eve of his departure from Judea, Albinus seeks to ingratiate himself with the people of Jerusalem. He clears the prisons by executing the worst criminals and releasing others after payment of a bribe. As a result, the Judean countryside becomes a lawless land of bandits and gangs.

AD64
A20.11.1
W2.14.2

Gessius Florus, arguably the worst Roman governor of all, begins his two-year campaign of violence and corruption. He seizes property as though "he had been sent as an executioner to punish condemned malefactors." His atrocities ultimately provoke the Jews to take up arms and rebel against Rome.

Passover
AD66
W2.14.3

Cestius Gallus, the Roman procurator of Syria, visits Jerusalem and is met by crowds denouncing Florus as the bane of their country. Florus laughs dismissively. However, Cestius promises the people that he will keep Florus on a tighter leash. Florus, worrying that the Jews might accuse him before Caesar, decides that a Jewish rebellion is needed to cover up his crimes.

May
AD66

An incident in Caesarea provides Florus with a pretext for war. Some Greeks provoke the Jews over a minor building conflict, but Florus ignores Jewish calls for justice. The Jews pay him a bribe, and he promises to help, but after another incident, he throws the Jews in jail.

June 3
AD66
W2.14.3–6

The Jews of Jerusalem are outraged but do nothing. Determined to provoke them further Florus demands seventeen talents of silver from the temple treasury. Already impoverished from decades of heavy Roman taxation, the Jews mock greedy Florus. He reacts by crucifying some prominent citizens and giving his soldiers permission to plunder the city. The soldiers break into homes and kill 3,600 people, including women and infants.

W2.17.2

Eleazar, the son of Ananias the high priest, persuades temple officials to receive no gift or sacrifice from foreigners. Josephus records that "this was the true beginning of the war with the Romans" since customary sacrifices offered on behalf of the emperor were now rejected.

Aug.
AD66
W2.17.6

Not wishing to antagonize Rome, the leading citizens of Jerusalem appeal to Florus and Agrippa to crush the nascent rebellion. The governor ignores them but King Agrippa, anxious to save the city, sends 2,000 cavalries. For a week the two sides clash. Then the rebels join forces with the *Sicarii* and repel the royal troops.

W2.17.7 The rebels, along with members of the *Sicarii*, attack the Roman garrison in the Antonia Tower killing the soldiers and setting it on fire.

W2.18.1 Racial tensions flare up in Caesarea. In one hour Greek-speaking Caesareans slaughter 20,000 Jews. Those that flee are caught by Florus and sent in bonds to the galleys. In one day the city is emptied of Jews.

W2.18
W2.20.2 Infuriated, the Jews retaliate by attacking more than a dozen foreign cities. However, their enemies slaughter 50,000 Jews in Alexandria and 10,000 in Damascus. Massacres also take place in Joppa (8,400 dead), Ashkelon (2,500), and Ptolemais (2,000).

W2.18.3 In Scythopolis the attacking Jews find their own people armed in defense of the city. The Scythopolitan Jews fight so fiercely that their neighbors fear they may repent for opposing the Jewish cause and turn against them. They demand the Jews demonstrate their fidelity by taking their families to a nearby grove where 13,000 of them are treacherously slain in one night.

W2.18.9 Cestius Gallus marches south from Antioch with a massive army consisting of the Twelfth Legion, cohorts and cavalry troops from other legions, and 16,000 men contributed by other kings including Herod Agrippa, the last king of Judea. (This is the same king the apostle Paul addressed in Acts 26.) Along the way, he collects large numbers of auxiliary troops from the free cities. These additional troops are not professional soldiers, but any deficiencies in martial skills are offset by their intense hatred of the Jews.

Oct.
AD66
W2.19.2 After slaughtering the inhabitants of Joppa and subduing Galilean outlaws, Cestius proceeds to Jerusalem. However, while his army is divided and camped either side of the pass of Bethoron, he is attacked by the Jews at both ends. The Romans lose 400 infantry and 115 horsemen to the Jews' loss of 22. Leading the attack on the Roman rear is Simon the son of Giora. Simon captures many of the beasts used to haul Roman weapons of war.

W2.19.3 With the Roman position precarious, Agrippa sends two envoys to negotiate with the Jews. He offers amnesty to the Jewish rebels on the condition that they will lay down their weapons. But the rebel leaders, fearing the people will listen to Agrippa, attempt to kill the messengers.

Nov. AD66 W2.19	Sensing disunity among the Jews, Cestius pushes on to Jerusalem. However, after just nine days and on the verge of victory, he pulls up stakes and heads for home. His departure emboldens the Jews, and they pursue and harass his rear. At Bethoron they give him a humiliating defeat. He loses his siege machines, and the Twelfth Legion is all but destroyed.
AD67	The Jews and Romans prepare for war. On the Jewish side, the temple leaders elect generals such as Joseph son of Matthias, the future Flavius Josephus and chronicler of the war. On the Roman side, Nero appoints as commander the seasoned campaigner Titus Flavius Vespasianus, a.k.a. Vespasian. Militias led by peasant leaders also emerge. The most notable of these is a crafty olive oil merchant named Yohanan Ben-Levi, better known as John Levi. He and Josephus clash in the Galilean countryside.
Spring AD67 W3.4.2	Vespasian marshals his troops at Ptolemais. With him are the legions he has brought from Antioch along with another his son Titus has brought up from Egypt. In addition, he has twenty-three cohorts plus auxiliaries supplied by Agrippa and three other client kings. Altogether, he has 60,000 soldiers plus servants with military training.
W3.7.1, 31 W3.10.9	War! Vespasian begins his campaign by sending his legions to different parts of Galilee. Vespasian takes Gadara and puts to death every male of fighting age. In Japha, 12,000 Galileans are caught between the walls of their city and the merciless Romans. In Tiberius, the townsfolk are marshaled into the stadium where the young are taken to be sold as slaves, while the old and infirm are put to death.
Summer AD67 W3.7–9	At the mountain stronghold of Jotapata, the Romans raise an embankment to starve the city into submission. After eight weeks they take the city at a cost of 40,000 Jewish lives. Among the presumed dead is General Josephus. The Jews of Jerusalem mourn his loss but become furious when they learn Josephus is alive and has surrendered. While in Roman captivity, Josephus prophecies that Vespasian will become Caesar. Vespasian doesn't believe it, but when he learns that Josephus correctly predicted his city would fall on the 47th day of the siege, he bestows his prisoner with gifts.[4]
Nov. AD67 W4.2	Only one Galilean town remains to be subdued – Giscala. Titus marches on the town offering pardon. In the town, John Levi accepts the Roman's terms but asks for a day's grace since it is the Sabbath. Titus agrees and during the night John and many others slip away. Learning of this duplicity the following morning, Titus and sends a squadron of cavalry in pursuit. Of those who fled, 6,000 are killed and 3,000 are captured. However, John and his men make it safely to Jerusalem.

By the end of the year, the rebellion in Galilee has been brutally suppressed giving those in Jerusalem a clear picture of what to expect.

AD68 Judea is torn apart by civil war. In the towns battles rage between those fond of war and those desiring peace. In the countryside outlaw gangs engage in acts of barbarism.

W4.3.4–8 In Jerusalem, a fanatical sect known as the Zealots execute the relatives of King Agrippa for talking to the Romans about the surrender of the city. The Zealots move into the temple. They cast lots to choose a new high priest to replace the one appointed by the Herodians. The lot falls to a yokel who doesn't know what a high priest is. Nevertheless, the Zealots install him with pomp and ceremony, angering the priests.

W4.3.10–12 Ananus, the oldest of the former high priests, denounces the Zealots and their abominations. He encourages the people of Jerusalem to kick the "impious wretches" out of the temple. A battle ensues. It starts with stones and javelins flung at a distance but degenerates into hand-to-hand combat. A terrible slaughter takes place before the Zealots retreat into the inner courts of the temple.

W4.3.14 John Levi, recently arrived and having ingratiated himself among the
W4.4.1–2 prominent citizens of Jerusalem, is chosen to negotiate with the Zealots. However, John betrays Ananus by telling the Zealots the priest is doing deals with the Romans. The Zealots call for help, and 20,000 Idumean soldiers (Edomites) come marching up from the south.

Feb. Fearing they have come under wrong pretenses, Ananus locks the
AD68 Idumeans out of the city and sends a mediator to talk to them. However,
W4.4.3 the offended Idumeans refuse to listen. That night, during a fierce storm
W4.5.2 and earthquake, the Zealots open the gates to the city. Initially thinking
W4.4.7 Ananus is coming with an army to attack them, the Idumeans go on a killing spree slaying 8,500 citizens. Then they hunt and kill Ananus. According to Josephus, the death of the old high priest marks the beginning of the end of Jerusalem.

W4.5.3 With no opposition, the Zealots and Idumeans begin a campaign of
W4.6.3 terror in Jerusalem that results in the deaths of 12,000 people. Every day people try to flee the city, but the Zealots guard the exits and slay those they catch.

W4.6.2 Learning about the unrest in Jerusalem, Vespasian decides to let the city simmer in its own juices. After wintering in Caesarea, he turns his attention to the Jordan Valley in the east.

W4.7.1   Aspiring to take total control of Jerusalem, John Levi and the Galileans withdraw from their alliance with the Judean Zealots. The two groups don't fight but separately pillage the populace. In return for their support, John gives his followers license to loot the houses of the rich. For amusement, the Galileans dress up as women, engage in unlawful pleasures, and run their swords through many.

W4.9.7   With an army of 20,000, Simon, son of Giora, captures Hebron in the Idumean south. This is no mean feat because the Idumeans have a sizeable army of their own, but the Idumeans are betrayed. Simon's army ravages the countryside like a plague of locusts and plunders "a vast quantity of fruit."

W4.9.7–8   The Zealots in Jerusalem are scared witless of Simon and his army, so they lay ambushes and kidnap his wife. They return to Jerusalem feeling smug, "as if they had taken Simon himself captive." For some inconceivable reason, the Zealots expect that Simon will react by laying down his arms. Instead, the warlord comes to the walls of Jerusalem like a wild, wounded beast tormenting anyone he can get his hands on. Simon cuts the hands off many people and sends them into the city with threats and curses. The Zealots, more terrified than ever, return Simon's wife.

W4.9.10   His wife restored, Simon returns to his southern campaign of fruit stealing and eating everything in sight. Idumean refugees flee to Jerusalem and Simon follows them like a shark after a school of fish. For the second time he camps outside the city wall slaying those who are coming and going.

Summer AD68 W4.9.2   With a Roman garrison now installed in Jericho, Vespasian is ready to move on Jerusalem. But before he proceeds news comes from Rome: Nero has committed suicide. Vespasian again decides to postpone the siege.

April AD69 W4.9.10   The situation in Jerusalem is grim. Those who try to flee the assassins inside the city are killed or maimed by Simon outside the city.

W4.9.12   John is now master of Jerusalem, but his hold on power is tenuous. The Idumeans and wealthy citizens are fed up with him, so the chief priest, Matthias, asks Simon to defend Jerusalem against John. Simon enters the city and is welcomed by the populace as a savior. However, Simon ignores them and plunders the Zealots' stores to feed his insatiable army. Simon becomes master of Jerusalem.

W5.1.2 Meanwhile, Eleazar, bristling at John's tyranny, moves to regain control of the Zealots. Soon the city is torn apart by a three-way war between John, Simon, and Eleazar.

June
AD69
W4.9.9
W4.11.4
Vespasian rides with his cavalry to the walls of Jerusalem, while Cerealis, commander of the Fifth Legion, captures Idumean territory that had previously been taken by Simon. Jerusalem is effectively surrounded. But civil war has broken out in Rome, and the empire is in turmoil. Vespasian's soldiers proclaim him as emperor, and he departs, leaving his son Titus in charge. Again Jerusalem gets a reprieve.

Dec.
AD69
W4.10.7
In Rome Vespasian is declared the new emperor. The man who predicted it, Josephus, is released from his bonds.

AD70
W5.1.2-3
At the start of its final year, the city of Jerusalem is split three ways between the Zealots led by Eleazar, John Levi and his private army of cross-dressing Galileans, and the local force led by Simon bar Giora. Eleazar, with the smallest army, controls the high ground of the temple's inner courts. Simon, with the largest army, controls the upper and much of the lower city. John, with his psychopathic army, is sandwiched between them in the outer courts of the temple compound. During this three-way warfare, sacrifices continue to be made at the temple. But worshiping has become a risky business owing to the darts fired over the walls by the engines of war. Jews and circumcised Gentiles alike are killed by the missiles, and the bodies of the priests and the profane lie together amidst lakes of blood.

W5.1.4-5 John's and Simon's forces burn each other's grain supplies. Food that could have sustained the defenders for years goes up in smoke just weeks before the siege. The situation within the city has deteriorated so much that the elderly long for the Romans and an external war to deliver them from their domestic miseries.

W5.1.6 Titus marches from Caesarea with the three legions his father had commanded – the Fifth, Tenth, and Fifteenth – and a reconstituted Twelfth Legion thirsting for revenge. With them are the armies of several allied kings. The Romans march on Jerusalem from three directions: the Fifth Legion approaches from Emmaus in the west, the Tenth approaches from Jericho in the east, while Titus and the rest approach from Mt. Scopus in the north.

April
AD70
W6.9.4
The population of Jerusalem swells on account of the Passover feast. Drawing his net around the city, Titus allows pilgrims to enter the city but he does not allow them to leave. In this way he entraps the entire

nation "as in a prison." Apart from a few skirmishes, battle does not immediately commence as it takes time for the Romans to erect earthworks and assemble their siege towers and machines of war.

W5.3.1   Inside the city, Eleazar opens the temple for Passover celebrations. John Levi and his men enter the temple with hidden swords and overpower the Zealots. Thus the last Passover celebrated in the temple is marred by violence and betrayal.

W5.6.1   At the start of the siege the city is split into two factions: John and his army (6,000 armed men) along with the Zealots (2,400 men) control the temple precinct in the east and adjacent parts, while Simon and his army (10,000 armed men plus 5,000 Idumeans) hold the upper city, including the fortress of Herod's Palace, and part of the lower city to the south. In the new quarter to the north, between the outer and second walls, countless Passover pilgrims are trapped.

May   The Romans attack the north walls of the city using massive siege tow-
AD70   ers and battering rams. Only as the darts and stones start flying do the
W5.6.4 two rebel factions unite in their defense of the city.

W5.7.1   After fifteen days the outer or third wall is breached. The second wall
W5.8.1–2 falls five days later. In the city, the Roman attackers and Jewish defenders engage in fierce street-to-street fighting with neither side backing down.

W5.9.1–4 A stalemate follows during which Titus holds a four-day military parade in an attempt to awe the defenders. Josephus, the former Jewish general now working for the Romans, makes speeches to induce the city to surrender. The Jews are unimpressed, and the battle resumes.

W5.10   With nothing to eat in the city, families fight over food. Children take food from their fathers' mouths; mothers snatch food from their infants. Rebel fighters steal from everyone and torture those thought to be concealing food.

W5.11.1   Titus learns that the city is running out of food. Using stones taken from the outer wall, he builds fortified embankments about the city. Starvation drives many Jews over the wall, but those who are caught are crucified atop the Roman embankment. This barbarism is meant to frighten the defenders into surrender, but the rebel leaders refuse to yield. Many of the poor continue to flee preferring a brutal death by crucifixion, to the slow death of starvation. The Romans crucify hundreds a day until they run out of wood.

June AD70 W5.12.2–3 W5.13.4 W5.13.7	Seeing the Jews won't surrender, Titus decides to enclose the city within his wall. Construction moves at a dazzling pace, and the city is encircled by an unbroken five-mile wall within three days. With no hope of escape, people scavenge among the sewers and dunghills for food. The famine kills many and houses are filled with the dead and dying. More than 600,000 bodies are carried out the gate. Some of those who slip away to the Romans have their bellies slit by soldiers looking for swallowed gold. On a single night, 2,000 deserters are dissected in this manner.
W5.13.1–2 W6.8.2	The tyrants ruling Jerusalem also kill many defenders. Simon accuses Matthias of having Roman sympathies and has him executed without trial. Simon also slays the priest Ananias and sixteen prominent men. When he learns that the men keeping a certain tower are thinking of deserting to the Romans, Simon has them killed before throwing their mangled bodies over the wall. The Idumeans, thinking to surrender, send five emissaries to Titus. Hearing this, Simon kills the emissaries.
W5.13.3	Josephus makes another speech outside the wall and is hit on the head with a rock. The Jews rejoice thinking the old turncoat is dead. However, Josephus recovers and shouts that it won't be long before those who attacked him get their comeuppance.
W6.3.3–4	The food shortage is so severe that people eat things animals wouldn't touch. Defenders chew their shoes and the leather on their shields. Close friends fight over morsels. Starving robbers prowl "like mad dogs" breaking into the same houses two or three times a day. A once-wealthy woman called Mary is so exasperated that she slays and cooks her infant son. The thieves smell the roasting meat and break into her house. She shows them her half-eaten child and dares them to take the rest. The men leave trembling and empty-handed. The city is so horrified by the story that many of those who live wish to die, while those who are already dead are esteemed blessed to be spared such miseries.
July AD70 W6.1	The Romans capture the strategically significant Tower of Antonia, the fortress overlooking the temple compound.[5]
Aug. 30 AD70 W6.5.1	The Romans take the temple. Ten thousand defenders are slain without mercy, both "children and old men, and profane persons and priests." Against Titus' wishes, the temple is plundered and destroyed in a mighty conflagration. The sound of the fire combines with the shouts of the Romans and the cries of the defeated make a terrific noise.

W6.5.2 The Romans burn all the temple buildings including the treasury chambers. In one portico 6,000 women and children have taken refuge because a false prophet promised divine deliverance. Before Titus can decide what to do with these people, soldiers set the portico on fire. None survive.

W6.6.1 The Romans set their ensigns against the eastern gate of the temple and make sacrifices to them.

W6.6.3 The Romans now have the upper hand, but the defenders refuse to surrender. Titus, weary of negotiating with stubborn Jews, cancels all standing offers. He orders his soldiers to burn the city and slay all deserters.

W6.9.4
W7.2.1 The rebel leaders, John and Simon, hide in the caverns but are eventually captured. Simon is later executed in Rome while John is imprisoned, presumably for life.

Sept. 26
AD70
W6.9.3
W7.1.1 Titus becomes master of Jerusalem. The siege has left more than a million Jews dead. Titus takes 97,000 Jews into captivity and orders the demolition of the city and temple.

Jerusalem is no more. The Romans depart leaving nothing behind except for three towers of Herod's palace, and part of the western wall of the temple precinct. These are preserved for posterity to show the strength of the defenses that had yielded to Roman might. And "this was the end of Jerusalem ... a city otherwise of great magnificence, and of mighty fame among all mankind."

---

[1] Eusebius records this famine as occurring during the reign of Emperor Claudius (*Church History*, 2.8.2).

[2] This figure comes from Josephus' account in *Wars*, 2.12.1. However, in his later retelling of the story in *Antiquities*, 20.5.3, he puts the number of dead at 20,000.

[3] This Jonathan was high priest immediately after the Caiaphas of Biblical fame. He was also the son of the former high priest Ananus (or Annas) who had questioned Jesus (John 18:19–24). Jonathan's brother Ananus, also a high priest, was behind the sham trial that resulted in the death of James the Just in AD62.

[4] Vespasian originally planned to send Josephus to Nero. Hearing this, the captured general replied in language worthy of Shakespeare, "Why? Thou, O Vespasian, are Caesar and emperor, thou, and this thy son. Bind me now still faster, and keep me for thyself, for thou, O Caesar, art not only lord over me, but over the land and the sea, and all mankind" (*Wars*, 3.8.9).

[5] This was the same fortress or barracks from where the Apostle Paul addressed the Jewish mob in Acts 21:37, less than fifteen years earlier.

APPENDIX 2: TEN THEOLOGIANS SUPPORTING DIVINE VENGEANCE

Can the destruction of Jerusalem be attributed to a vengeful God punishing the Jews for the murder of his Son? Was AD70 the result of God destroying an offensive religious system and his removal of the old covenant? As we saw in Chapter 22, such notions are inconsistent with the gospel of Jesus. However, for 2,000 years the traditional view has been that God *was* executing vengeance upon the Jews. Below is a partial list of scholars and theologians who have made this claim.

1.   Eusebius (~260–340)

In his *Church History*, the church historian Eusebius wrote that the Jews met "with destruction at the hands of divine justice" for their crime against Christ. "The judgment of God at length overtook those who had committed such outrages against Christ and his apostles, and totally destroyed that generation of impious men." Eusebius wrote about the Jews' misfortunes so that "those who read this work may have some means of knowing that God was not long in executing vengeance upon them for their wickedness against the Christ of God."[1]

2.   Chrysostom (349–407)

In his *Homily LXXVI*, John Chrysostom, the Archbishop of Constantinople, asks why the Jews experienced "wrath from God intolerable," and concludes that it was for their rejection of Christ's work. From "whence came upon them so grievous wrath from heaven more woeful than all that had come upon them before? Plainly it was because of the desperate crime and the denial of the Cross."[2]

3.   John Calvin (1509–1564)

In his *Commentary on Matthew, Mark, Luke: Volume 3*, John Calvin, the French Reformer, wrote that the Jews suffered because "God determined, by this dreadful example, to take vengeance on that nation, for having rejected his Son, and despised the grace which was brought by him."[3]

4.   Matthew Henry (1662–1714)

The Welsh churchman Matthew Henry believed AD70 was "when Christ came to destroy the Jewish nation by the Roman armies ..." In his commentary on Luke 21:5–28, he wrote: "So fully did the Divine judgements come upon the Jews, that their city is set as an example before us, to show that sins will not pass unpunished; and that the terrors of the Lord, and his threatenings against impenitent sinners, will all come to pass, even as his word was true, and his wrath great upon Jerusalem."[4]

5. John Gill (1697–1771)

The English theologian John Gill interpreted Luke's days of vengeance as referring to "God's vengeance on the Jewish nation, for their rejection and crucifixion of the Messiah."[5]

6. William Newcome (1729–1800)

Bishop William Newcome, the English cleric, in his *Harmony of the Gospels*, said the Jews reaped "the awakened vengeance of heaven" not solely for killing Jesus, but for "the blood of all the prophets, which had been shed from the foundation of the world."[6]

7. Joseph Benson (1749–1821)

In his commentary on Matthew 24, Joseph Benson, the English Methodist minister, wrote that the phrase "coming in the clouds of heaven," signified God interposing "to execute vengeance on a wicked generation." He noted that "the destruction of Jerusalem and of the Jewish state, civil and religious, would be such a remarkable instance of divine vengeance … that all the Jewish tribes should mourn, and many should be led from thence to acknowledge him for the true Messiah."[7]

8. Adam Clarke (1760–1832)

In his commentary on Matthew 24, Adam Clarke, the British theologian, said that the destruction of Jerusalem was "a remarkable instance of Divine vengeance" and "a signal manifestation of Christ's power and glory." In his commentary on Hebrews 6 he wrote, "God visited and avenged the innocent blood of Christ upon the Jews and they continue to be monuments of his displeasure to the present day."[8]

9. George Peter Holford (1769–1839)

George Holford, an English parliamentarian, made no distinction between Roman and divine vengeance in his 1805 oft-reprinted book *The Destruction of Jerusalem*. He wrote of the dire and heavy vengeance "accumulating in the vials of divine displeasure." Holford wrote about the fall of Jerusalem so that nominal Christians might "receive a salutary admonition from that exemplary vengeance which was inflicted by the Almighty upon the whole Jewish nation." In other words, watch out lest God pour out his vials of divine wrath upon you.[9]

10. Albert Barnes (1798–1870)

In his commentary on Matthew 24:30, Albert Barnes, the American theologian, wrote that the sign of the Son of Man mentioned in verse 30, possibly referred to his "coming to destroy the city of Jerusalem."[10]

[1] Eusebius, *Church History*, 3.5.6 and 3.7.9.

[2] John Chrysostom, *Homily, LXXVI*, source: www.ccel.org/ccel/schaff/npnf110.iii.LXXIII.-html, accessed June 29, 2016. The second quote is found in the *Catena Aurea - Gospel of Matthew*, by Thomas Aquinas. Source: www.ccel.org/ccel/aquinas/catena1.ii.xxiv.html

[3] John Calvin, *Commentary on Matthew, Mark, Luke: Volume 3*, Christian Classics Ethereal Library, p.95. Website: www.ccel.org/ccel/calvin/calcom33.pdf.

[4] Matthew Henry (1706), "Luke 17," *Commentary on the Whole Bible*. Source: http://biblehub.-com/commentaries/mhc/luke/17.htm. The second quote is from Henry's commentary on Luke 21. Source: http://biblehub.com/commentaries/mhc/luke/21.htm.

[5] John Gill (1748), "Luke 21," *An Exposition of the New Testament*. Source: http://biblehub.-com/commentaries/gill/luke/21.htm.

[6] William Newcombe (1778), *Harmony of the Gospels*, quoted in "Jerusalem, AD70: The Worst Desolation Ever?" Website: www.ukapologetics.net/09/AD70.htm, accessed June 29, 2016.

[7] Joseph Benson (1818), "Matthew 24," *Commentary of the Old and New Testaments*. Source: http://biblehub.com/commentaries/benson/matthew/24.htm.

[8] Adam Clarke (1832), "Matthew 24," *Commentary on the Whole Bible*. Source: www.study-light.org/commentaries/acc/matthew-24.html. The second quotes is from his "Commentary on Hebrews 6," source: www.studylight.org/commentaries/acc/hebrews-6.html.

[9] George Holford (1805), *The Destruction of Jerusalem*. Source: www.bible.ca/pre-destruction-70AD-george-holford-1805AD.htm

[10] Albert Barnes (1832), "Matthew 24," *Notes on the New Testament: Explanatory and Practical. Vol. I – Matthew and Mark*. Source: http://biblehub.com/commentaries/barnes/matthew/24.htm

SCRIPTURE INDEX

Scripture Index

IMAGE CREDITS

Unless otherwise stated, all images are public domain, Creative Commons license, or considered fair use. Public domain images come from sources such as Wikimedia Commons and the Providence Lithographic Company. (Introduction) "Flavius Josephus," is a colorized image based on a 18th-century woodcut by an unknown artist, (Part A) "The destruction of the Temple of Jerusalem," by Francesco Hayez (1791–1882), (Chapter 1) "Herod's Temple," by Najla Kay, (Chapter 3) "Paul arrested in Jerusalem (Acts 21:40)," by unknown artist, (Chapter 5) "Saint Paul being let down in a basket," by unknown artist, (Chapter 6) "Paul Starts on a Great Trip," by unknown artist, (Chapter 7) "Destruction of Jerusalem foretold," by unknown artist, (Chapter 8) Detail from "Destruction of Jerusalem," by Wilhelm von Kaulbach (1805–1874), "Romans on the coastal plain" map by Rémi Torralba, (Chapter 9) "Vespasian and Titus," by Najla Kay, "Romans plundering the treasures," by Najla Kay based on the "Spoils of Jerusalem" detail from the Arch of Titus, (Chapter 10) "Assault on Jerusalem" map by Rémi Torralba, (Chapter 12) "Roman Aquila," by Rémi Torralba, (Chapter 13) "Night falls on Israel," by Najla Kay, (Chapter 14) "Jesus ascending to his heavenly home," from Standard Bible Story Readers, Book Two by Lillie A. Faris (1925), (Part B) detail from "The Four Horsemen of the Apocalypse," by Viktor Vasnetsov (1848–1926), (Chapter 21) "Woe unto You, Scribes and Pharisees," by James Tissot (1836–1902), (Chapter 24) "Parable of the Talents," by unknown artist, (Chapter 28) "Annas and Caiaphas," by James Tissot (1836–1902), (Chapter 29) "The torn curtain," by Santanu Mitra, (Chapter 31) "The Pharisees question Jesus," by James Tissot (1836–1902), (Chapter 32) "Pope Sylvester II" from *The Lives and Times of the Popes*, by Chevalier Artaud de Montor, New York: The Catholic Publication Society of America, (1842/1911), (Chapter 36) "Wise and Foolish Virgins," by unknown artist, (Appendices) "First-century Palestine," map by Rémi Torralba, "Herod's Temple and precincts," by Najla Kay.

ACKNOWLEDGEMENTS

Over the past few years, many people have asked for my thoughts on preterism and the events of AD70. In response to these questions, and my own eschatological uncertainties, I decided to dig deep into the prophecies and parables of Jesus. This book is the fruit of that study. I am grateful to Escape to Reality readers who regularly nudge me towards exciting projects such as this.

Eschatology is a controversial subject with more questions than answers. I wrote this book knowing that I could be wrong about many things. More than with my other books I sought input from people who might have a different perspective. I am hugely grateful for the encouragement and feedback received on early drafts from Dave Orrison, Ryan Rufus, Rick Manis, Mark Machen, Chad Mansbridge, Tony Ide, Leopoldo Solis, Clint Byars, and Peter Sze. Extracts from draft chapters were also published on my blog attracting hundreds of comments. I'm grateful to everyone who took the time to provide feedback. I heard from extreme preterists, full-on futurists, and everyone in between. Needless to say the views and errors expressed in this book are my own.

I am blessed to be married to a woman who provides me with a sounding board for all my ideas, and who reads everything I write. Camilla also checked the 500+ scriptures in this book. But most of all I am grateful for the peaceful writing space she provides inside a house full of children – no mean feat!

I knew from the start that a book such as this needed pictures and maps. I am grateful to Najla Kay and Santanu Mitra who contributed original artwork and Rémi Torralba who made all the maps. Shelly Davis did a superb job with the proofreading.

Finally, I am grateful to the following people without whose support (via Patreon) books like this would not be possible: Andrew and Margaret Robertson, Charles and Sheilla van Wijk, Ben Dailey, Terry Maupin, Bill Fowler, Debra Hamilton, Randy and Julee Armstrong, Richard Bradford, Doug Hignell, Swee Heng Chee, Henry Yeo, Scott and Christine Engell, Rachmat Permana, Amanda Henderson, Ray Williams, Low Jer Wei and Carmen Ng Wai Yin, Ian and Norma Anderson, Don Beeson, Melissa and Adam Kensell, James Young, Anne Hoover, Tim Brasic, Anita Sheridan, Joe Merchant, Patti McPike, Kindall Nelson, Agnes Tan, Jean-Paul Parenteau,

Rose Simmons, Yeo Wee Khin, Rose Hayden, James Smith, Lee Ping Tung, Erik Grangaard, Karen Moffett, Bill Schanuel, Kyle Defoe, Kundayi Bernard Mugabe, Jason Kim, Justin Hopper, Michael and Kimberly Vizza, Ted and Georgie Nelson, Prince and Sandra Osei-Gyamfi, Michael and Julie Lipparelli, Peter Hanson, Klaus and Erika Degen, Keith Forwith, Cecilia Villanobles Lim, James Tuttle, Helen Brown, Leroy Herring, Jessica Carpenter, Rebekah Watson, Gideon Caranzo, Gerry Macabuhay, Marisa Raynaldo, Janelle and Terry Myers, Jan Kiel, Keith Pinke, Miguel, Stephanie and Estelle Gonzalez, John Ross, Mikael Jonsson, Mary Anne Tango, Nagy Andrea Eva, Jeremy Pelfrey, David Dunham, Jerry Williams, Derrick Darden, David Edwardds, and Cornerstone Bible Church in Crofton, KY. I am also grateful for the support and friendship of my fellow Kiwis; Robbie and Dollice Tan, Richie and Mandy Lewis, and Mel and Clare Sanders.

ESCAPE TO REALITY

If you have questions about the last days and the gospel of grace, you can find answers at Paul's website. Visit escapetoreality.org and you will discover:

- 500+ grace-based articles covering 1000+ scriptures
- reviews of 50 outstanding grace books
- resources for private study and small group discussion
- hundreds of stories of lives radically changed by grace

Other books by Paul Ellis

The good news may be the best news you never heard!

Discover the secret to walking in divine favor and experiencing freedom in every aspect of your life. Learn who you really are and why you were born. This book will take you to the heavenly treasure rooms of grace leaving you awestruck at the stunning goodness of God.

A good question can change your life!

Questions are keys to treasure and doorways to discovery. The questions in this book will take you places. They will cause you to dance on the uplands of your Father's favor and lead you to a deeper relationship with Jesus, the greatest Answer of all.

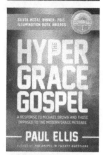

God's love for you is greater than you know!

Drawing on insights gleaned from more than forty grace preachers, *The Hyper-Grace Gospel* addresses common misperceptions some have about the message of grace. This book will leave you marveling at the relentless love of your Father.

Gold Medal Winner (IBA), Book of the Year (CSPA)

Stuff Jesus Never Said shatters the myth of the angry, faultfinding God and celebrates the God that Christ revealed—a God who wants you to prosper and live well.

AVAILABLE NOW!

Amazon, BAM!, Barnes & Noble, Book Depository, Booktopia, Eden.co.uk, Kinokuniya, Loot.co.za, Nile.com.au, Waterstones, W.H. Smith, and other good retailers.

www.KingsPress.org

CPSIA information can be obtained
at www.ICGtesting.com
Printed in the USA
BVHW011938261218
536462BV00005B/147/P

9 781927 230411